PETER KENT'S
BIG BOOK OF
ARMOUR

KINGFISHER

First published 2010 by Kingfisher
an imprint of Macmillan Children's Books
a division of Macmillan Publishers Limited
20 New Wharf Road, London N1 9RR
Basingstoke and Oxford
Associated companies throughout the world
www.panmacmillan.com

Illustrations by Peter Kent

ISBN 978-0-7534-3164-1

9 8 7 6 5 4 3 2
2TBP/0610/WKT/UNT/157MA/C

A CIP catalogue record for this book
is available from the British Library.

Printed in China

Picture credit: p6–7 Shutterstock/mehmetsait

The website addresses listed in this book are correct at the
time of publishing. However, due to the ever-changing nature
of the internet, website addresses and content can change.
Websites can contain links that are unsuitable for children.
The publisher cannot be held responsible for changes in
website addresses or content, or for information obtained
through third-party websites. We strongly advise that
internet searches should be supervised by an adult.

Contents

Introduction	4
Earth's armour	6
Coastal defence	8
Animal armour	10
Plant armour	11
Primitive protection	12
Ancient armour	13
Classical armour	14
Medieval armour	16
Making armour	18
Bloody battle	20
Fighting for fun	21
Asian armour	22
Armour in decline	24
Armour makes a comeback	26
Modern armour	28
Athletic armour	30
Industrial armour	32
Safety suits	33
War wagons	34
Birth of the tank	36
Modern tanks	38
Armoured trains	40
Early armoured ships	42
Battle of the ironclads: USS *Monitor* v CSS *Virginia*	44
Modern battleships	46
Deep-sea diving vessels	48
Armoured planes	50
Armoured buildings	52
Iron island	54
Forts on land	56
Magic armour	58
Private armour	59
Glossary	60
Further information	62
Index	64

INTRODUCTION

When most people think of armour they imagine a clanking suit, the kind of clothing worn by a man whose tailor is a blacksmith, but there is more to it than that. Armour is defensive covering, something that protects the wearer from harm but not just in war. There are many more dangers to people than battleaxes, bullets and bombs. Most people put on some sort of armour every day, whether it's a bicycle helmet, shin pads or safety goggles. And it's not only people that wear it – just look at a tortoise, or the aptly named armadillo. Whenever something needs protection, there you'll find armour. From a battleship to a beetle, there's nothing like armour to keep it safe.

Strong plastic knee and elbow pads with a helmet keep this scooter-rider safe. They were unknown 30 years ago when grazed knees were universal.

Legs are in danger in a game of football with all those boots hacking at the ball. Pads save shins from cuts and bruises.

The shining knight in a polished suit on his equally well-protected horse is most people's idea of what armour looks like.

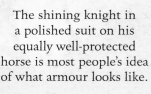

DIY can be lethal, too. Safety requires a pair of ear defenders, safety goggles and a dust mask.

The kitchen can be a dangerous place. An apron and oven gloves protect the cook from spitting fat and hot trays.

Strange concrete objects such as this are part of the sea coast's armour, defending it against the waves.

Soldiers long dreamed of armoured vehicles to keep them safe on the battlefield. This armoured war cart was used by Hussites from Bohemia in the 15th century.

Building sites can be almost as dangerous as battlefields, so builders wear helmets and steel-capped boots.

A helmet with a visor to protect his eyes against a toxic spray is standard wear for today's security guard.

Factor 50 sun cream acts as invisible armour, filtering out the harmful ultraviolet rays in sunlight.

Animals have worn armour long before there were humans. The hard plates covering an armadillo protect it against teeth and claws.

Even plants have armour. This spiny, outer layer covers the shiny, hard conker inside.

Insects live inside a complete suit of armour as they have their skeleton on the outside. The hard outer casing is, for their size, very strong.

EARTH'S ARMOUR

The atmosphere is an envelope of gases that surrounds the Earth – without it, no life would be possible. As the Earth moves through space, the atmosphere acts both as a shield, giving protection from most of the deadly rays and meteorites that continually bombard us, and container, stopping the air from escaping into space.

The atmosphere, which is about 700km thick, does not work like a normal sheet of armour – lumps of rock do not simply bounce off. A solid object piercing the atmosphere creates friction as its surface drags through the air, and more speed means more friction and more heat. Meteorites either burn up entirely, or only small fragments reach the ground. Only the very biggest meteor or asteroid could pass through the atmosphere in one large piece. The atmosphere also acts as a filter to radiation, only letting through sunlight, heat and some less harmful rays.

Solar shield

The exosphere is the very top layer. It starts at about 650km above the Earth and finally merges into space at about 8,000km.

Most meteorites burn up in the mesosphere at about 60–80km above Earth, where the air is thick enough to cause friction.

Although it is made of nothing but gas, the atmosphere is immensely heavy, weighing about 5,000 million million tonnes.

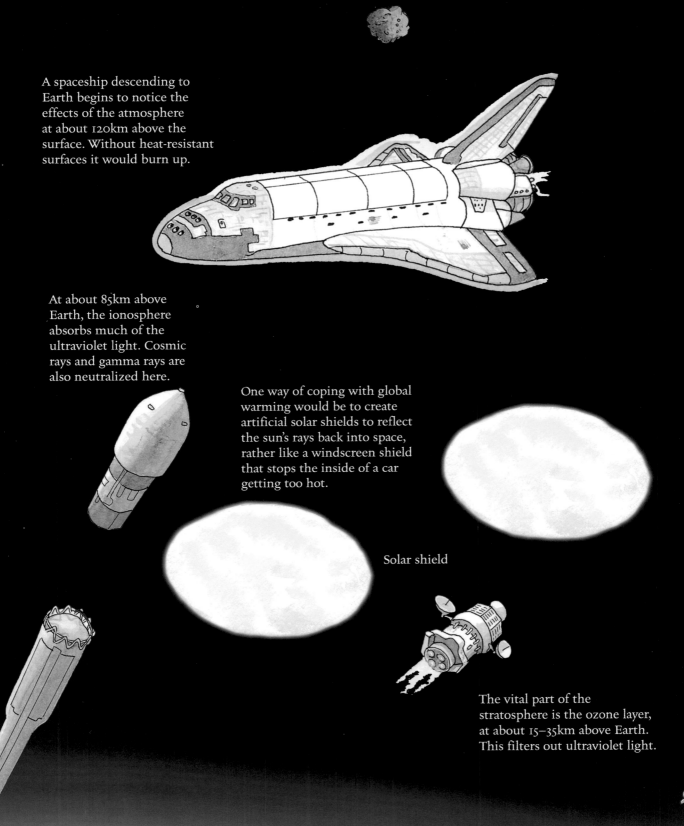

A spaceship descending to Earth begins to notice the effects of the atmosphere at about 120km above the surface. Without heat-resistant surfaces it would burn up.

At about 85km above Earth, the ionosphere absorbs much of the ultraviolet light. Cosmic rays and gamma rays are also neutralized here.

One way of coping with global warming would be to create artificial solar shields to reflect the sun's rays back into space, rather like a windscreen shield that stops the inside of a car getting too hot.

Solar shield

The vital part of the stratosphere is the ozone layer, at about 15–35km above Earth. This filters out ultraviolet light.

The lowest layer of the atmosphere is the troposphere. About 80 per cent of all the gases in the atmosphere are in this layer. This is where oxygen is thickest, and where the final filtering of harmful rays takes place.

COASTAL DEFENCE

When you are walking on a beach or scrambling up cliffs, you are playing on the gigantic suit of armour protecting the land in its everlasting battle with the sea. There are natural defences against the waves: hard, such as cliffs, and soft, such as sand dunes, but still the coast is washed away. Ever since people began to live by the sea they have been defending their homes and harbours against the waves. The Romans were the first to build built breakwaters, but it was the Dutch who started building sea defences on a large scale. For the Netherlands and other countries that lie below sea level, their sea defences are vital armour.

Gabions are a way of making large rocks by scooping up smaller ones and packing them in boxes made of wire mesh.

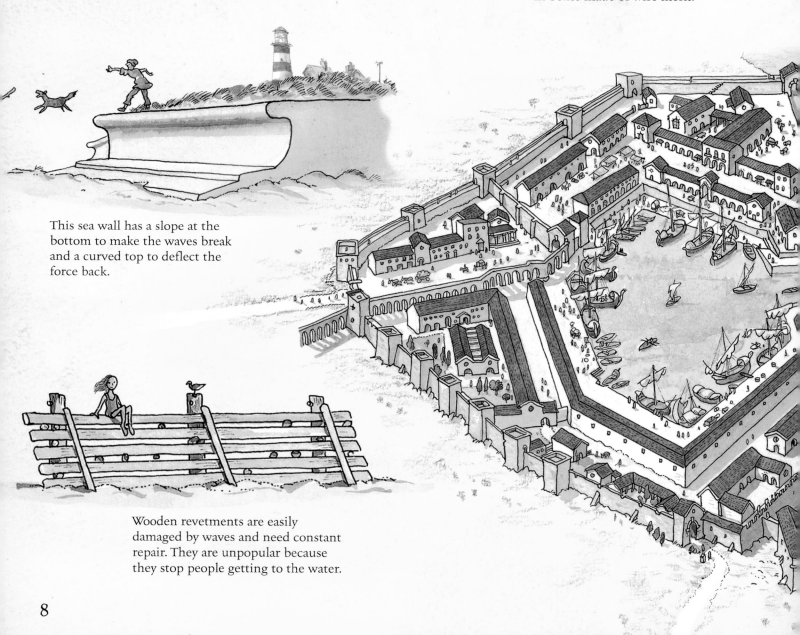

This sea wall has a slope at the bottom to make the waves break and a curved top to deflect the force back.

Wooden revetments are easily damaged by waves and need constant repair. They are unpopular because they stop people getting to the water.

8

CONCRETE BLOCKS

Interlocking concrete shapes make a great sea defence. These are made to many different designs but the most common is the 'dolos'. The legs lock together so they form an immovable barrier, while the spaces in between allow the water to wash through and lose most of its energy.

Xbloc

Accropod

Tetrapod

A-jack

Dolos

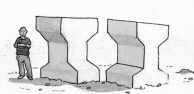
Akmon

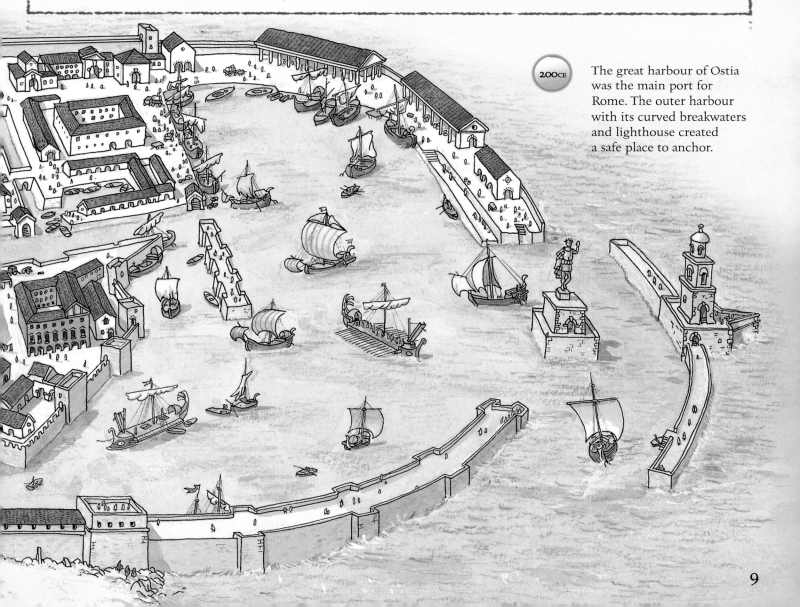

200ce The great harbour of Ostia was the main port for Rome. The outer harbour with its curved breakwaters and lighthouse created a safe place to anchor.

9

ANIMAL ARMOUR

Millions of years before there were human designers of armour, nature had evolved the basic ways of providing bodily protection, for nearly every animal has an enemy that wants to kill it. The animal without any defence is soon extinct. The best defence is to run away or hide but for those who can't, nature has provided armour in the form of shells, scales and thick skins. The more dangerous an animal's enemies are, the more complete its armour has to be.

HORNS

The basic forms of weapons are clubs that crush, spears that stab and swords that cut. The horns of animals are the equivalent of spears.

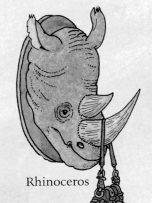

Rhinoceros

TEETH

Animals' teeth are designed to cut and tear. The terrible fangs of Tyrannosaurus rex and the tiger's huge canines are the classic weapons of the predator.

Moose

Narwhal

Tiger

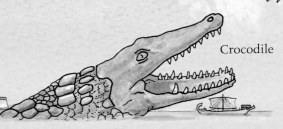

Crocodile

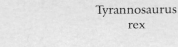

Tyrannosaurus rex

NATURAL ARMOUR

The strongest form of armour is a shell. Its continuous surface can resist heavy blows but it is heavy and restricts movement. The most flexible form of armour is a strong hide like that of an elephant or a hippopotamus, but to be effective it must be very thick.

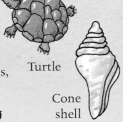

Turtle

Cone shell

Conch shell

Ladybird

Elephant

Hippopotamus

A coat of bony plates or scales is easier to move in. It is strong but there are weak places in the joints.

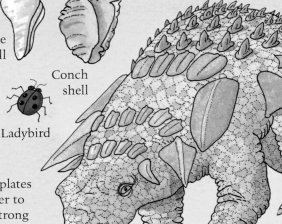

Ankylosaurus

Pangolin

CLAWS

The paw of a grizzly bear is like a spiked club. The crab's claws and the golden eagle's talons are used to crush and grip their prey.

Bear

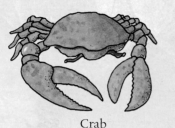

Crab

Golden eagle

BEAKS

Birds' beaks have many uses: the macaw's cracks open nuts; the woodpecker's chisels wood; the heron's spears fish; and the vulture's tears its prey.

Macaw

Woodpecker

Heron

Vulture

PLANT ARMOUR

Most of the world's creatures are vegetarians and, in order to survive, plants have evolved ways to protect themselves. Trees need a hard, outer layer to protect the growing wood inside and seeds need a case to protect them long enough for them to ripen. But the defences cannot be too good. Plants need to be eaten – if their armour was completely effective, animals would be unable to feed and would starve.

Bark protects the tree against cold, keeps in moisture, keeps out insects and prevents injury. It is continually renewed from within as the inner bark dies.

The seeds of the Bhutan pine are inside this cone made of woody plates.

The bark of the cork tree can be over a metre thick. It is mainly harvested to provide the corks for wine bottles.

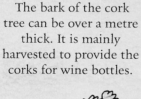

The hardened cases of seeds are the most common form of plant armour. The horse chestnut seed is contained within the hard shell used for playing conkers.

The cone of the maritime pine is made of woody scales reinforced with sharp prickles.

As coconut trees are very tall, their seedcases need to be very strong to avoid breaking when hitting the ground.

PRIMITIVE PROTECTION

T he first pieces of armour were made from natural materials: shields were formed from woven twigs, wood or animal hide. Body armour used the natural toughness of skins and hide. Other primitive armour was made from hoops of wood, strips of bark, slats of wood or bone sewn into fabric, and rope woven into a stiff suit. Some shields and helmets were made from tortoise shells. All these 'green' forms of armour were no longer used as soon as metal was easily available.

20,000 BCE All basic armour must defend against stabbing and blows to the head.

1890 CE The first armour was probably like this Dayak armour from Borneo, made of goat hides.

1850 This Inuit wears a breastplate of walrus ivory plates laced together with rawhide.

1800 On the South Pacific Islands, strong armour was fashioned from coconut fibre rope and woven cane.

1780 Wood bent into hoops and covered in hide made armour for Chukchi warriors from Siberia.

1400 The Aztecs wore very effective armour of padded linen. Knights wore suits to make them look like jaguars or eagles.

ANCIENT ARMOUR

It was in Egypt, the Middle East and China that civilization in cities and states first appeared. Quarrels between them led to fighting on a large scale, with properly organized armies, but it was the discovery of metal – first copper, then bronze and finally iron – that truly revolutionized warfare. Metal weapons cut with deadly efficiency, so more protection was necessary. The first armour was made of leather and thick cloth, sometimes reinforced with small metal plates.

1275 BCE Only the Egyptian pharaoh could afford a coat of bronze plates sewn on leather; soldiers wore armour of thick leather, hippopotamus hide or padded linen.

3000 BCE The first Egyptian soldiers fought savage tribes armed only with primitive weapons. They did not need to wear armour and carried only large cowhide shields.

900 BCE These strange decorated bronze helmets were worn more for show than for serious fighting.

1020 BCE The Bible says that the giant Philistine, Goliath, wore armour of brass, but it was more likely to have been bronze.

750 BCE Assyrians wore armour of bronze scales laced together, and a well-designed helmet with cheek pieces.

1300 BCE The Hittites were the first to use iron swords and helmets.

2500 BCE Sumerians wore long, thick leather cloaks strengthened with bronze discs in the same way as their wooden shields. Their helmets were made of leather or copper.

CLASSICAL ARMOUR

The most beautiful and elegant armour was made by the ancient Greeks, as you might expect from the people who built the Parthenon. Armour was so important to them they even had a god, Hephaistos, dedicated to metal working. A few centuries later, Rome was the greatest power in the western world. The Roman empire, stretching from the Arabian desert to the far north of Britain, was defended by a superb professional army.

1200 BCE At the siege of Troy warriors wore helmets made of boar tusks and carried huge cowhide shields.

1450 BCE Charioteers who didn't need to walk could wear heavy bronze suits made up of 15 individual pieces.

490 BCE Greek soldiers or hoplites wore bronze or leather body armour with bronze helmets and bronze greaves on their legs.

420 BCE Greek hoplites formed a solid mass called a phalanx. Each man was protected by a large shield and carried a long spear.

GREEK HELMETS

Greek helmets were beautifully shaped and skilfully made by hammering out a single sheet of bronze. Each city had its own distinctively shaped helmet.

Illyrian helmet

Spartan helmet

Corinthian helmet

Chalcidian helmet

Boeotian helmet

Thracian helmet

CELTIC WARRIORS

Most of the Romans' Celtic enemies wore no armour. Some even fought naked. No wonder the Romans nearly always won!

100 CE Roman soldiers or legionaries wore a standardized armour of metal plates with a helmet that defended cheeks and neck. An apron of metal discs gave extra protection.

35 CE Flexible plate armour was introduced in the reign of Tiberius. The plates were an effective defence but were light and easy to wear.

55 BCE Legionaries in Caesar's time wore a chain-mail shirt and a bronze helmet. Officers wore a bronze cuirass which mimicked the muscles of the abdomen.

100 CE The rectangular shields could be formed into a *testudo*, or tortoise, to make an instant and very effective 'tank'. It was used to attack walls and ramparts while under heavy bombardment.

Medieval armour

When the Roman Emperor was deposed in 456CE, Europe entered a period known as the Dark Ages. The continent splintered into a chaos of warring barbarian tribes. The peoples that replaced the Romans – the Saxons, Franks, Goths, Vandals and Lombards – were brave and fierce but very backward in military technology. They thought the Romans' armour made of metal plates was too complicated. The barbarian kings, nobles and warriors wore mail shirts and richly decorated helmets. Common soldiers had to make do with leather jerkins.

 400CE

The Saxons were called after their saxes (long knives) and the Lombards after their long axes.

 750

This noble is wearing a magnificent helmet decorated with gold. Most helmets of the Dark Ages are known as *spagenhelm*.

1120

The crusaders wore linen surcoats to protect them from the fierce heat. Their great battle helmets were very uncomfortable and very hard to see out of.

1400

Common soldiers wore leather jerkins called jacks. They were often strengthened with small plates of metal or horn. Their helmets were known as pots.

1400

Every knight needed a squire and a couple of servants to help him dress and to keep his armour clean.

1200
Suits of armour were still mainly made of mail, but plates of boiled leather were added to vulnerable parts.

1350
This is typical armour of the 100 Years War, with metal plates added to chain mail. The wasp waist look was very fashionable.

1500
A good horse was expensive and needed protection: a knight didn't want it to be killed under him or he would have to fight on foot.

800
The Vikings never wore helmets with horns. They did have ones that looked as if they were wearing spectacles, but the nose bar was more common.

1450
By the 1400s knights wore a suit completely made of plate armour, weighing about 35kg.

1066
The Normans wore mail shirts and helmets like the Vikings but added kite shields. These protected the legs as well as the body.

MAKING ARMOUR

Armourers were the most famous and best-paid medieval craftsmen in the Middle Ages. The best armour was made in Germany and Italy. Learning the skill of making complicated armour by hand took four years as an apprentice, and then another four as a paid workman. After passing an examination by making a special piece – his masterpiece – the workman became a master. Armourers combined to form a guild, which set prices and inspected work to make sure it was of the highest quality.

I The master armourer took the order, measured the client and discussed what he wanted. Some clients left wax models of their limbs with their armourer, so he could make replacements without seeing them again.

2 A bar of wrought iron or soft steel was hammered flat, at first by a water-powered hammer and then by hand.

3 This reduced the bar to a thin sheet about 4mm thick.

4 The metal was cut into flat shapes with shears, following a pattern.

5 The parts were hammered into shape on a wooden mould. This was the most skilled part of the making process.

6 The parts were heated in a furnace to harden the surface. Every armourer had a secret recipe for this process. One smeared the surface of the metal with rancid pork lard, and wrapped it in goatskin covered in clay.

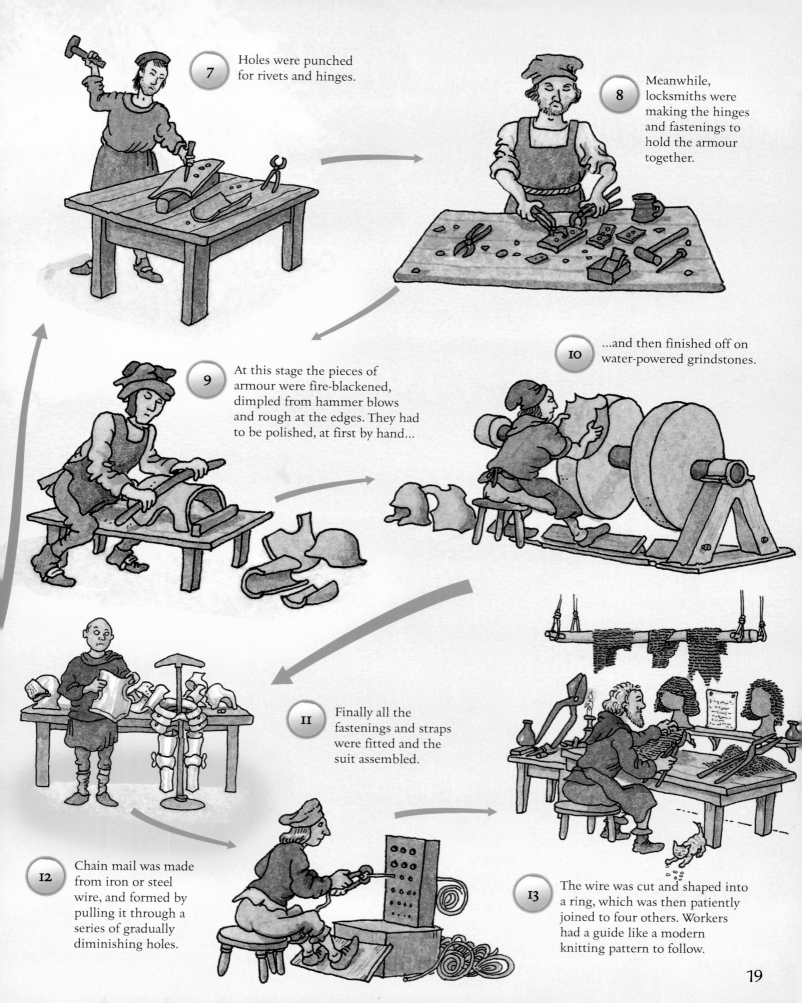

7 Holes were punched for rivets and hinges.

8 Meanwhile, locksmiths were making the hinges and fastenings to hold the armour together.

9 At this stage the pieces of armour were fire-blackened, dimpled from hammer blows and rough at the edges. They had to be polished, at first by hand...

10 ...and then finished off on water-powered grindstones.

11 Finally all the fastenings and straps were fitted and the suit assembled.

12 Chain mail was made from iron or steel wire, and formed by pulling it through a series of gradually diminishing holes.

13 The wire was cut and shaped into a ring, which was then patiently joined to four others. Workers had a guide like a modern knitting pattern to follow.

19

BLOODY BATTLE

Medieval battles were dreadful, muddled, bloody affairs. Once the fighting began the commanders had no control over their armies. They could not send messages and, even if they did, their soldiers would not have heard above the din of thousands of men yelling and the clanging of weapons on armour. It must have sounded like a football match in which every spectator was banging a metal bucket with a poker and shouting too.

The fighting did not last long. No man was strong and fit enough to fight for hours wearing armour and wielding a heavy weapon. Usually one army charged and there was a struggle until one side or the other turned and ran. Medieval soldiers only took prisoners who were noble and could pay a ransom to buy their freedom.

FIGHTING FOR FUN

Tournaments or mock battles were, along with hunting, the only sport of knights. They began in the 1100s as one-to-one combats and then developed into mock battles, called mêlées, that were so dangerous that many knights were killed. A safer sport was devised where two knights rode at each other, trying to unhorse one another or score points by hitting each other's shields.

A tournament was the chance for a knight to show off all his martial skills before an admiring crowd of noble ladies: the applause of common peasants was of no account even if they were allowed to watch in the first place. A tournament looked and sounded thrillingly warlike, but in reality it was no more dangerous than a game of rugby.

Asian armour

India was often invaded from the north by armies of horsemen, so cavalry (soldiers who fought on horseback) became the most important part of Indian armies. The last invaders were the Muslim Mughals who set up an empire in Delhi.

Indian soldiers wore suits of chain mail and helmets richly decorated with gold and brass. Plates of iron were added to the body and arms. Helmets were conical and pointed, like the roofs of mosques, and had adjustable nose guards. Horses and elephants were armoured, too.

Japanese warriors, or samurai, were like the medieval knights of Europe in spirit, but their armour was very different. It was lighter and more flexible than European armour, designed to absorb the shock of a blow rather than break it. A suit of armour was made of hundreds of thin strips of steel laced together with silk threads. The Japanese seemed deliberately to make their armour as complicated as possible. Each suit had dozens of parts with many different names for each of them, and there are more sorts of Japanese chain mail than from all of the rest of the world put together.

22

1300 CE As well as iron, Chinese armour was made from bronze, leather, wicker and even paper.

1640 Swallow-tailed shields were popular. The archer wears a leather coat studded with steel plates.

1400 Dogs and other animals carrying fire bombs were used to spread confusion amongst the enemy.

1100 The impressive armour of this heavy cavalryman and his horse is made of bronze scales.

1400 Thin strips of steel laced together were called lamellar armour. It was always light and flexible.

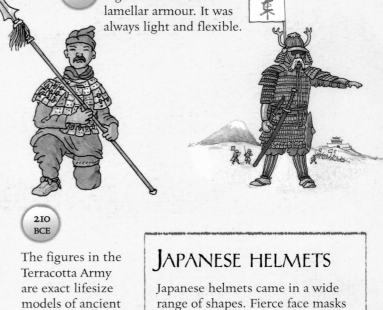

1600 More modern Japanese armour was made from larger steel plates, and was much less complicated.

210 BCE The figures in the Terracotta Army are exact lifesize models of ancient Chinese soldiers, such as this one.

JAPANESE HELMETS

Japanese helmets came in a wide range of shapes. Fierce face masks were worn to frighten the enemy as well as for protection.

1640 This soldier's armour is very simple and cheap. The string of bags round his neck contain rice.

ARMOUR IN DECLINE

As soon as handguns became widely used, armour became increasingly unpopular. It had to be made thicker to stop bullets, which made it too heavy and uncomfortable to wear. Ordinary soldiers refused to wear armour unless they were paid extra and were not made to march more than 16km a day.

It was not just guns – crossbows could also pierce armour plate – but a powerful combination of new infantry tactics and new weapons that made the knight obsolete. Swiss, German and Czech infantry learnt to fight in great squares bristling with lances, rather like the Greek phalanx. In the square were handgunners and crossbowmen who, safe amongst the spears that kept the attacking cavalry at bay, picked off the riders.

By the middle of the 16th century, armour, particularly for the infantry, was reduced to a helmet, a breastplate and a back plate with thigh protection. Men armed with muskets did not usually bother with body armour. It got in the way when they were firing, and was an extra weight to carry when added to that of their heavy gun.

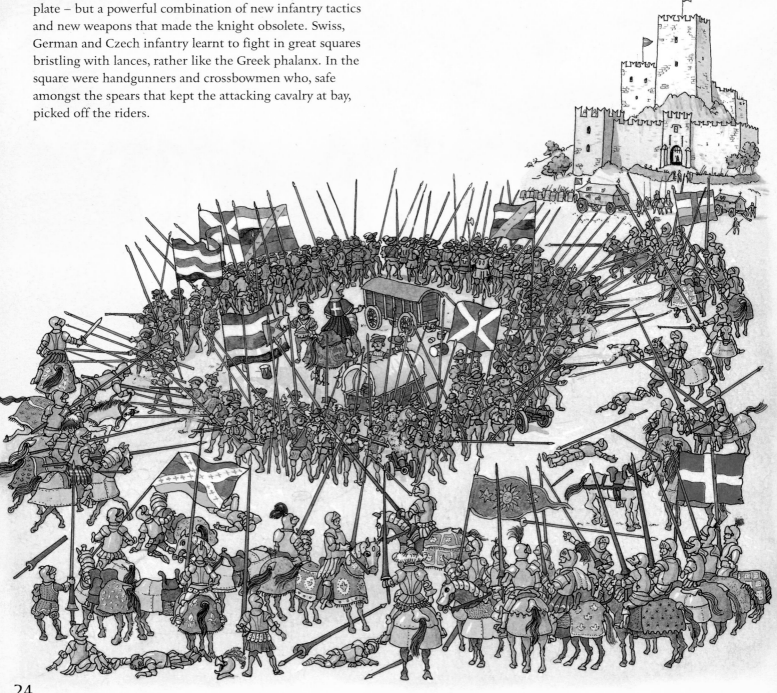

24

1670 CE Kings and generals still wore a suit of armour for their portraits, as it made them look stern and warlike.

1848 Engineers digging trenches close to a fortress wore heavy helmets right into the 19th century.

1520 German mercenary

1560 Polish officer

1600 Pikeman

1645 A Roundhead cavalry trooper of the English Civil War.

1798 Armour finally shrank to nothing more than the small steel plate at this officer's throat.

1760 Prussian cavalry wore breast and back plates, heavy boots and a hat reinforced with iron.

1861 A few officers in the American Civil War wore steel breastplates disguised as uniform waistcoats.

1815 The armour of the French cuirassiers was not much use against cannon at the Battle of Waterloo.

ARMOUR MAKES A COMEBACK

In the First World War many soldiers died of head wounds, and it was soon realized that a steel helmet could save lives. The French army was the first to have them in 1915 and all other armies soon followed. Body armour was designed too, but it was too heavy to use comfortably. In the Second World War all soldiers wore helmets, but body armour was only used by bomber crews. As the men were sitting or lying down, weight was not a problem.

1918 CE German body armour was very heavy and worn only by soldiers guarding dangerous places.

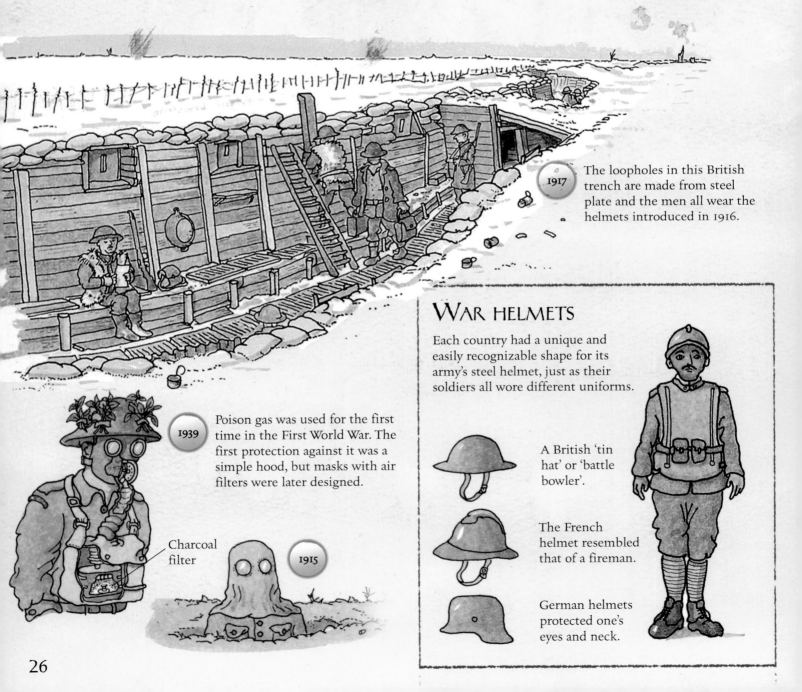

1917 The loopholes in this British trench are made from steel plate and the men all wear the helmets introduced in 1916.

1939 Poison gas was used for the first time in the First World War. The first protection against it was a simple hood, but masks with air filters were later designed.

Charcoal filter

1915

WAR HELMETS

Each country had a unique and easily recognizable shape for its army's steel helmet, just as their soldiers all wore different uniforms.

A British 'tin hat' or 'battle bowler'.

The French helmet resembled that of a fireman.

German helmets protected one's eyes and neck.

26

1918 Sailors wore gloves and hoods of flameproof fabric to protect them from the flash of an explosion.

1916 These Austrian messenger dogs in their hoods are safe from gas.

1917 This British body armour consisted of a metal plate inside felt lining, with padding behind.

1944 Gunners in American bombers wore a steel helmet and full body armour. Headphones in the helmet allowed communication with the pilot.

1940 This set of armour included a spade on the chest for extra protection and steel goggles.

1940 Bomb-aimers lay flat on the floor of the aircraft and often made improvised body armour from the hubcap of a car.

1969 Rioters in Northern Ireland threw rocks at the soldiers' unprotected ankles. They responded with armour made from baked bean tins.

27

MODERN ARMOUR

If a knight travelled from 1400 to 1900 he would have been surprised and alarmed to see that soldiers no longer wore armour. Then, if he were to resume his time travel forward another 100 years, he would be amazed to see soldiers in armour that looked remarkably like his. Armour, made from lighter materials than steel, staged a big comeback in the late 20th century. From soldiers and police to security guards, everyone is wearing it now.

Medieval and modern soldiers look similar in their helmets and body armour – only the materials are different.

Riot police wear helmets with plastic visors, body armour and flameproof overalls. Their shields are made of clear, high-impact plastic.

Police and guards at check points carry mini-shields in the form of bullet-proof clipboards.

Even community police officers have to wear knifeproof vests made from kevlar, just in case.

American soldiers in the Vietnam War were the first in modern times to wear armour in battle.

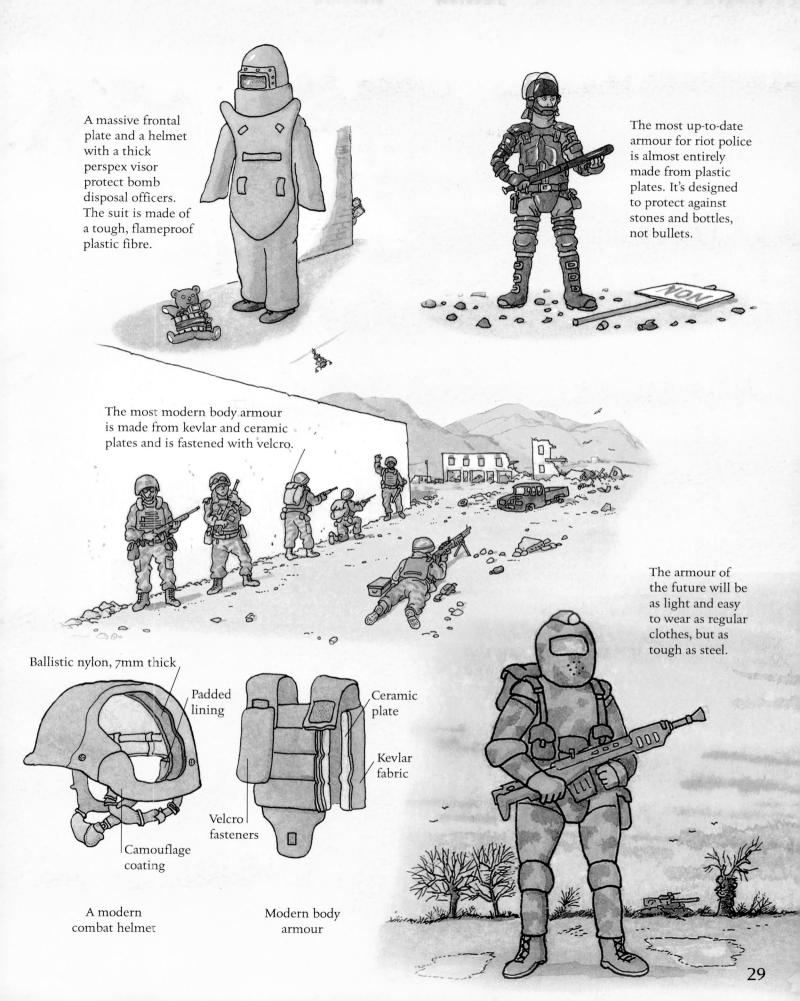

A massive frontal plate and a helmet with a thick perspex visor protect bomb disposal officers. The suit is made of a tough, flameproof plastic fibre.

The most up-to-date armour for riot police is almost entirely made from plastic plates. It's designed to protect against stones and bottles, not bullets.

The most modern body armour is made from kevlar and ceramic plates and is fastened with velcro.

The armour of the future will be as light and easy to wear as regular clothes, but as tough as steel.

Ballistic nylon, 7mm thick

Padded lining

Ceramic plate

Kevlar fabric

Velcro fasteners

Camouflage coating

A modern combat helmet

Modern body armour

29

ATHLETIC ARMOUR

All popular sports have an element of danger, and some people love dicing with death. A game with hard balls thrown at great speed is always going to be more exciting than netball, ice hockey is more exhilarating than show jumping and it is a boring motor race that does not have at least one crash. But even the most daring athlete needs some protection...

150 CE In Roman times there were many types of gladiators, each with a specific style of armour and weapons. Two similar gladiators never fought each other. The crowd liked to see two different types, pitting their individual skills against each other.

1400 The Aztecs wore padding on their elbows and waists to play a fast and dangerous game with a solid rubber ball.

Motorcyclists wear helmets and suits of leather and kevlar with high-impact plastic inserts to protect their knees, elbows, shoulders and backs.

Fencers wear face masks of stainless steel and a jacket made of closely woven nylon.

The puck in ice hockey is hard and travels very fast. The goalkeeper is padded and protected like a medieval knight.

In the Middle Ages, hunting dogs often wore leather armour with metal studs to protect them from wild boars' tusks.

A cricket ball can travel at 175km/h, so players must wear shin pads, a helmet and thick, padded gloves.

American footballers wear helmets with face guards and elaborate body armour with shoulder pads to absorb the shocks of the game.

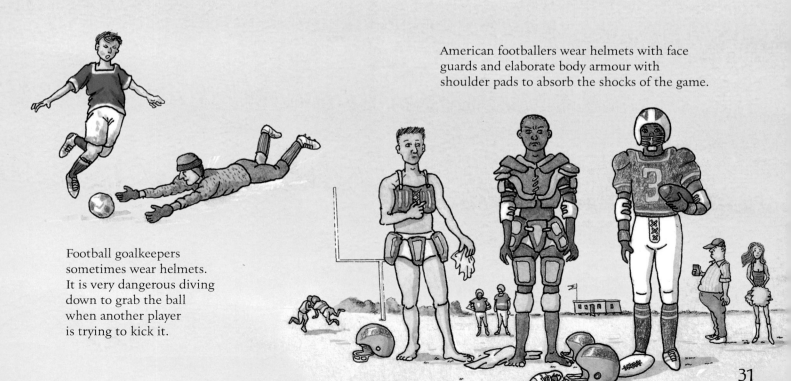

Football goalkeepers sometimes wear helmets. It is very dangerous diving down to grab the ball when another player is trying to kick it.

INDUSTRIAL ARMOUR

Industry has always been dangerous. Workers are threatened by extreme heat, poisonous fumes and falling objects. In the last 50 years, even more deadly jobs have been created. The crew of some rockets handle fuel that can dissolve them; a nuclear reactor is lethally radioactive. Specialized clothing now protects most workers in dangerous jobs. This is just as much armour as the metal suit of the knight. If there is a gap in the protection, the result is just as deadly.

Miners' helmets are made of metal, fibreglass or plastic and are usually equipped with a lamp.

Workers cutting fish or meat wear chain mail gloves and aprons as well as arm guards.

Welders must wear a smoked glass mask to protect their eyes from the intense heat and light.

Gloves made of kevlar are used by workers where there is a danger of cuts or piercing.

Workers in foundries need flameproof hoods and aprons, thick gloves and reinforced boots.

In the 19th century, shining brass helmets were popular with firemen but they were too heavy and too tall to be practical.

This inflatable radiation suit (left) was made by a tyre manufacturer. Sealed suits are used wherever there is radioactivity.

SAFETY SUITS

Space and the depths of the sea are dangerous. In space it is extremely cold, and full of deadly cosmic rays, whizzing rocks and specks of space dust. The deep sea, too, is freezing and the pressure of the water increases with depth. To walk in space you must have a very special suit, and the only way to dive comfortably is to wear armoured diving gear. At 60m down the pressure of the water is five times greater than at the surface, so a diving suit must be very strong to resist it.

1962 CE The first space suits were only designed for use inside the spacecraft, so they weren't very tough.

1990 This suit is for space walks, made of a mixture of kevlar and synthetic fabric to resist space dust.

2010 The latest space suit is made of strong plastic and metal alloys. Ball-and-socket joints allow mobility.

1800 This diving suit is made of thick, rubberized canvas. Only the brass helmet is armoured.

1920 This diving suit did not work. The water pressure at 100m collapsed the flexible limbs, making them immovable.

2005 The newest diving suits have plastic helmets and thruster motors to give them mobility. They can dive to 650m.

1865 This was the first attempt at a fully armoured diving suit, so the diver could breathe air at normal pressure.

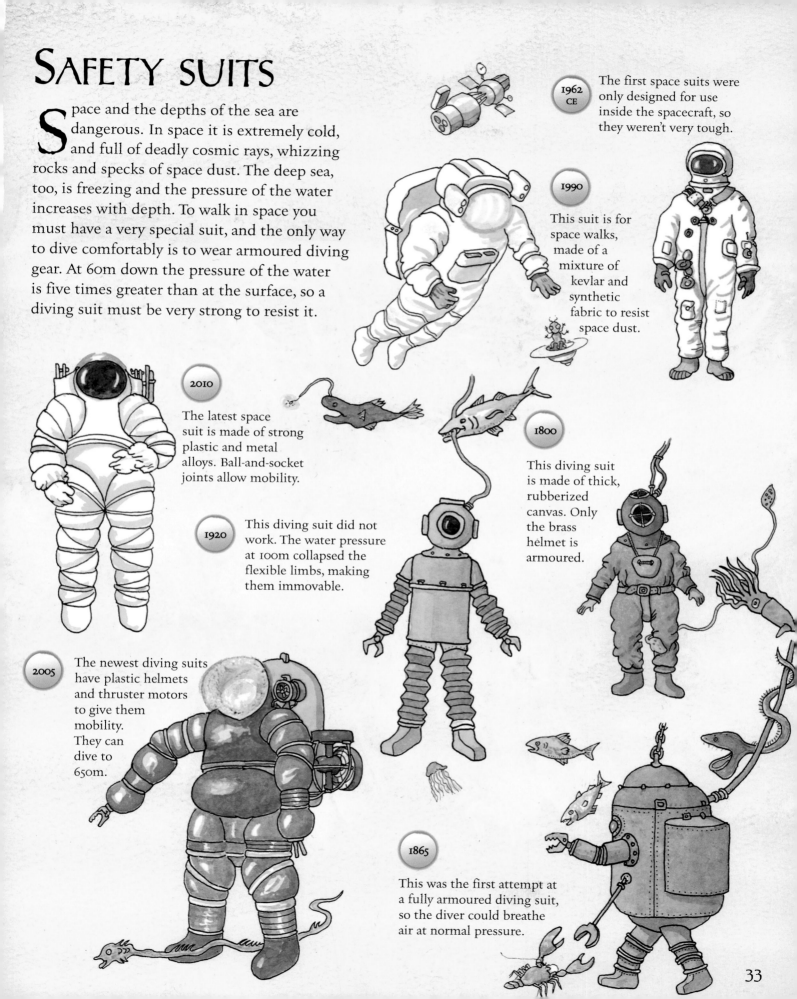

33

WAR WAGONS

Soldiers have dreamed of war chariots or armoured carts that could move about the battlefield since ancient times. The problem was always how to power them. Men weren't strong enough and horses pulling from outside could be killed. Horses inside took up too much room, and in any case weren't powerful enough to move a heavy vehicle over rough ground. It wasn't until the invention of small powerful engines 120 years ago that a true armoured fighting vehicle became possible.

100 CE

The Romans and the Greeks built siege towers to attack walled towns. Sometimes they were coated with plates made of iron or bronze.

900 BCE This battering ram was used by the Assyrians to attack cities. It was protected by leather skins and the sides were made of wicker, rather like a basket.

1425 The Hussite armies in what is now the Czech Republic would draw their war carts in a circle and chain them together to make a fortress. The carts mounted many small guns and they always defeated the knights that attacked them.

1300 This was a common sight at a siege in the Middle Ages. The battering ram hung from the roof of a shed on wheels, which was protected by strong boards covered in animal hides.

34

c.1500 Leonardo da Vinci was a great inventor as well as an artist. He drew plans for this circular war vehicle which was powered by men turning crank handles inside. It was never built, though.

1530 If you ignore the fancy dress, this is quite a sensible siege tower. It moved forward on skids by winching itself on a pulley attached to a strong post.

1560 Guido Ramelli designed this ingenious amphibious armoured car. It was powered by four men turning the paddle wheels. When it reached dry land they changed gears to turn the four land wheels.

1580 A couple of horses inside this cart pushed it forward. But they could only have pushed it forward on firm, level ground. It couldn't cross ploughed fields.

1795 The French were about to invade England. To defend the open beaches, Captain Adam Elliott proposed a land sloop, armed with a six-pounder gun, six muskets and scythes on the wheels. It could travel at 10km/h but only if the wind was blowing!

35

BIRTH OF THE TANK

Armoured carts failed because no engine could move them fast enough and their wheels sank into mud. Petrol engines and caterpillar tracks solved these problems in time for the First World War. When soldiers fought from trenches protected by barbed wire, it was impossible to cross the space between them without being hit. A bulletproof machine was needed that could crawl over the rough ground and crush the wire. The British were the first to design and send tanks into action in 1916.

1770 CE Richard Edgeworth invented the first caterpillar track. To stop thin wheels sinking into mud, the weight was spread on wooden pads.

1854 This proposed armour-plated steam locomotive was armed with eight small cannon and scythes like Boudicca's chariot.

1900 This bulletproof traction engine and wagons carried soldiers and supplies during the Boer War in South Africa. It had a top speed of 16km/h on a good road.

1902 Fred Simms built one of the first 'motor war cars'. It had armour 6mm thick, a top speed of 15km/h and three machine guns, but the British army still wasn't interested.

1903 H. G. Wells wrote a story, *The Land Ironclads*, describing huge armoured vehicles running on wheels fitted with pads. They had automatic rifles and could easily cross trenches.

1903 The first armoured cars were fine on good roads, but they were useless going cross-country.

 1904 The Russian army was one of the first to buy an armoured car, but no more were ordered because it frightened the horses.

1914 The British army was already using tractors running on caterpillar tracks to pull heavy guns.

1915 Soon a tractor was turned into an armoured vehicle. This was the very first tank, called 'Little Willie'.

1916 The British were the first to use tanks in action. They had a gun on each side and caterpillar tracks that ran over and under the body. The spoked wheels helped them to steer.

1917 Man-propelled mini-tanks seemed a good idea – on smooth ground – but the soldier's legs were dangerously exposed.

Modern tanks

When British tanks first appeared, the French and Germans quickly made their own designs. They were all crude machines that now look very odd. After the war, armies experimented with different sorts of tank. Some wanted swarms of light, fast tanks, others very heavy tanks. By 1939 the classic shape of the tank had evolved, with a single turret on an armoured hull. The only difference now is that tanks have thicker armour and bigger guns.

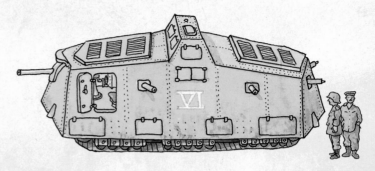

1918 CE The Germans' answer to the tank was the lumbering 32 tonne Sturmpanzerwagen with a crew of 18, six machine-guns and one small cannon. It was very slow, unable to cross ditches and so top-heavy it often fell over.

1917 France produced this clumsy tank weighing 22 tonnes and armed with a field gun and four machine guns. Its petrol/electric engine pushed it along at a crawl. It didn't fall over but got its nose stuck in ditches.

1918 The French Renault light tank weighed only 6 tonnes and was, at 10km/h, the fastest tank of the war. It carried two men and a small cannon in a revolving turret.

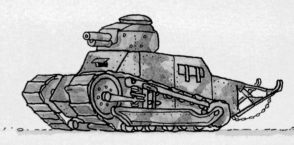

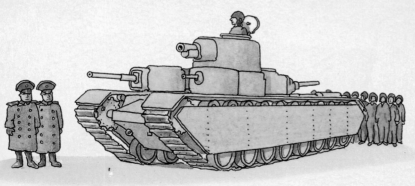

1930 This Mercedes was the first armoured car. The windows were protected by steel plates that sprang up when needed. The driver had a small vision slit; the passengers used a periscope.

1933 The Russians in the 1930s favoured very heavy battle tanks. The giant T-35 weighed 50 tonnes, had five turrets and a large crew of 11.

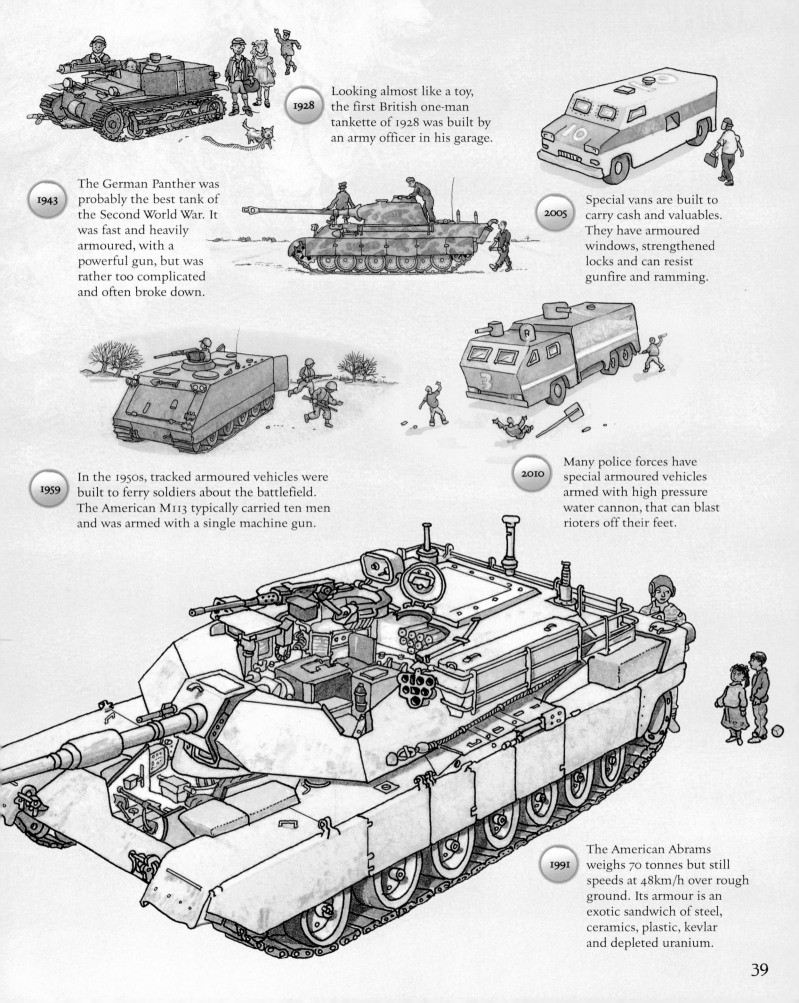

1928 Looking almost like a toy, the first British one-man tankette of 1928 was built by an army officer in his garage.

1943 The German Panther was probably the best tank of the Second World War. It was fast and heavily armoured, with a powerful gun, but was rather too complicated and often broke down.

2005 Special vans are built to carry cash and valuables. They have armoured windows, strengthened locks and can resist gunfire and ramming.

1959 In the 1950s, tracked armoured vehicles were built to ferry soldiers about the battlefield. The American M113 typically carried ten men and was armed with a single machine gun.

2010 Many police forces have special armoured vehicles armed with high pressure water cannon, that can blast rioters off their feet.

1991 The American Abrams weighs 70 tonnes but still speeds at 48km/h over rough ground. Its armour is an exotic sandwich of steel, ceramics, plastic, kevlar and depleted uranium.

ARMOURED TRAINS

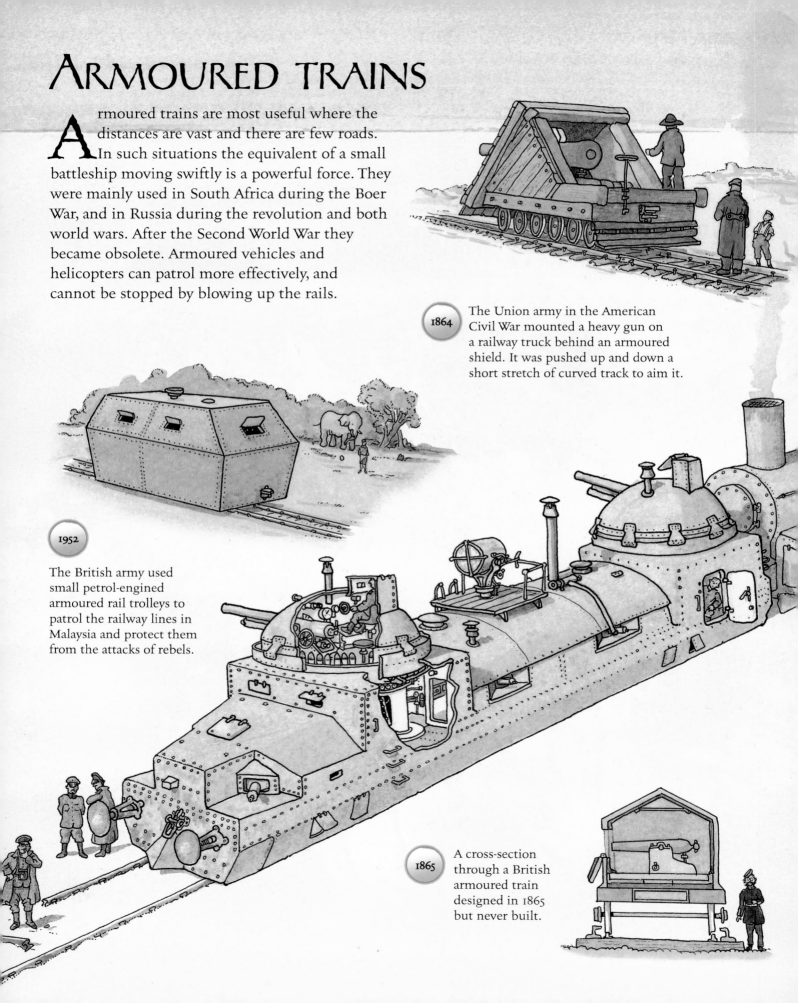

Armoured trains are most useful where the distances are vast and there are few roads. In such situations the equivalent of a small battleship moving swiftly is a powerful force. They were mainly used in South Africa during the Boer War, and in Russia during the revolution and both world wars. After the Second World War they became obsolete. Armoured vehicles and helicopters can patrol more effectively, and cannot be stopped by blowing up the rails.

1864
The Union army in the American Civil War mounted a heavy gun on a railway truck behind an armoured shield. It was pushed up and down a short stretch of curved track to aim it.

1952
The British army used small petrol-engined armoured rail trolleys to patrol the railway lines in Malaysia and protect them from the attacks of rebels.

1865
A cross-section through a British armoured train designed in 1865 but never built.

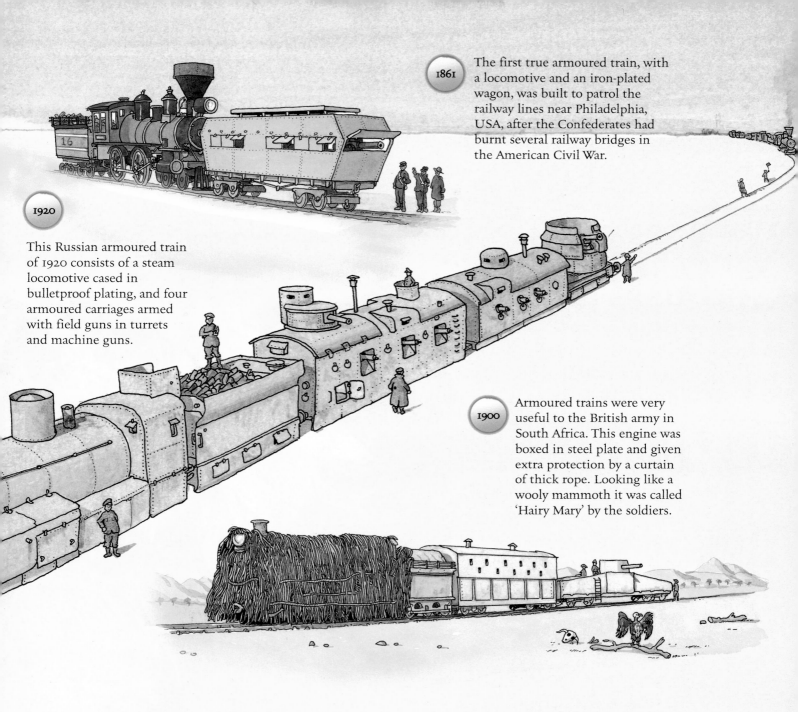

1861 The first true armoured train, with a locomotive and an iron-plated wagon, was built to patrol the railway lines near Philadelphia, USA, after the Confederates had burnt several railway bridges in the American Civil War.

1920 This Russian armoured train of 1920 consists of a steam locomotive cased in bulletproof plating, and four armoured carriages armed with field guns in turrets and machine guns.

1900 Armoured trains were very useful to the British army in South Africa. This engine was boxed in steel plate and given extra protection by a curtain of thick rope. Looking like a wooly mammoth it was called 'Hairy Mary' by the soldiers.

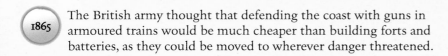

1865 The British army thought that defending the coast with guns in armoured trains would be much cheaper than building forts and batteries, as they could be moved to wherever danger threatened.

Early armoured ships

The Romans and the Chinese sometimes put iron or brass plates on their warships, but there was no urgent need for armour until guns firing explosive shells were used in the 1840s. Shells were much more dangerous than solid cannonballs, which were usually stopped by a ship's thick timbers. The solution was to fix iron plates to the hull, and the new warships built in the second half of the 19th century became known as 'ironclads'. They were too heavy to use sail power alone and all had steam engines.

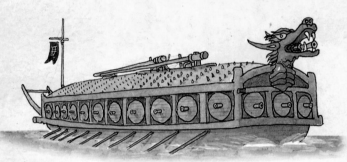

1592 The Koreans built several turtle ships to fight the Japanese. The spiked iron roof protected the crew from arrows and bullets but, most importantly, made the ship impossible to board.

1483 This fanciful floating fortress was originally drawn in 1483. The crew are armed with spears, halberds, crossbows and primitive handguns. As they are all wearing armour, they must be very confident that the ship will not be sunk.

1859 France launched the first seagoing armoured ship in 1859: the *Gloire*. She was 78m long and weighed 5,630 tonnes. Her armour was 121mm thick and she was armed with 36 guns.

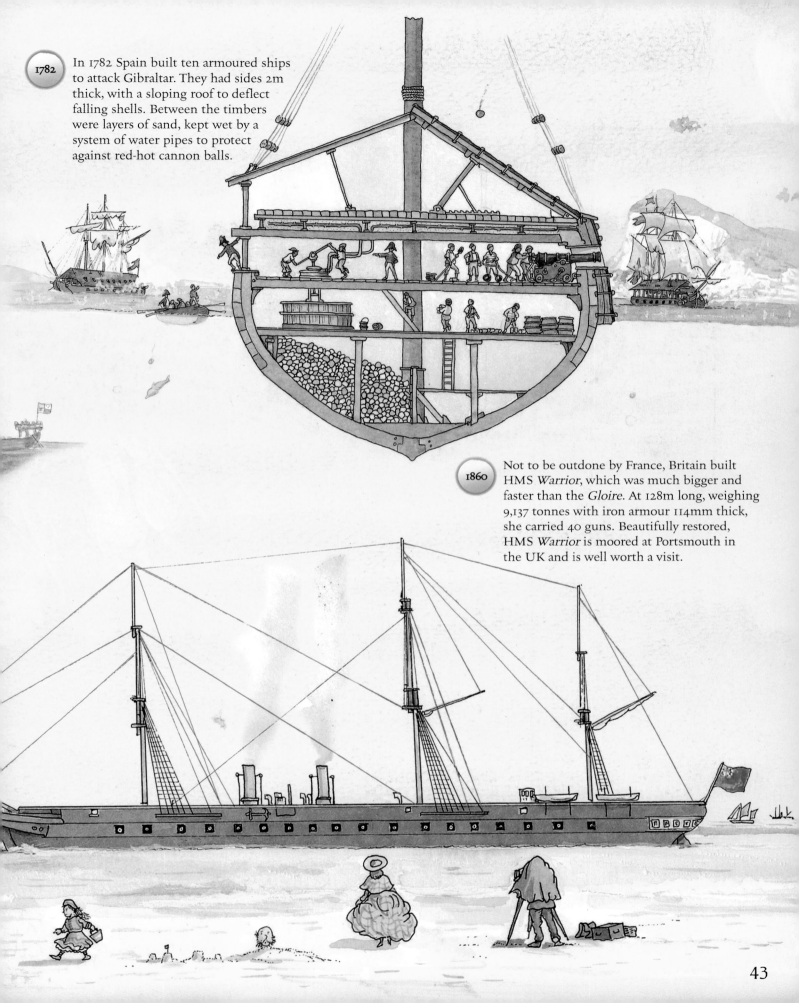

1782 In 1782 Spain built ten armoured ships to attack Gibraltar. They had sides 2m thick, with a sloping roof to deflect falling shells. Between the timbers were layers of sand, kept wet by a system of water pipes to protect against red-hot cannon balls.

1860 Not to be outdone by France, Britain built HMS *Warrior*, which was much bigger and faster than the *Gloire*. At 128m long, weighing 9,137 tonnes with iron armour 114mm thick, she carried 40 guns. Beautifully restored, HMS *Warrior* is moored at Portsmouth in the UK and is well worth a visit.

BATTLE OF THE IRONCLADS: USS MONITOR v CSS VIRGINIA

When the American Civil War began, the Union navy blockaded the Confederate coast to stop them getting supplies. The Confederates decided to build an armoured ship to destroy the wooden Union ships. They took the hull of a frigate, renamed her *Virginia*, and cut the sides down to within half a metre of the water. On the deck they built a casemate (an armoured enclosure for guns) with thick, sloping wooden sides covered with iron plates.

On 7 March 1862 the *Virginia* steamed into the estuary of Hampton Roads. The Union ships fired furiously, but their shot and shell bounced off the *Virginia* as she slowly advanced to sink two warships and force another aground.

The next day, the *Virginia* sailed out to finish off the rest of the Union fleet only to be met by another, even weirder ship. Looking like 'a cheese box on a plank', the USS *Monitor* was truly revolutionary: the first ship to mount guns in a revolving turret. The historic first battle between armoured ships lasted four hours. *Virginia* was hit 41 times and *Monitor* 21, but neither could injure the other. The fight was a draw, but the overall battle was a victory for the *Monitor* because she saved the rest of the fleet.

Grilles in the deck helped ventilation.

The first layer of 50mm-thick plates was laid vertically over the second layer rather than horizontally. The wood backing was 600mm thick.

178mm muzzle-loading rifled cannon

Steering chains

Armoured porthole cover

The engines of the *Virginia* were always breaking down and she could only steam at a speed of 6km/h. Her armour was 100mm thick and made from railway tracks that had been heated and rolled into plates.

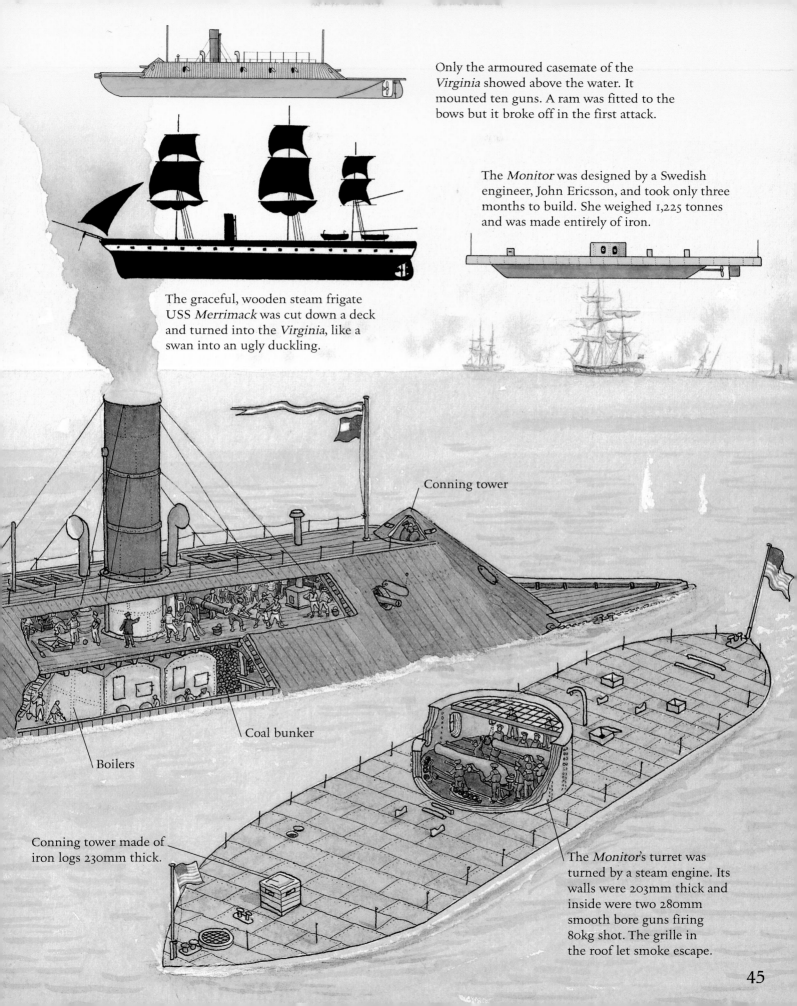

Only the armoured casemate of the *Virginia* showed above the water. It mounted ten guns. A ram was fitted to the bows but it broke off in the first attack.

The *Monitor* was designed by a Swedish engineer, John Ericsson, and took only three months to build. She weighed 1,225 tonnes and was made entirely of iron.

The graceful, wooden steam frigate USS *Merrimack* was cut down a deck and turned into the *Virginia*, like a swan into an ugly duckling.

Conning tower

Coal bunker

Boilers

Conning tower made of iron logs 230mm thick.

The *Monitor*'s turret was turned by a steam engine. Its walls were 203mm thick and inside were two 280mm smooth bore guns firing 80kg shot. The grille in the roof let smoke escape.

45

MODERN BATTLESHIPS

The first ironclads mounted their guns in rows along the sides or in turrets. It was not obvious which was best. The rest of the 19th century was a time of experimentation, and many odd designs were tried out until the turret was accepted. Although all battleships were powered by steam, most carried sails until the 1890s. The classic modern battleship of the last century carried enormous guns in three or four turrets, with armour up to 400mm thick.

0   50m

1865
The turret ship *Huascar* was built in Britain for Peru. She was captured by Chile in 1879 and still survives as a museum ship.

1867
The German *Kronprinz* was a typical broadside ironclad of the 1860s, with sails and a ram bow. She had armour 127mm thick and carried 16 guns.

1872
The Royal Navy's *Thunderer* was the first battleship without sails. She carried four 305mm guns in two turrets. There was a terrible accident aboard when a gun was loaded twice by mistake and exploded.

0   50m

0   50m

1944
USS *Missouri*, 1944, was the fastest ever battleship with a speed of 61km/h. She carried nine 406mm guns and last saw action in the Gulf War of 1991 before retiring the following year.

0   50m

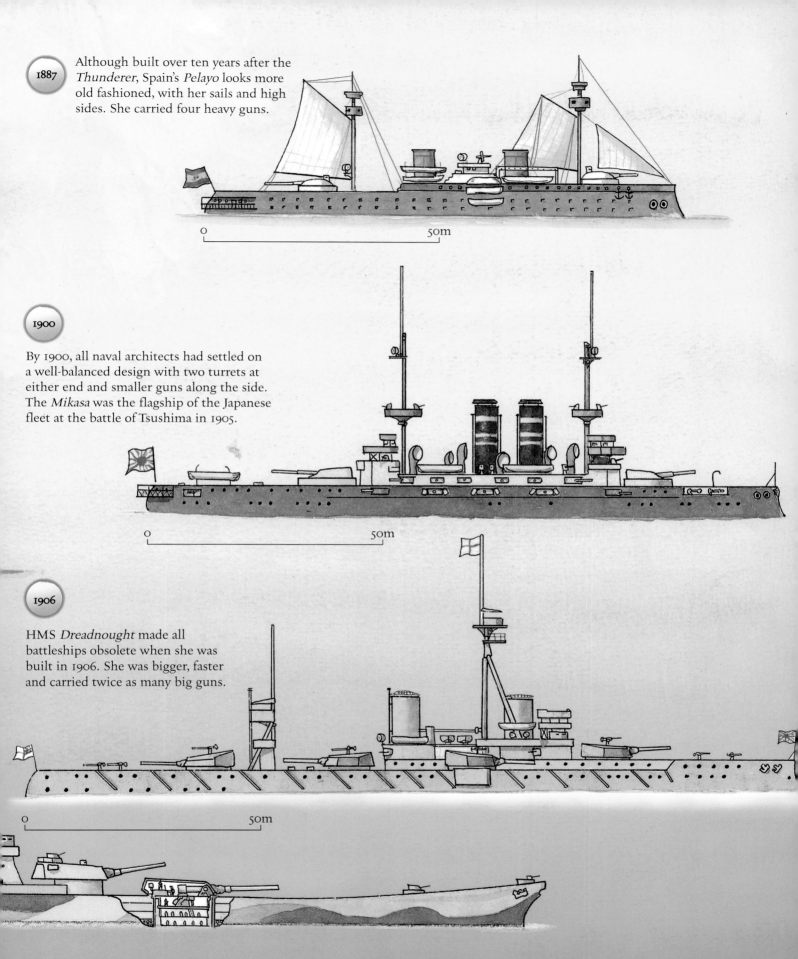

1887 Although built over ten years after the *Thunderer*, Spain's *Pelayo* looks more old fashioned, with her sails and high sides. She carried four heavy guns.

0   50m

1900

By 1900, all naval architects had settled on a well-balanced design with two turrets at either end and smaller guns along the side. The *Mikasa* was the flagship of the Japanese fleet at the battle of Tsushima in 1905.

0   50m

1906

HMS *Dreadnought* made all battleships obsolete when she was built in 1906. She was bigger, faster and carried twice as many big guns.

0   50m

DEEP-SEA DIVING VESSELS

Some of the most heavily armoured ships are not protected against the sudden blow of a shell but from the slow, steady, terrible crushing pressure of the depths of the sea. Water is very heavy, and the deeper an object sinks the greater the pressure on it. Thousands of metres down, tonnes press on every square centimetre. A vessel designed to explore the still-mysterious ocean deeps has to be immensely strong.

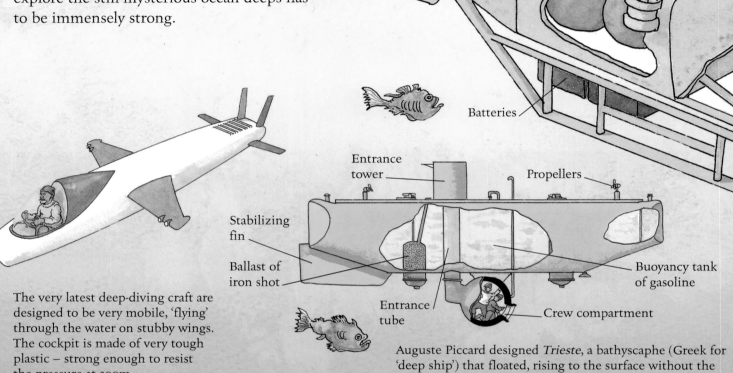

Thruster

Ballast spheres

Batteries

Entrance tower

Propellers

Stabilizing fin

Ballast of iron shot

Buoyancy tank of gasoline

Entrance tube

Crew compartment

The very latest deep-diving craft are designed to be very mobile, 'flying' through the water on stubby wings. The cockpit is made of very tough plastic – strong enough to resist the pressure at 300m.

Auguste Piccard designed *Trieste*, a bathyscaphe (Greek for 'deep ship') that floated, rising to the surface without the need for a heavy cable, and with propellers so it could move.

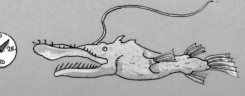

As the submarine sinks deeper the pressure increases and, once beyond the safe limit, something will give way and water will cascade in. But once the submarine is full of water, the pressure will equalize and, however deep it sinks, it will not be squashed any further.

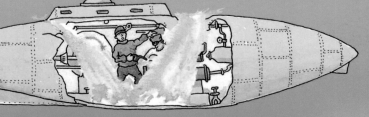

A submarine is safe as long as it doesn't go below its designated safe depth. That depth depends on the strength of the hull.

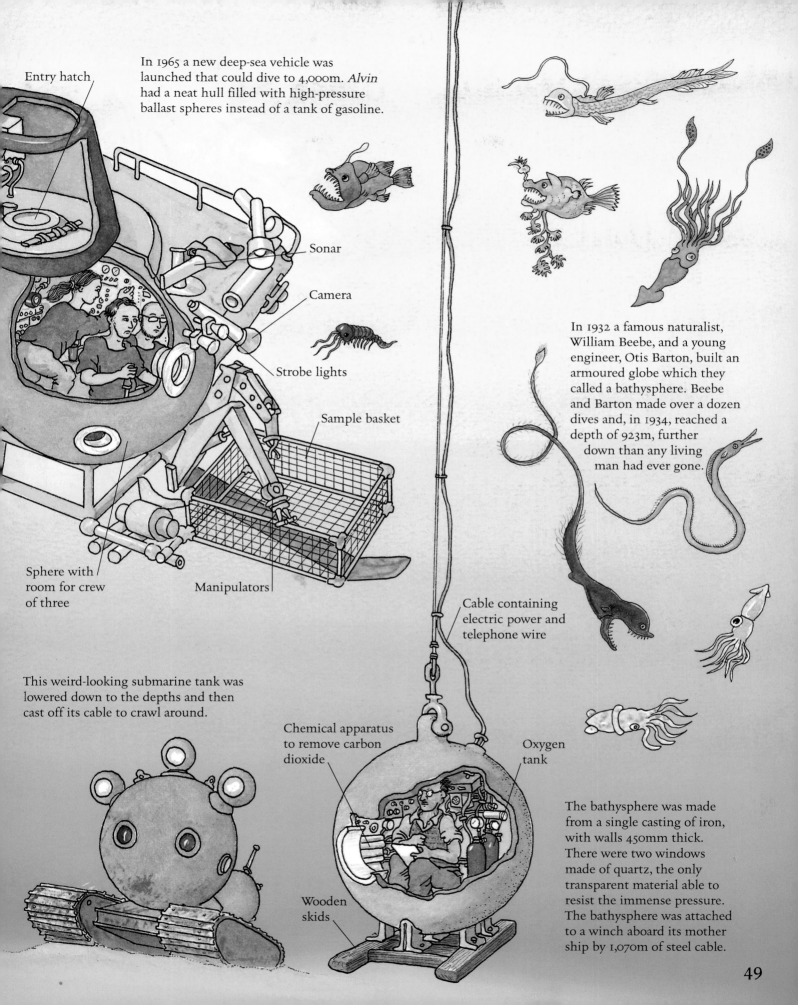

Entry hatch

In 1965 a new deep-sea vehicle was launched that could dive to 4,000m. *Alvin* had a neat hull filled with high-pressure ballast spheres instead of a tank of gasoline.

Sonar

Camera

Strobe lights

Sample basket

Sphere with room for crew of three

Manipulators

This weird-looking submarine tank was lowered down to the depths and then cast off its cable to crawl around.

In 1932 a famous naturalist, William Beebe, and a young engineer, Otis Barton, built an armoured globe which they called a bathysphere. Beebe and Barton made over a dozen dives and, in 1934, reached a depth of 923m, further down than any living man had ever gone.

Cable containing electric power and telephone wire

Chemical apparatus to remove carbon dioxide

Oxygen tank

Wooden skids

The bathysphere was made from a single casting of iron, with walls 450mm thick. There were two windows made of quartz, the only transparent material able to resist the immense pressure. The bathysphere was attached to a winch aboard its mother ship by 1,070m of steel cable.

49

ARMOURED PLANES

During the First World War, aircraft started flying low to attack targets on the ground. Many were shot down, so designers produced rugged metal planes fitted with armour. Many Second World War fighters had armour around the cockpit and bombers had armoured seats for the pilots. Today, jets fly so fast that armour is unnecessary except for ground attack aircraft. The danger to passenger planes is more often from inside. Flight deck doors have strong locks and strengthened luggage containers lessen the damage caused by a bomb smuggled into a suitcase.

1918
The German Junkers J-4 was the first all-metal biplane. The crew, engine and petrol tank were all protected by sheets of 5mm armour.

1974
The A-10 Thunderbolt was designed to fight Russian tanks. It has a 30mm anti-tank gun in the nose and the pilot sits in a bath of thick, light and tough titanium armour.

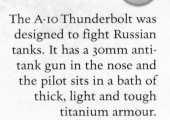

1941
The Russian Stormovik's nickname was 'The Flying Tank' because it was so heavily armoured. They flew close to the ground and destroyed thousands of German vehicles in the Second World War.

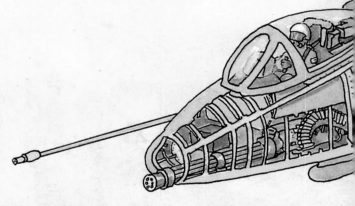

2010
Attack and troop-carrying helicopters have to fly low and slowly over the battlefield, so they are protected around the cockpit and engine with lightweight plastic and ceramic armour.

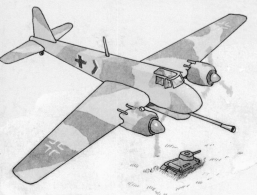

1942
The windscreen of the German Henschel Hs 129 was 75mm thick, and the cockpit was armour-plated. Its huge 75mm gun was deadly to Russian tanks.

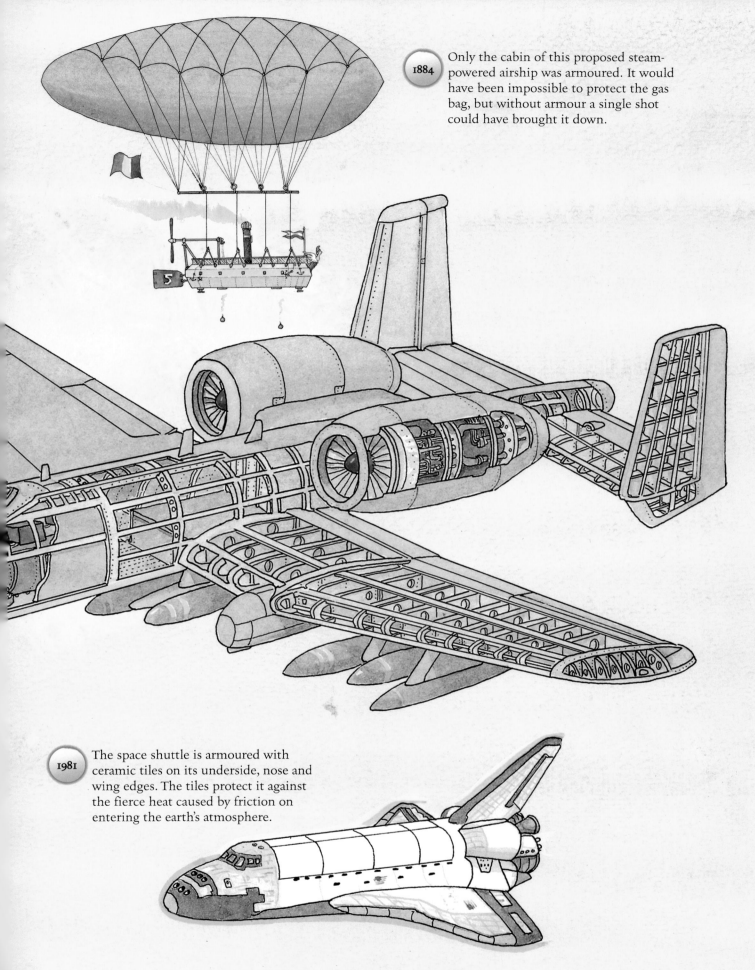

Only the cabin of this proposed steam-powered airship was armoured. It would have been impossible to protect the gas bag, but without armour a single shot could have brought it down.

1981 The space shuttle is armoured with ceramic tiles on its underside, nose and wing edges. The tiles protect it against the fierce heat caused by friction on entering the earth's atmosphere.

ARMOURED BUILDINGS

Doors and windows are the weakest point in any building. Since early times doors have been strengthened with bolts, and windows covered by bars. In modern cities many homes and offices have security grilles over their doors and windows. Some have armoured shutters and even bulletproof windows. The Oval Office of the US president has windows able to withstand a small missile.

This medieval door has its thick timbers bound with iron straps. A tiny barred window allows the doorkeeper to see who's knocking.

In warm countries, downstairs windows were covered by iron grilles so the house could be open to the air but not robbers or, in this picture, would-be suitors.

The strongest and heaviest doors are found in bank vaults, safes and strong rooms. Designed to resist attack by explosives and heat cutters, they have very complicated locks.

The 'Impregnable Iron Fortress', designed in England in 1860, had walls of iron blocks dovetailed together with portholes for 70 cannon. Three were proposed to guard the Thames estuary but were never built.

Some German forts were built with walls made from large iron plates. These were assembled like giant pieces of flat-pack furniture.

This Russian fort was built in 1897 to protect the entrance to Saint Petersburg harbour. The front wall is made of iron plate.

In 1940 Britain feared invasion by the German army from across the English Channel, and thousands of concrete pillboxes and gun batteries were quickly built. A cheap alternative was this small steel turret. Its machine gun could fire from the roof against aircraft or from the front against troops and tanks.

In the Second World War, railway workers and sentries were often caught out in an air-raid and needed to find shelter quickly. Steel one-man shelters like this were quick and simple to install and could be moved easily. Anyone inside was safe from everything except a direct hit.

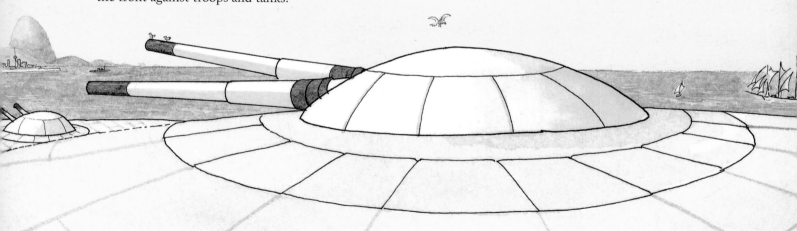

Fort Copacabana was built in 1914 to defend the entrance to Rio de Janeiro harbour, Brazil. All that can be seen is the concrete roof and the two gun turrets.

IRON ISLAND

This extraordinary iron fort sits in the sea a couple of kilometres away from Portsmouth, in England. It cost a fortune, took nearly 20 years to finish and never fired its guns at an enemy. So why was it built?

More than 150 years ago, cannon had a very short range. They could not hit anything much more than a kilometre away. This was a big problem for the army, who wanted to defend the approach to Portsmouth, which was Britain's most important naval base.

It was nearly 6.5km from Portsmouth across the stretch of water called the Solent to the Isle of Wight. Any ship sailing down the middle of the Solent would be quite safe; no gun on land could hit it. If only there was another island in the Solent, dreamed the army. Then, ingenious Victorian engineers solved the problem and built artificial islands in the sea with a fort on each. Work started in 1861.

Crane for lifting supplies

Winch

Small crane

Landing stage

The biggest of the forts was called No Man's Land. It was completely circular and armed with 49 heavy guns. The bottom floors were made of hard granite, but the top two storeys were built of iron. The outside wall was a sandwich of armour plate and especially hard iron concrete 400mm thick. The fort's skin weighed 2,500 tonnes, probably the heaviest suit of armour ever made. And probably the most expensive: the fort cost the enormous sum (in those days) of around half a million pounds.

It was painted in a chequered pattern of black and yellow squares, with a lighthouse on top to warn ships. The fort had its own bakery and fresh water from a well. The garrison of 300 soldiers exercised by running around the roof, swimming and hauling the heavy shells to the guns.

But almost as soon as the fort was finished, new guns were invented that could fire up to 16km, and No Man's Land was rendered useless.

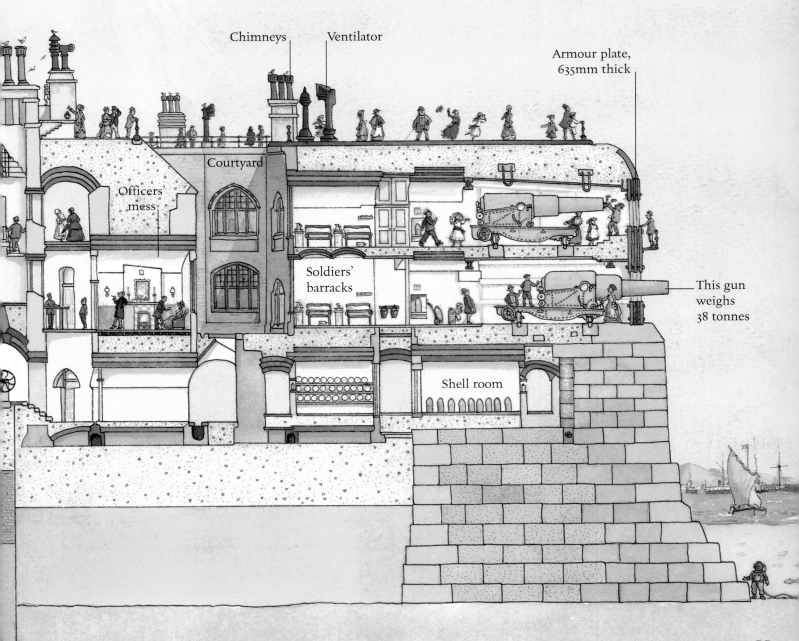

Chimneys   Ventilator

Armour plate, 635mm thick

Officers' mess

Courtyard

Soldiers' barracks

This gun weighs 38 tonnes

Shell room

FORTS ON LAND

In the late 19th century, guns firing high explosive shells forced a redesign of all forts on land. The new underground forts were made of concrete and covered with earth. All the guns were in armoured turrets that could fire in any direction, so a fort needed fewer guns to cover the same area and the guns were completely protected. All that could be seen from a distance was a low mound with a few metal domes showing above the grass.

In the 1930s, the French built a chain of forts called the Maginot Line to defend the border with Germany. All that was visible above ground were gun turrets that popped up to fire, and steel lookout and machine gun turrets like this. Underneath was virtually a small town, with stores, barracks, a power station and even an underground railway.

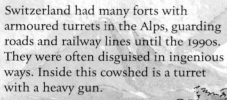

Switzerland had many forts with armoured turrets in the Alps, guarding roads and railway lines until the 1990s. They were often disguised in ingenious ways. Inside this cowshed is a turret with a heavy gun.

During the Second World War, the Japanese used small steel pillboxes to defend islands in the Pacific. They were light enough to be moved to wherever they were needed.

These mobile armoured turrets were used in the fortifications of Romania. The wheels were only used to move them to a prepared position.

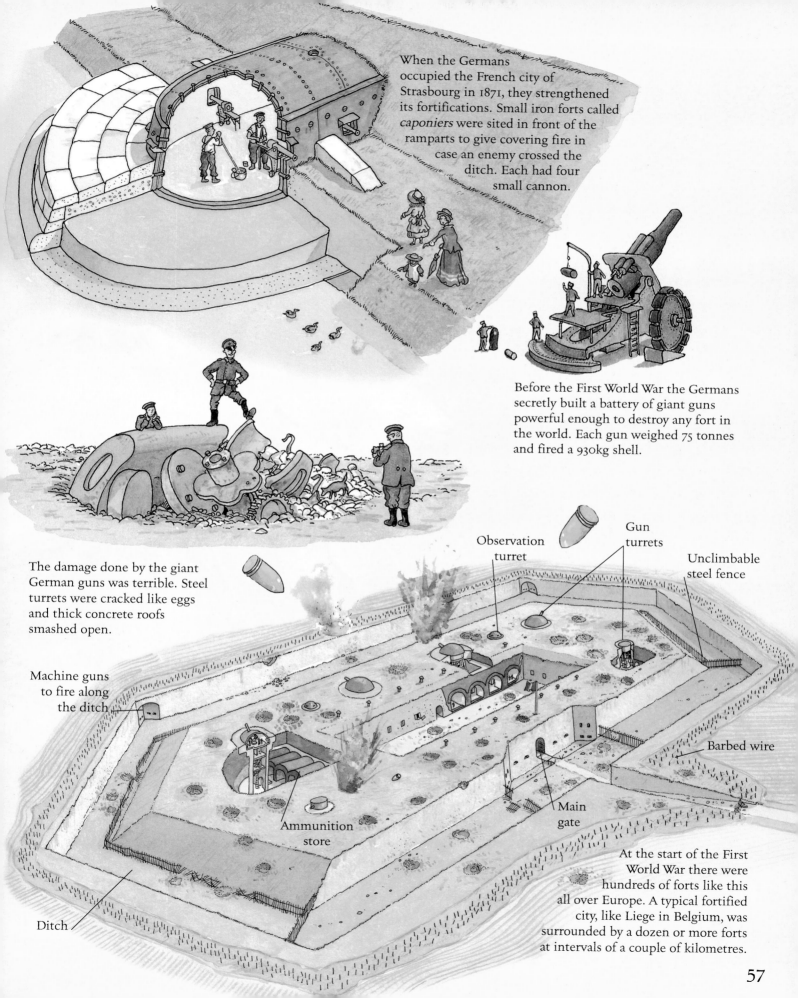

When the Germans occupied the French city of Strasbourg in 1871, they strengthened its fortifications. Small iron forts called *caponiers* were sited in front of the ramparts to give covering fire in case an enemy crossed the ditch. Each had four small cannon.

Before the First World War the Germans secretly built a battery of giant guns powerful enough to destroy any fort in the world. Each gun weighed 75 tonnes and fired a 930kg shell.

The damage done by the giant German guns was terrible. Steel turrets were cracked like eggs and thick concrete roofs smashed open.

Observation turret

Gun turrets

Unclimbable steel fence

Machine guns to fire along the ditch

Barbed wire

Ammunition store

Main gate

Ditch

At the start of the First World War there were hundreds of forts like this all over Europe. A typical fortified city, like Liege in Belgium, was surrounded by a dozen or more forts at intervals of a couple of kilometres.

MAGIC ARMOUR

Every warrior's dream was for some magic defence; an invisible layer that would deflect arrows and sword cuts and make him invulnerable. That sort of magic only exists in legends of gods and heroes, but soldiers have always gone into battle hoping to be kept safe by heavenly means as well as earthly. Spells and prayers have always been recited over armour to give it extra strength and, even today, priests sprinkle modern battle tanks with holy water.

Most armour was blessed in the Middle Ages. Some armour had a holy relic fixed to it in the pious hope that the saints would make extra efforts to protect the wearer.

When Achilles, the Greek hero of the Trojan Wars, was a baby, his mother dipped him into the magic waters of the River Styx so that no weapon could ever harm him. Unfortunately she forgot about his heel, which she held as she dunked him. It was here that he was later hit by an arrow and killed.

Some Celtic warriors fought naked to show how brave they were. They painted their bodies with blue woad in magic patterns, in the belief that this would protect them.

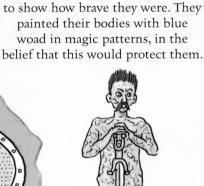

Native American warriors who had taken part in a special religious ceremony – the Ghost Dance – wore a buckskin shirt decorated with magic symbols. Unfortunately it was no use at all against the bullets of the US cavalry.

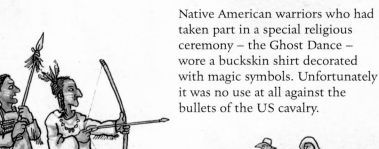

Dervishes, the followers of the Mahdi (a spiritual leader) in the Sudan, wore quilted cotton robes called *jibbahs*. They believed the special cotton patches and their faith would keep them safe from bullets. They were wrong.

PRIVATE ARMOUR

Armour is not just for soldiers. Anybody who feels in danger wants to be protected, but steel armour is too heavy and can't be worn with ordinary clothes. Bulletproof vests made out of silk and cotton were developed in the late 1800s and were surprisingly effective. Politicians and royalty who feared assassination were eager to buy them.

John Bradshaw, the judge at King Charles I of England's trial, was so frightened of being shot by an angry royalist that he wore a hat reinforced with iron and a breastplate under his robes.

Ned Kelly and his gang of Australian bandits wore suits of armour made from plough blades. They were bulletproof but did not cover the legs, so that was where the police shot Kelly.

The 1920s were a violent time in some American cities. Gangsters and private detectives were the best customers for bulletproof vests.

These stylish steel spectacles were on sale at the beginning of the Second World War.

As the threat of war loomed in 1938, this armoured gas-proof pram went on sale. Very few were bought because, unsurprisingly, nobody wanted to take their baby out in an air-raid.

Mums worried by the threat of drive-by shootings on the mean streets of the USA can keep their baby safe in this armoured buggy, guaranteed proof against machine gun bullets.

GLOSSARY

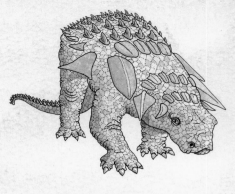

amphibious Having the ability to move equally well on land and water. Amphibious vehicles have been around since the 16th century.

Assyria A fierce and warlike power that dominated the Middle East from 900–600BCE.

ball and socket joint A flexible joint formed by one part ending in a ball and the other in a curved socket to hold the ball. A natural version of this is where the leg joins the hip.

brass A metal made from mixing copper with zinc. Copper is a very soft metal and zinc makes it harder.

breech-loading Loading a gun from the breech, or opposite end from the muzzle. This method is easier, faster and safer than muzzle-loading.

bronze A metal made from copper and tin.

cast iron When iron melts, it can be formed or cast into almost any shape by being poured into a mould.

ceramic A material made from non-metallic elements by the application of heat, such as a tile, a brick or a pot. Ceramic plates can be very strong and are lighter than metal ones.

Confederate In 1861, the 11 southern states of the USA split from the northern states to form their own country, which they called the Confederate States of America. This led to a civil war between the Confederates and the remaining states, who were known as the Federals, or the Union. The Confederates were defeated in 1865 and rejoined the USA.

cuirass Armour protecting the upper body, consisting of a breast and back plate.

cuirassier A cavalryman wearing a cuirass and helmet.

cupola A small, rounded dome on a fort used either for observation or to protect guns.

Dayak A group of tribes who live by the rivers in Borneo and Sarawak, in Malaysia. They used to be famous for headhunting.

depleted uranium A very dense metal – almost twice as heavy as lead – that is used to make armour and bullets.

fibreglass A metal made from glass spun into fine threads. Mixed with plastic resin, it makes a strong material that is easily moulded into shape.

gauntlet A heavy glove of leather or steel.

halberd A fearsome weapon with a combined axe blade, spear and hook mounted on the end of a long pole.

Hittite An appropriate name for the fierce and warlike people who were the dominant power in what is now Turkey from 1750–1200BCE.

Hussites The followers of the religious leader Jan Huss (c.1369–1415) in what is now the Czech Republic. They wanted their own national church and fought for many years against the armies of the German Emperor, who wanted to make them part of the Roman Catholic Church.

ironclad The first armoured ships were actually wooden ships with an outer layer of iron plate, hence the name 'ironclad'. Later all armoured ship were called ironclads even though they were built of, and armoured with, steel.

kevlar A very strong synthetic material made from spun plastic fibres. It is woven into sheets to make modern body armour and protective clothing.

loophole A narrow slit window in a castle or fort from which bows or guns are fired.

muzzle The dangerous end of a gun from which the bullet emerges.

muzzle-loading A cannon that is loaded from the end of the muzzle. This is always a slower process than breech-loading.

pike A very long spear.

red-hot shot Solid cannon balls heated in a furnace then fired at wooden ships to set them ablaze.

rifled cannon A cannon with twisting grooves cut inside the barrel. These spin the shell as it is fired to make it go further and with greater accuracy.

rubberized Describes materials such as cloth or canvas that have been treated with a rubber solution to make them waterproof.

shell A projectile filled with explosive. At first they were round like solid cannon balls, but those fired from rifled cannon were cylinders with a pointed end.

sloop A small sailing ship with a single mast.

smooth bore A cannon with no grooves inside the barrel.

sonar SOund Navigation And Ranging – a machine that sends out sound waves to measure the depth of water or detect obstacles and other vessels.

steel An alloy or mixture of mainly iron, with a tiny amount of carbon to add strength. It is much stronger and more flexible than pure iron.

strobe A very bright light flashing at a regular frequency, e.g. 50 times a second.

Sumerian Sumer was the first civilization where people lived in cities. It flourished in Mesopotamia or what is now modern Iraq from about 3000–1900BCE.

synthetic An artificial material made by putting together separate elements. Rubber is a natural material produced by trees, but synthetic rubber can be made from chemicals.

titanium A metal that is much stronger than steel but weighs only half as much.

Union During the American Civil War the northern states were known as the Union, as they were still part of the United States of America.

visor The moveable part of a helmet covering the face.

wrought iron Iron is wrought when hammered into shape while red hot – think of a blacksmith shaping a horseshoe – rather than melted and poured into a mould.

61

FURTHER INFORMATION

Where to see armour

Many museums have small collections of armour or the odd piece, but those listed here are some of the very best, with beautiful examples of the armourers' skill. Many museums hold regular events with mock fights and tournaments, and some even let you try on the armour.

Austria
The Armoury of the State of Styria, Graz (www.zeughaus.at)
Art History Museum, Vienna (www.khm.at)

Belgium
Army and Military History Museum, Brussels (www.klm-mra.be)

Canada
The Royal Ontario Museum, Toronto (http://images.rom.on.ca/public/index.php?function=browse&action=selected&tbl=aa&filter=aa_cat&fid=1&sid=&ccid=)

Denmark
The Royal Arsenal Museum, Copenhagen (www.thm.dk)

France
Army Museum, Les Invalides, Paris (www.invalides.org)

Germany
The Baden State Museum, Karlsruhe (www.landesmuseum.de/website)
The Bavarian National Museum, Munich (www.bayerisches-nationalmuseum.de)
The Bavarian Army Museum, Ingoldstadt (www.bayerisches-armeemuseum.de)
The Imperial Castle, Nuremberg (www.schloesser.bayern.de/englisch/palace/objects/nbg_burg.htm)

Italy
Churburg Castle, Churburg (www.churburg.com/willkommen_engl/index.html)
Bargello, Florence (www.polomuseale.firenze.it/english/musei/bargello)
Royal Armoury, Turin (www.artito.arti.beniculturali.it/Armeria%20Reale/DefaultArmeria.htm)

Japan
National Museum, Tokyo (www.tnm.go.jp)

The Netherlands
Army Museum, Delft (www.armymuseum.nl)

Russia
Kremlin Museum, Moscow (www.kreml.ru/en/main/museums/)
State Hermitage Museum, St Petersburg (www.hermitagemuseum.org)

Spain
Royal Armoury, Madrid (www.patrimonionacional.es/Home/Palacios-Reales/Palacio-Real-de-Madrid.aspx)

Sweden
The Royal Armoury, Stockholm (www.livrustkammaren.se)

Switzerland
National Museum, Zurich (www.musee-suisse.com)
Museum of History, Berne (www.bhm.ch)

UK
Fitzwilliam Museum, Cambridge (www.fitzmuseum.cam.ac.uk)
Art Gallery and Museum, Glasgow (www.glasgowmuseums.com)
Royal Armouries, Leeds (www.royalarmouries.org)
British Museum, London (www.britishmuseum.org/default.aspx)
National Army Museum, London (www.national-army-museum.ac.uk)
Tower of London, London (www.hrp.org.uk/TowerOfLondon)
The Wallace Collection, London (www.wallacecollection.org)
Victoria and Albert Museum, London (www.vam.ac.uk)
Warwick Castle, Warwick (www.warwick-castle.co.uk)

USA
The Art Institute of Chicago, Chicago (www.artic.edu/aic)
Museum of Art, Cleveland (www.clemusart.com)
Metropolitan Museum of Art, New York (www.metmuseum.org)
The Higgins Armory Museum, Worcester (www.higgins.org)

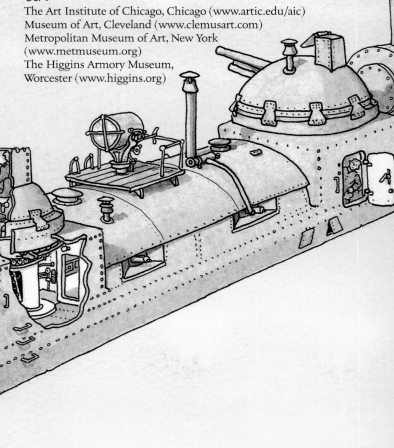

Where to see amoured ships

From 1860 to 1944, hundreds of armoured warships were built but hardly more than a dozen have been preserved. The USA has the most, but Britain has the oldest, HMS *Warrior*, still afloat at Portsmouth.

Chile
Huascar (1865), Talcahuano (www.oz.net/markhow/pre-dred/huascar.htm)

Greece
Georgios Averoff (1910), Faliron, Athens (www.bsaverof.com)

Japan
HIJMS *Mikasa* (1902), Yokosuka
(www.midwaysailor.com/mikasa/index.html)

The Netherlands
HNLMS *Schorpioen* (1868), The Dutch Navy Museum, Den Helder
(www.hnsa.org/ships/schorpioen.htm)
HNMLS *Buffel* (1868), Maritime Museum, Rotterdam
(www.hnsa.org/ships/buffel.htm)

UK
HMS *Warrior* (1860), Portsmouth (www.hmswarrior.org)

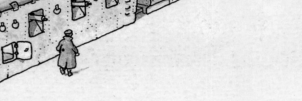

USA
USS *Olympia* (1895), Independence Seaport Museum, Philadelphia
(www.phillyseaport.org/ships_olympia.shtml)
USS *Texas* (1910), Houston, Texas (www.usstexasbb35.com)
USS *North Carolina* (1940), Wilmington, North Carolina
(www.battleshipnc.com)
USS *Massachusetts* (1942), Fall River, Massachusetts
(www.battleshipcove.org)
USS *Alabama* (1942), Mobile, Alabama (www.ussalabama.com)
USS *New Jersey* (1942), Camden, New Jersey
(www.battleshipnewjersey.org)
USS *Missouri* (1944), Pearl Harbor, Hawaii (www.ussmissouri.com)

Where to see tanks
Austria
Museum of Military History, Vienna (www.hgm.or.at/eng)

France
Museum of Armoured Vehicles, Saumur (www.museedesblindes.fr)

Germany
German Tank Museum, Munster (www.germantankmuseum.de)

Israel
Israeli Tank Museum, Latrun (www.yadlashiryon.com)

Russia
Kubinka Tank Museum, Moscow
(www.kubinka.ru/newindex.php?id=3&lang=2)

UK
Bovington Tank Museum, Dorset (www.tankmuseum.org)
The Imperial War Museum, London (http://london.iwm.org.uk)

USA
US Army Ordnance Museum, Aberdeen Proving Ground, Maryland
(www.peachmountain.com/5star/US_Army_Ordnance_Museum.aspx)

Where to see amoured trains
Finland
The Armour Museum, Parola (www.panssarimuseo.fi/nayttelyt.html)

Russia
Kubinka Tank Museum, Moscow (www.tankmuseum.ru/train4.html)

Where to see amoured forts
Belgium
Fort Loncin, Liege (www.palmerstonforts.org.uk/gall/loncin.php)
Fort Eben-Emael, near Maastricht (www.fort-eben-emael.be/home.php)

Brazil
Fort Copacabana, Rio de Janeiro (www.fortedecopacabana.com)

Finland
Fort Kuivasaari, Helsinki (www.nortfort.ru/coastal/foto_kvs3_e.html)

France
Fort de Fermont, near Longwy (www.ligne-maginot-fort-de-fermont.asso.fr/)
Fort du Hackenberg, near Thionville (www.maginot-hackenberg.com)

Italy
Fort Montecchio, Colic, Lake Como (www.fortemontecchionord.it)

Switzerland
Fort Verein-Magletsch, Oberschan (www.afom.ch)
Fort Airolo, St Gotthard (www.unterirdischeschweiz.ch/10001s.html)

INDEX

A
American Civil
 War 25, 40, 44–5
ancient armour 13
animals 5, 10–11
armourers 18–19
Asia 22–3
athletic armour 30–1
atmosphere 6–7

B
battles 20, 34–7
battleships 35, 42–7
birds 11
body armour 12, 14,
 24, 26–9, 59
Boer War 36, 40, 41
bomb disposal 29
buildings 52–3

C
Celts 14, 58
chain mail 19
coastal defence 8–9
cricketers 31
crusaders 16

D
Dark Ages 16–17
diving suits 33
dogs 23, 27, 31

E
English Civil War 25

F
fencers 31
First World War 26,
 36, 50, 57
fish 10
forts 54–7
Franks 16

G
Goliath 13
Goths 16
Greeks 14, 34, 58

H
helicopters 50
helmets 4, 12–14,
 26, 29, 31–3
horses 17, 21, 23
Hussites 5, 34

I
India 22–3
industrial armour 32
insects 5, 10

K
kings 25
knights 4, 16–17,
 21, 24

L
Lombards 16

M
magic armour 58
making armour 18–19
Middle Ages 16–17,
 20, 34, 52, 58
mock battles 21
motorcyclists 31
Mughals 22

N
Native Americans 58
Normans 17
Northern Ireland 27

O
ozone layer 7

P
pikemen 25
planes 27, 50–1
plants 5, 11
poison gas 26
police 28, 29, 39
primitive armour 12
private armour 59

R
Romans 8, 9, 14–16,
 30, 34, 42
Roundheads 25

S
safety suits 33
sailors 27

samurai 22
Saxons 16
sea battles 35, 42–7
sea defences 8–9
Second World War 26,
 38–9, 40, 50, 53, 56, 59
shields 12–14, 16–17,
 23, 28
ships 35, 42–7
space 6, 7, 33, 51
Spain 43
submarines 48–9

T
tanks 36–8
tournaments 21
trains 40–1
trenches 25, 26

V
Vandals 16
vehicles 5, 27, 34–8,
 40–1, 48–51
Vietnam War 28
Vikings 17

W
war wagons 34–5
weapons 10, 12–13, 24

SUMMER
FLOWERS
from seed

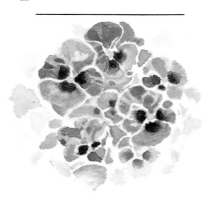

SUMMER
FLOWERS
from seed

ALAN TOOGOOD

In Association with
Unwins Seeds

Executive Managers	Kelly Flynn
	Susan Egerton-Jones
Art Editor	Sue Hall
Production	Peter Phillips

This edition produced exclusively
for W H Smith
Created in association with Unwins (Seeds) Ltd
Edited and designed by the Artists House
Division of Mitchell Beazley International Ltd
Artists House
14–15 Manette Street
London W1V 5LB

ISBN 0 86134 104 X

Typeset by Hourds Typographica, Stafford.
Reproduction by La Cromolito s.n.c., Milan.
Printed in Spain by Printer Industria Grafica SA, Barcelona.
D.L.B. 811-1987

Contents

INTRODUCTION   6

Site Planning
Suitable Sites   9
The Principles of Using Colour   9
The Colour Wheel   9
Harmony   10
Contrast   11
Using Colour Effectively: 12
Perspective   13
Restricted Use of Colours: 14
The Rainbow Effect   16
Separating Strong Colours   16
Using Multi-Coloured Flowers   17
Planning Tips   17
Planting Schemes: 18
Borders   18
Beds   21
Containers   26
Hanging Baskets   27
Rock Gardens and Paved Areas   28
Specimen Plants   28
Walls and Fences   29
Wild Areas   29

Catalogue of Annuals and Biennials
Key to Symbols   30
Green   31
White   34
Yellow   38
Orange   47
Red   50
Pink   58
Purple   63
Blue   66
Multi-Colour   77

Flower Gardeners' Reference
Soils   104
Raising and Growing Hardy Annuals   105
Raising and Growing Half-Hardy Annuals   106
Raising and Growing Hardy Biennials   108
Pests, Diseases and Weeds   109

INDEX   110

Introduction

There is no faster way of providing masses of colour in a garden than raising hardy annuals, half-hardy annuals and hardy biennials from seed. These are the plants which form the basis of this book.

All are short-term plants – that is, they are discarded when their display is over. Most are grown for colourful flowers although some are noted for spectacular foliage. Leaf colour and interest should not be ignored in planting schemes for it makes a marvellous contrast for blooms.

As most plants in these three groups are easily raised from seed they have special appeal to newcomers to gardening while many advanced gardeners grow a good range of them as a matter of course.

Annuals complete their life cycle within one growing season. They grow from seed, produce their blooms, set a crop of seeds and then they die. All of this takes place well within one year. Some annuals live for only a few months, others for many months and generally we use those annuals with the longest life cycles for our garden displays.

Hardy annuals (HA) are able to survive frosts and cold weather to a greater or lesser extent according to species and the part of the world from which they originate. These are sown out of doors direct in their flowering positions between early and late spring. The hardiest of the hardy annuals can also be sown in the autumn. They overwinter as small plants and flower earlier the following year, than if they were sown in the spring. The majority of hardy annuals bloom in the summer.

Half-hardy annuals (HHA) are frost sensitive and will be damaged or killed if subjected to frosts. In climates with cold winters (and hence frosts) half-hardy annuals are raised in a frost-free environment in winter or spring (according to species) and are planted out in their flowering positions when all danger of frost is over. They flower throughout summer and into autumn but the display will be stopped by the first frosts of autumn.

Among the half-hardy annuals included here are some plants which are, correctly, perennials (plants which live for a number of years). However, they are more successfully grown when treated as half-hardy annuals anywhere which is not sub-tropical.

Half-hardy annuals are popularly called summer bedding plants. This is due to the fact that they are 'bedded out' (planted) for summer display.

Biennials take two growing seasons to complete their life cycle. In year one they are sown, usually in spring or early summer, and they grow for the rest of that year, overwintering outdoors. In year two they flower, in spring or summer according to species; then they set a crop of seeds and die. The hardy biennials (HB), the ones we are dealing with here, generally survive cold winters without protection, although some, like wallflowers, will not come through really severe winter weather without protection and cannot be overwintered outdoors in many parts of the USA. A few hardy perennials and also included under this heading because they are treated as biennials by gardeners. In theory these are capable of living for a number of years although they would quickly decline in vigour if kept.

Some of the spring-flowering biennials are popularly called spring bedding plants.

Why we grow these plants

Colour is the most important characteristic of the annuals and biennials so if you want masses of colour in your garden they should top the list of desirable plants. They are mass planted to provide really bold splashes of colour – to create great impact. These plants cannot be used sparingly – we want plenty of them, but this need not be expensive if you raise your own from seed.

Nowadays, it is, of course, possible to buy a wide variety of ready-to-plant half-hardy annuals and hardy biennials at garden centres and nurseries. They come in boxes or trays and sometimes in pots, ready for planting out. Spring sees the garden centres well-stocked with summer bedding plants while autumn is the time to buy plants for spring bedding.

Seeds are cheap, comparatively and packets of seeds of many of the plants described and illustrated in this book will be found in garden centres and shops in the winter and spring. The more unusual species and varieties will have to be bought mail-order from seedsmen, who produce colourful and informative annual catalogues. Once you get on to the mailing lists of seedsmen and place an order you will automatically receive their catalogues each year – generally they are mailed in the autumn.

Some plants are easier to raise than others. Sowing hardy annuals and biennials direct in the open ground is straightforward enough and reommended for complete beginners. Raising plants from seeds in a greenhouse calls for a little more skill but most gardeners find they can quickly master it.

Annuals and biennials have many uses in the garden. Hardy annuals can be grown in their own special border; they can be used to fill gaps in mixed borders containing shrubs and hardy perennials; while small varieties can be used to provide colour on rock gardens and in paving.

Half-hardy annuals are normally used for more formal summer bedding displays, for example around the house, patio or terrace; they can be used to fill containers – urns, tubs, window boxes and hanging baskets – with summer colour; and they can also be used to fill spaces in mixed borders.

Some of the hardy biennials are used for formal spring bedding displays; others look at home in a cottage-garden border, perhaps alongside some hardy annuals; while some can be used to fill gaps in mixed borders. Spring bedding plants are also excellent for ornamental containers.

Some of the larger more dramatic plants can be used as focal points or accent plants to create different profiles and to lead the eye to some particular part. Good use, too, can be made of climbing plants clothing walls and fences, and there are several climbing hardy annuals to choose from.

Some of the plants selected here are excellent for cut flowers. A few could be grown specially for cutting in a spare part of the garden.

Site
Planning

Suitable Sites

The majority of plants here should be sown or planted in full sun or in positions which are in shade for only a small part of the day. There are some annuals and biennials which will also grow well in partial shade. Nevertheless, even these do enjoy some sunshine. Dappled shade as created by trees is an example of partial shade. Another example is a bed or border which receives sun for only about half the day.

If the full sun-loving plants are grown in shady spots they will become straggly and produce few if any flowers.

Most plants prefer a sheltered position, free from cold drying winds. Cold winter winds can cause a lot of damage to young plants by "scorching" their foliage, high winds in summer, often coupled with rain, can flatten tall thin-stemmed plants such as many of the hardy annuals. Bear in mind that less staking or supporting is necessary in a wind-sheltered garden.

Shelter can be provided by hedges and shrubs, and larger gardens can be protected by tall windbreaks of deciduous or evergreen trees or conifers. Temporary wind protection can also be used until permanent plantings become established. Windbreak netting supported on a system of wooden posts and horizontal wires can be every effective.

The Principles of Using Colour

The main reason for growing annuals and biennials is to provide masses of colour. Indeed one could say that this book is basically about creating colour with plants. But some thought has to be given to the use of colour just as it is when decorating one's rooms. Some people have a natural flare for this, being able to combine colours to great effect; others are not so blessed. But there is no need for them to despair, because happily in nature few colours clash or look absolutely awful together, so the risk of making serious mistakes is minimal.

Hopefully, though, I can tell you enough about using colour to enable you to get down to planning some delightful colour schemes for your beds and borders.

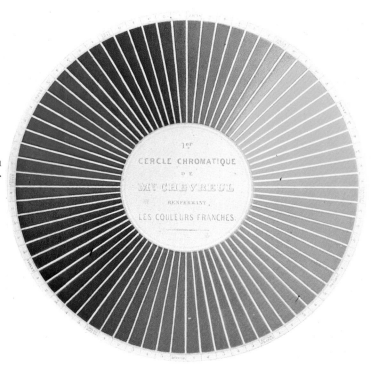

The Colour Wheel

The colour wheel will help you to combine colours effectively and can be used as a guide when planning your planting schemes. It comprises the three primary colours – red, blue and yellow. Between these are the intermediate colours which are obtained by mixing the primary colours. You could put this to the practical test by 'playing around' with a box of artist's watercolour paints.

On the colour wheel all complementary colours (those which combine well) face one another. To quote a few examples, red complements green, blue complements orange, yellow complements violet, and so on with the intermediate colours.

The paler shades of all these colours (including pastel colours) are obtained by mixing white with them (again experiment with your box of paints). For instance, pink is obtained by mixing white with red. Darker shades of the primary and intermediate colours are obtained by mixing black with them.

Harmony

Going a step further we should aim for colours which harmonize and/or contrast when planning planting schemes.

Subtle and 'restful' effects are achieved by combining harmonizing colours. But what are these?

They are the closest colours on the colour wheel – the closer the colours the better they harmonize. Thus we could combine the blue flowers of anchusas and lobelias with the blue-violets of heliotropes and pansies and the violet of *Verbena venosa*; or red-violet petunias with red *Salvia spendens* and orange-red amaranthus.

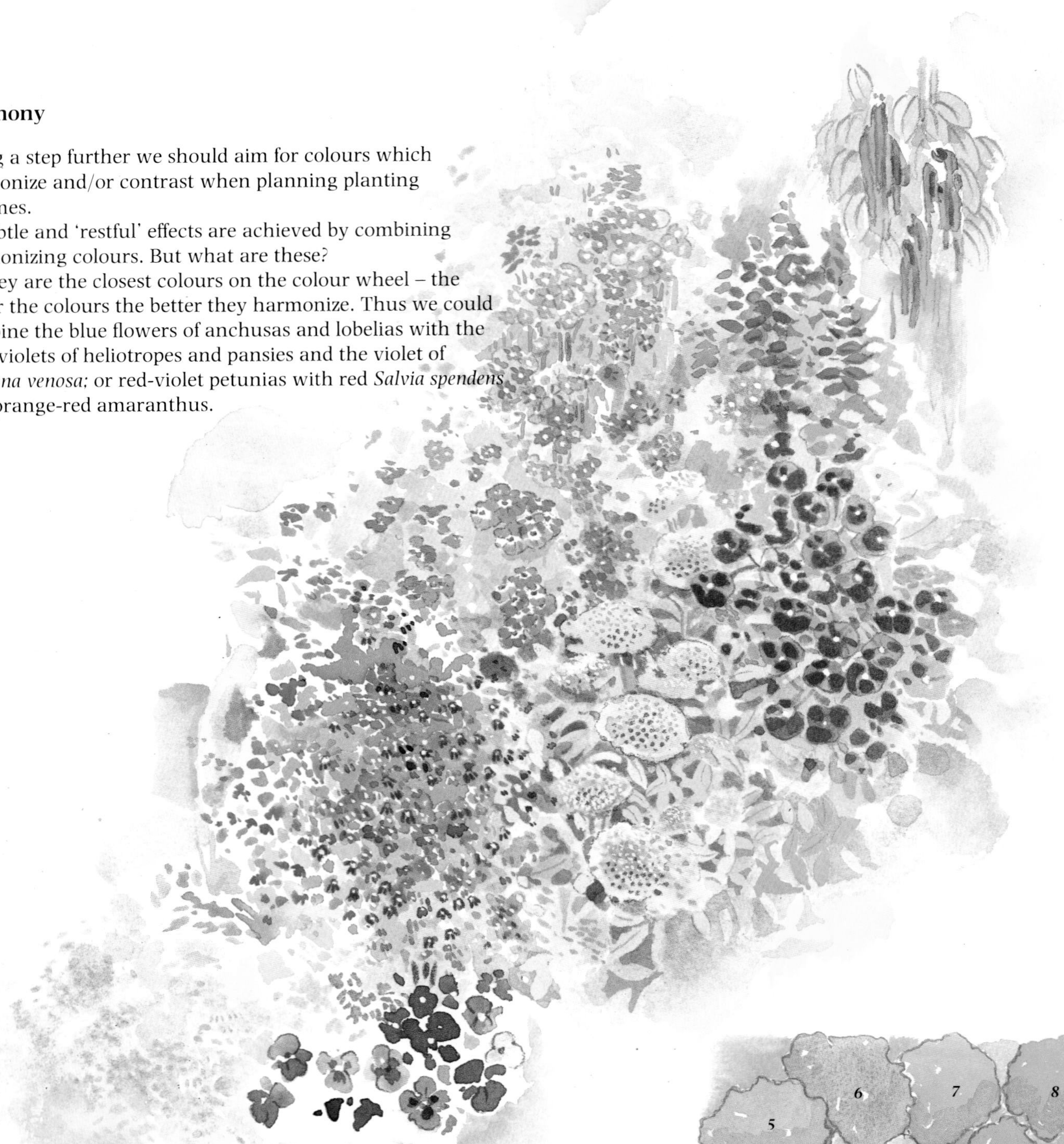

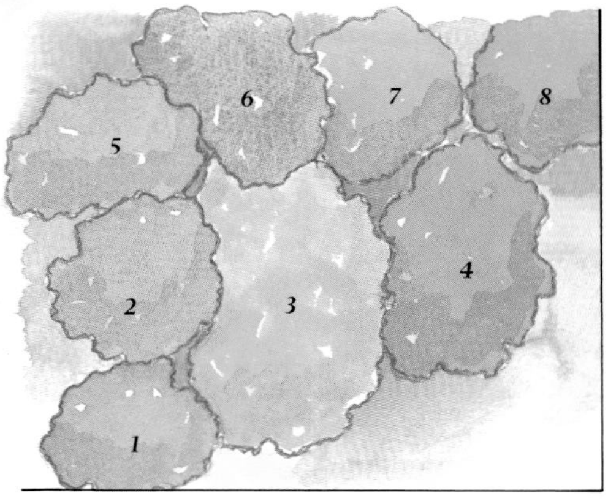

HARMONY

1 *Pansies*
2 *Lobelia erinus*
3 *Heliotrope*
4 *Petunia 'Plum Picotee'*
5 *Verbena venosa*
6 *Anchusa capensis*
7 *Salvia splendens*
8 *Amaranthus tricolor*

Contrast

Contrasting colours create more dramatic effects and are used if you want your beds and borders to have real impact. Looking at the colour wheel, examples of contrasting colours are blue and orange, which could be obtained by mixing blue nigella and convolvulus with orange calendulas or marigolds; yellow and violet (try yellow antirrhinums and African marigolds with violet heliotrope); and orange-yellow and blue-violet (try wallflowers and pansies in these colours).

Beware of overdoing planting schemes with contrasting colours – too many beds and borders planned in this way could result in a very unrestful garden.

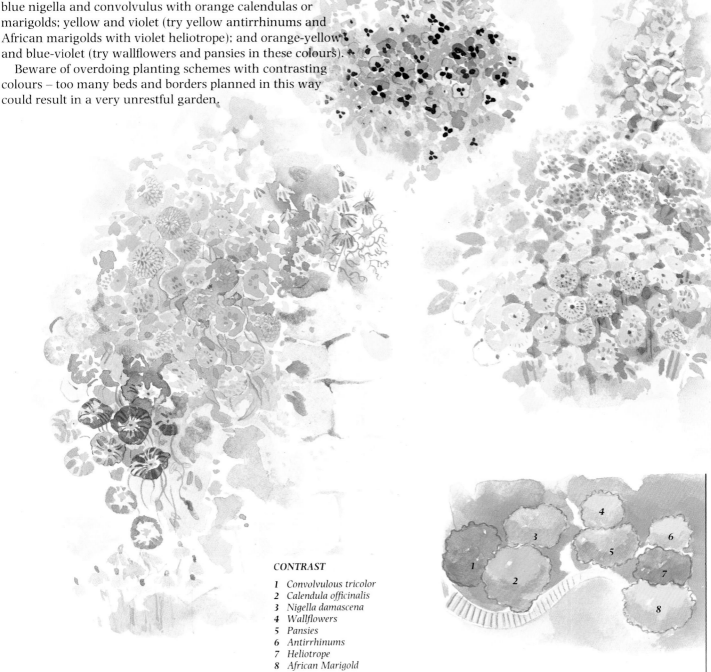

CONTRAST

1 *Convolvulous tricolor*
2 *Calendula officinalis*
3 *Nigella damascena*
4 *Wallflowers*
5 *Pansies*
6 *Antirrhinums*
7 *Heliotrope*
8 *African Marigold*

Using Colour Effectively

Each colour is capable of creating a 'mood' or atmosphere in a garden. Let's take a look at each colour and assess the effect it creates.

Green This is an important colour – indeed the basic colour of most gardens, provided by a permanent 'framework' of shrubs, trees, hedges and lawns. This green framework makes an excellent background and foil for brighter colours. You may think that a lot of green gives a dull effect but this is not so, for there are many 'greens': light, medium and dark; blue-greens; grey-greens; bronze-greens; silver-greens; and yellow-greens.

Green creates a cool restful atmosphere which is what most people desire in a garden. There are green-flowered annuals which could be used to further create this effect. Green-flowered plants are also useful for separating strong colours such as reds and scarlets.

White, silver and grey These create a cool atmosphere, and there are quite a few plants with white flowers and several with silver or grey foliage; all are extremely useful and should be used freely. Mix these plants with strong, dark or heavy colours to prevent a sombre or too powerful effect; use them also to lighten dark areas. They can be used with any other colour without fear of clashing and are especially useful for keeping apart strong colours.

Yellow This is a cheerful colour, bringing 'sunshine' to the garden. Dramatic contrasts can be created by combining with bright yellow such colours as violet, blue or purple; red or orange is often combined with yellow to create tremendous impact. Pale shades of yellow look lovely with strong purples, blues and violets.

Yellow really shows up in a garden and can be seen from a considerable distance; it is also very conspicuous at dusk.

Orange This is one of the colours that creates a 'warm' atmosphere in a garden, as do the yellows and reds. Indeed orange is a mixture of the two.

You can create a dramatic contrast by combining orange with blue. It can also be used with reds and yellows to create a really powerful effect. Like yellow, orange can be seen from a great distance.

Red This is a hot colour, useful for creating 'warmth' in a cool climate – particularly on dull summer days. Green complements red, which comes in several shades such as scarlet, orange and crimson (on the blue side). If you intend using a lot of red flowers provide a foil of green, white, silver or grey blooms and/or foliage. A large area of red without this relief can be overpowering. Try not to scatter red around the garden too much but keep it in one or two places. This ensures a more restful garden – you don't really want to 'see red' wherever you look.

Pink There are many shades of pink, on the blue side of red and on the orange side. It is an easy colour to use and very restful in the paler shades. It gives a warmish feeling to a planting scheme. Pale pinks look lovely with blues and yellow in pastel shades. Pinks of all shades combine beautifully with white, grey and silver. Use the shades of pink with blue in them with blue flowers, and the pinks with orange in them with orange or yellow flowers.

Purple and violet These are 'heavy' colours and if used on too large a scale can create a sombre effect. They come between red and blue on the colour wheel and can be used with both of them. Pale versions are mauve and lilac.

Purples and violets combine well with yellows and oranges, too. Some lovely effects can be created by combining whites and pale yellows with purple and violet flowers. Use white or pale yellow to separate these two deep colours from other strong colours if required.

Blue A lovely colour for a warm or hot climate, blue creates a cool atmosphere. Nevertheless it is also used a lot in cooler climates. For a dramatic contrast combine blue with orange. To liven up groups of blue flowers combine with them plants with yellow or white blooms. The blues blend well with purples and violets, but you should avoid overdoing it because it can create a sombre effect. A stimulating effect, bordering on a clashing combination, is blue and red. This is all too often overdone in summer bedding schemes; using red salvias or geraniums with blue lobelia looks quite good, but *not* everywhere!

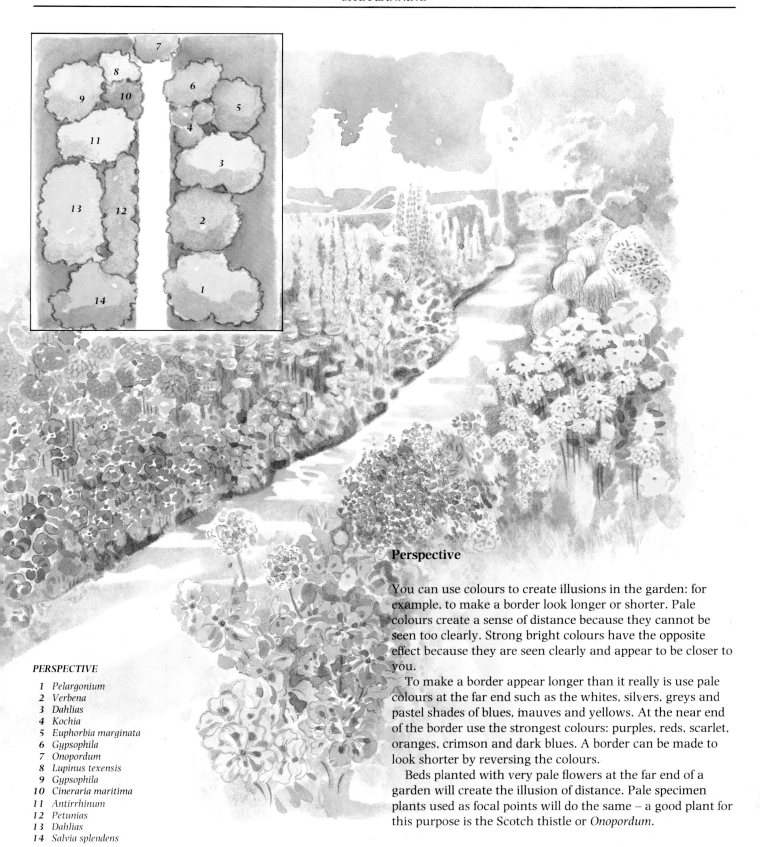

PERSPECTIVE

1 Pelargonium
2 Verbena
3 Dahlias
4 Kochia
5 Euphorbia marginata
6 Gypsophila
7 Onopordum
8 Lupinus texensis
9 Gypsophila
10 Cineraria maritima
11 Antirrhinum
12 Petunias
13 Dahlias
14 Salvia splendens

Perspective

You can use colours to create illusions in the garden: for example, to make a border look longer or shorter. Pale colours create a sense of distance because they cannot be seen too clearly. Strong bright colours have the opposite effect because they are seen clearly and appear to be closer to you.

To make a border appear longer than it really is use pale colours at the far end such as the whites, silvers, greys and pastel shades of blues, mauves and yellows. At the near end of the border use the strongest colours: purples, reds, scarlet, oranges, crimson and dark blues. A border can be made to look shorter by reversing the colours.

Beds planted with very pale flowers at the far end of a garden will create the illusion of distance. Pale specimen plants used as focal points will do the same – a good plant for this purpose is the Scotch thistle or *Onopordum*.

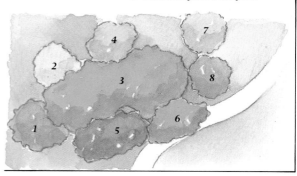

Restricted Use of Colours

Although they run in and out of fashion, borders consisting of plants in shades of one colour, or perhaps two colours, can be effective. You may not want to devote an entire large border to this so try it out in part of a border, or devote a small bed to a single-colour scheme.

RED BORDER

1 *Ricinus communis 'Gibsonii'*
2 *Coix lacryma-jobi*
3 *Dahlias*
4 *Canna*
5 *Nicotiana 'Domino Scarlet'*
6 *Linum grandiflorum*
7 *Briza maxima*
8 *Kochia scoparia trichophila*

Red border A lovely, warm scheme can be created with red, but don't make too large a feature. As well as the red-flowered varieties of dahlias, nicotianas and linums, incude some with bronze foliage such as *Ricinus communis* 'Gibsonii' and some of the cannas or Indian shot. Green foliage plants will help to tone down an otherwise overpowering effect and can include annual ornamental grasses and the burning bush or *Kochia scoparia* (this turns red later in the year).

Yellow border Yellow flowers and foliage create a bright sunny effect which will show up well at dusk. A bed or border of yellow plants will need a dark green background such as an evergreen hedge, otherwise the plants will not show up. There's no need to use all yellow plants: cream flowers could be included together with some plants with grey or silver foliage such as *Cineraria maritima, Onopordum acanthium* and *Verbascum bombyciferum*.

Blue border In a hot summer blue is a refreshing sight, but include some cream or white as well to prevent a 'cold' atmosphere. Don't forget, too, some plants with silver or grey foliage. Some lovely effects can be created by combining pale and dark blue, and even violet flowers.

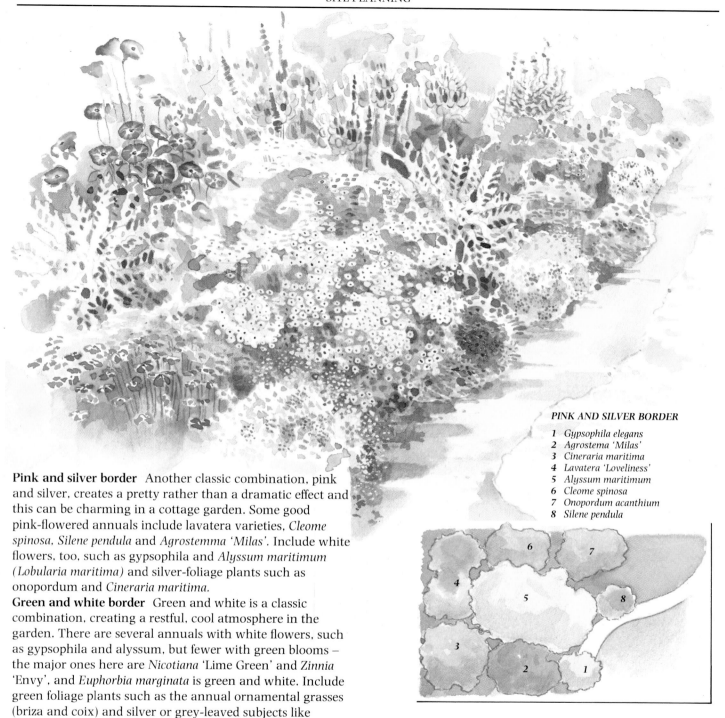

PINK AND SILVER BORDER

1 *Gypsophila elegans*
2 *Agrostema 'Milas'*
3 *Cineraria maritima*
4 *Lavatera 'Loveliness'*
5 *Alyssum maritimum*
6 *Cleome spinosa*
7 *Onopordum acanthium*
8 *Silene pendula*

Pink and silver border Another classic combination, pink and silver, creates a pretty rather than a dramatic effect and this can be charming in a cottage garden. Some good pink-flowered annuals include lavatera varieties, *Cleome spinosa*, *Silene pendula* and *Agrostemma 'Milas'*. Include white flowers, too, such as gypsophila and *Alyssum maritimum (Lobularia maritima)* and silver-foliage plants such as onopordum and *Cineraria maritima*.

Green and white border Green and white is a classic combination, creating a restful, cool atmosphere in the garden. There are several annuals with white flowers, such as gypsophila and alyssum, but fewer with green blooms – the major ones here are *Nicotiana* 'Lime Green' and *Zinnia* 'Envy', and *Euphorbia marginata* is green and white. Include green foliage plants such as the annual ornamental grasses (briza and coix) and silver or grey-leaved subjects like *Cineraria maritima*.

Strong colour Another idea is to use a few strong colours to create impact. You could follow the colour wheel around and have red, purple, blue, deep yellow and orange flowers.

Pastel colours Alternatively combine a few pastel colours, again following the colour wheel: pinks, mauves, pale blues and cream or pale yellow.

The Rainbow Effect

If you want to use many colours in a border then a 'safe' way to arrange them is in a progressive sequence popularly known as the rainbow effect. This prevents any possibility of unpleasant combinations and colour clashing.

A popular way of arranging the colours is to start at one end of the border with flowers in shades of blue; white flowers come next and then pale yellow followed by pink. Then continue on with the stronger colours: scarlet, orange and finally red. This is a good idea for a border of hardy annuals, some of which come in a range of colours that can be difficult to arrange effectively if you are not experienced in colour planning.

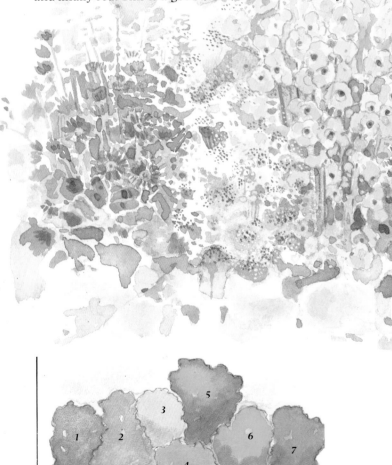

THE RAINBOW EFFECT

1 Centaurea cyanus
2 Gypsophila elegans
3 Verbascum bombyciferum
4 Helipterum roseum
5 Linum grandiflorum rubrum
6 Calendula officinalis
7 Alonsoa warscewiczii

Separating Strong Colours

Another way of playing safe to prevent possible colour clashes when using a wide range of colours in a bed or border is to separate strong colours such as the reds, oranges and bright pinks with white or green flowers. Or by using foliage plants of white, silver, grey or green.

Using Multi-Coloured Flowers

Many annuals and biennials are supplied by seedsmen as mixtures of a few or many colours. Some mixtures contain shades of one colour, others a lot of different colours such as reds, yellows and blues. And other annuals and biennials have two or more colours in the one flower, which ar known as bi-coloured flowers. The effects produced from these plants can be either harmonious or contrasting.

So how do we handle plants which come in mixtures? A complete bed of multi-coloured flowers can be very effective. A spring display of mixed wallflowers, pansies, polyanthus and double daisies is extremely lively. Plant each kind in a bold group, patch or drift.

Groups of multi-coloured flowers can also be combined with groups of single colours, again aiming for harmony or contrast.

Mixtures that contain shades of one colour should be treated as single colours for the purposes of colour planning.

It should be borne in mind that using too many multi-coloured flowers can create a fussy or spotty effect in the garden. Generally speaking, it is easier to use single colours when planning colour schemes.

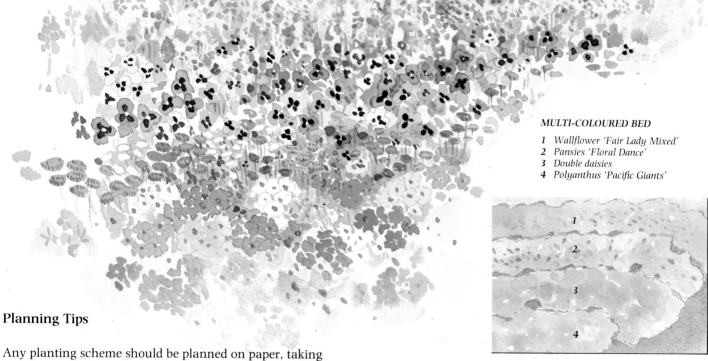

MULTI-COLOURED BED

1 *Wallflower 'Fair Lady Mixed'*
2 *Pansies 'Floral Dance'*
3 *Double daisies*
4 *Polyanthus 'Pacific Giants'*

Planning Tips

Any planting scheme should be planned on paper, taking into account colour, flowering time and height. If colour combinations are to be effective it goes without saying that all of the plants must flower at the same time. But do not stick too rigidly to the general rule of tall at the back, short at the front or you will end up with a border that is far too regimented. So bring the occasional group of tall plants and a few groups of shorter plants towards the centre of the border. In a bed that is viewed from all sides the taller plants should be grouped in the centre.

Prepare a colour sketch of the planting scheme, to show whether the colour combinations work. If they look pleasing to your eye, that's fine. Colour planning is, after all, a personal business. There is no need to go into elaborate detail here so don't worry if you are not much of an artist. Have a go with a box of artist's watercolour paints or with coloured felt-tipped pens.

Planting Schemes

Specific planting schemes using hardy and half-hardy annuals and biennials have many uses in the garden and can be grown in all kinds of places. Those shown here should be treated as starting points for individual imaginations to take over.

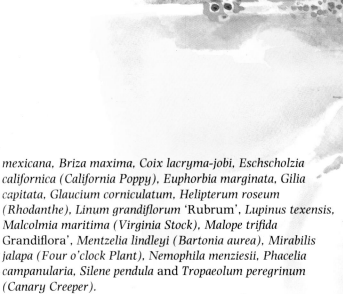

Borders

Traditional annuals borders Hardy annuals are traditionally grown in their own border, which makes a highly colourful feature in the summer. The border should ideally be backed by a dark green hedge. A wall or a dark fence would also make a suitable background. If there is a lawn in front of this border the annuals will show up really well.

The traditional annual border is nowhere near as popular today as it was in the past because gardens are now much smaller and there is not the space available to devote a whole bed to one type of plant. However it is an idea that might appeal to owners of brand new gardens because it is a quick and cheap way of providing colour and filling bare ground. Later, it can be turned gradually into a mixed border.

How do we plan an annual border? One way is to arrange the plants in a progressive rainbow sequence, as mentioned earlier. Or the colours could be mixed, taking into account harmony and contrast.

Each variety should be sown in bold informal splashes as it is far more pleasing to have fewer larger groups. So, if you have a small border, choose only a few varieties.

Mixed borders Many gardens today have mixed borders containing all kinds of plants. And this is sensible if you have a small garden. The main framework of a mixed border consists of shrubs, both deciduous and evergreen (a good balance is one-third evergreens to two-thirds deciduous) and, ideally, flowers and foliage will determine the varieties selected.

Among the shrubs are planted herbaceous perennials, bulbs, hardy annuals, half-hardy annuals and biennials. Here, too, the rule stands firm – bold groups or drifts for best effect.

When choosing plants for a mixed border it is important that they associate well with the shrubs – not all plants do so by any means.

With hardy annuals I prefer to use species plants rather than man-made hybrids, some of which are too flamboyant and just do not look right. Hardy annuals are particularly useful for filling any gaps, and there may be quite a few for the first few years.

Suitable hardy annuals for a mixed border are: *Argemone*

mexicana, Briza maxima, Coix lacryma-jobi, Eschscholzia californica (California Poppy), Euphorbia marginata, Gilia capitata, Glaucium corniculatum, Helipterum roseum (Rhodanthe), Linum grandiflorum 'Rubrum', *Lupinus texensis, Malcolmia maritima (Virginia Stock), Malope trifida* Grandiflora', *Mentzelia lindleyi (Bartonia aurea), Mirabilis jalapa (Four o'clock Plant), Nemophila menziesii, Phacelia campanularia, Silene pendula* and *Tropaeolum peregrinum (Canary Creeper).*

Half-hardy annuals are only planted in the mixed border when all danger of frost is over. Again they are useful for filling any gaps and should not be excessively flamboyant. I particularly recommend the following: *Ageratum houstonianum,* makes a good edging; *Amaranthus caudatus* (Love Lies Bleeding); *Begonia semperflorens,* looks good planted in drifts at the front of the border; *Cleome spinosa; Dahlia variabilis,* preferably in single colours, the dwarf ones being ideal for the front of the border; *Heliotropium arborescens (Heliotrope); Lobelia erinus,* which looks lovely planted in bold informal drifts at the front; *Nicotiana alata (Ornamental Tobacco),* particularly the variety 'Lime Green', *Ricinus communis,* for foliage effect; *Verbena x hybrida,* planted in drifts at the front; and *Zea mays,* for foliage effect.

Many hardy biennials are suitable for the mixed border including double daisies or *Bellis perennis,* which can be used

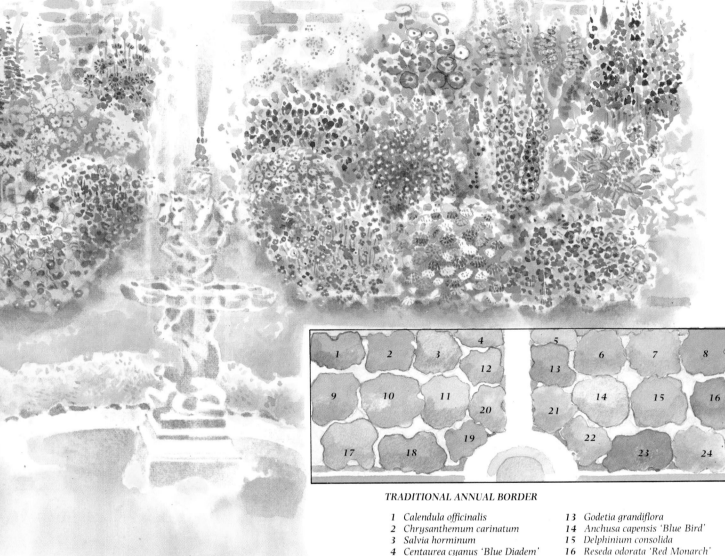

TRADITIONAL ANNUAL BORDER

1	*Calendula officinalis*	13	*Godetia grandiflora*
2	*Chrysanthemum carinatum*	14	*Anchusa capensis 'Blue Bird'*
3	*Salvia horminum*	15	*Delphinium consolida*
4	*Centaurea cyanus 'Blue Diadem'*	16	*Reseda odorata 'Red Monarch'*
5	*Gypsophila elegans*	17	*Dianthus chinensis*
6	*Lavatera trimestris 'Silver Cup'*	18	*Nemophila menziesii*
7	*Helianthus annuus*	19	*Eschscholzia californica*
8	*Clarkia elegans*	20	*Phacelia campanularia*
9	*Lupinus texensis*	21	*Silene pendula*
10	*Papaver nudicaule*	22	*Malcolmia maritima*
11	*Nigella damascena 'Miss Jekyll'*	23	*Iberis umbellata*
12	*Mentzelia lindleyi*	24	*Linum grandiflorum 'Rubrum'*

as edging or planted in bold drifts at the front; *Campanula medium* or Canterbury bells; sweet williams or *Dianthus barbatus*; foxgloves or *Digitalis purpurea*, particularly the 'Excelsior Strain', for the back of the border; *Lunaria annua* or honesty; *Myosotis sylvatica* planted in drifts; *Onopordum acanthium*, the Scotch thistle grown for its striking foliage and which should be planted at the back of the border; polyanthus or *Primula polyantha* which can be drifted among shrubs; and pansies or varieties of *Viola x wittrockiana* which should again be planted in bold drifts at the front – blue or yellow shades look particularly effective.

To create 'themes' in the mixed border, group plants by their flowering seasons. For example for a spring display

plant spring-flowering biennials such as polyanthus, honesty and forget-me-nots around spring-flowering shrubs such as forsythia.

Summer-flowering plants such as dahlias and nicotiana can be grouped around summer-flowering shrubs and are also particularly effective combined with coloured-foliage shrubs such as purple cotinus or berberis or golden philadelphus.

Foxgloves makes marvellous companions for the early summer flowering philadelphus or mock orange.

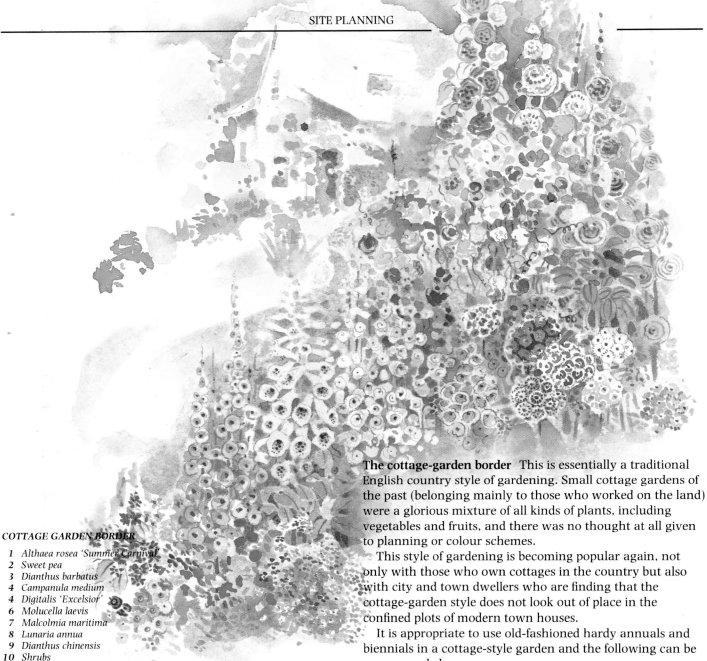

COTTAGE GARDEN BORDER

1 *Althaea rosea 'Summer Carnival'*
2 *Sweet pea*
3 *Dianthus barbatus*
4 *Campanula medium*
4 *Digitalis 'Excelsior'*
6 *Molucella laevis*
7 *Malcolmia maritima*
8 *Lunaria annua*
9 *Dianthus chinensis*
10 *Shrubs*

The cottage-garden border This is essentially a traditional English country style of gardening. Small cottage gardens of the past (belonging mainly to those who worked on the land) were a glorious mixture of all kinds of plants, including vegetables and fruits, and there was no thought at all given to planning or colour schemes.

This style of gardening is becoming popular again, not only with those who own cottages in the country but also with city and town dwellers who are finding that the cottage-garden style does not look out of place in the confined plots of modern town houses.

It is appropriate to use old-fashioned hardy annuals and biennials in a cottage-style garden and the following can be recommended:

Althaea rosea (Hollyhocks), *Calendula officinalis* (Marigolds), *Campanula medium* (Canterbury Bells), *Centaurea cyanus* (Cornflowers), *Cheiranthus cheiri* (Wallflowers), *Delphinium consolida* (Larkspurs), *Dianthus barbatus* (Sweet Williams), *Dianthus chinensis*, *Digitalis purpurea* (Foxgloves), *Iberis umbellata* (Candytufts), *Lathyrus odoratus* (Sweet Peas), *Lunaria annua* (Honesty), *Malcolmia maritima* (Virginia Stocks), *Matthiola incana* (Stocks), *Molucella laevis* (Bells of Ireland), *Myosotis sylvatica* (Forget-me-nots), *Nigella damascena* (Love in a Mist), *Reseda odorata* (Mignonette), *Scabiosa atropurpurea* (Scabious), *Tropaeolum majus* (Nasturtiums), *Verbascum bombyciferum* and *Viola x wittrockiana* (Pansies), particularly the small-flowered viola types.

Beds

Sub-tropical bedding This is a very popular form of summer bedding using half-hardy annuals – mainly foliage kinds – but a few flowering types too. The idea is to create a sub-tropical atmosphere – for instance, around a patio. Plants should be arranged informally in bold groups. Foliage kinds include *Ricinus communis, Canna x generalis, Amaranthus tricolor* varieties and *Coleus blumei*. For a sub-tropical scheme, choose exotic-looking flowers such as *Begonia semperflorens, Impatiens wallerana* (Busy Lizzie), *Amaranthus caudatus* (Love lies Bleeding) and *Celosia plumosa* (Prince of Wales' Feathers).

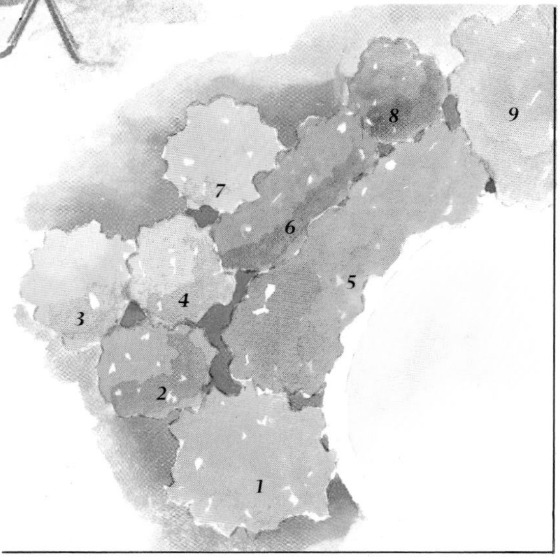

SUB-TROPICAL BED

1 *Begonia semperflorens*
2 *Amaranthus caudatus*
3 *Celosia plumosa*
4 *Amaranthus tricolor*
   'Illumination'
5 *Begonia semperflorens*

6 *Impatiens wallerana*
7 *Canna x generalis*
8 *Ricinus communis 'Impala'*
9 *Coleus blumei*

Summer bedding schemes The most popular use of half-hardy annuals is in summer bedding schemes. The plants are mass planted in formal beds that are often sited close to the house and/or patio. The purpose here is to provide a mass of bright colour.

There is a tried and tested way of arranging the plants. First there is the main carpet of plants which can cover most or all of the bed. This can consist of one type of plant or several intermixed and normally low growing. For example you could have a carpet of *Begonia semperflorens*; a mix of

zonal or bedding geraniums and petunias; scarlet salvias; or marigolds combined with *Verbena venosa*.

Then there is an edging to the carpet, again using a low-growing subject that contrasts with the main carpet. To be effective an edging needs to be reasonably wide – about 30cm (12in). Typical edging plants are ageratum, *Alyssum maritimum*, lobelia and golden pyrethrum.

A carpet of plants with strongly coloured flowers (such as scarlet salvias or bedding geraniums) needs relieving in some way otherwise the effect can be overpowering, so we plant at

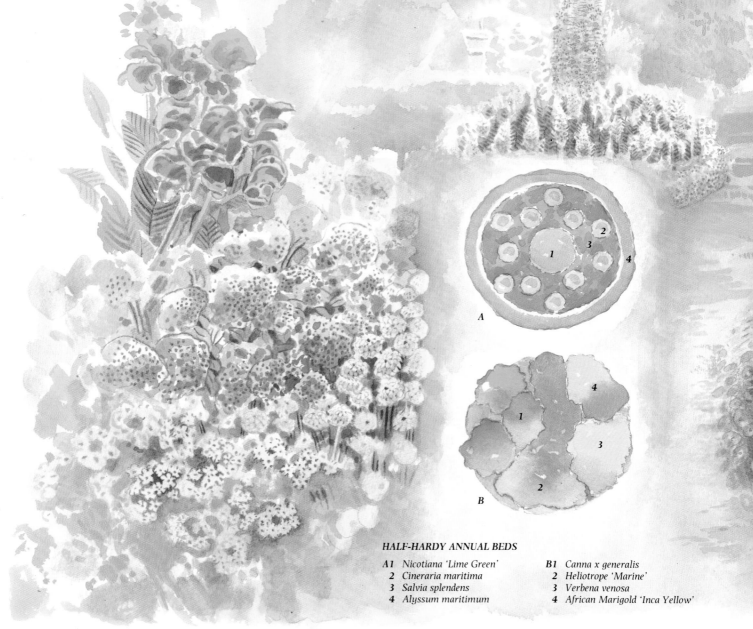

HALF-HARDY ANNUAL BEDS

A1 *Nicotiana 'Lime Green'*
  2 *Cineraria maritima*
  3 *Salvia splendens*
  4 *Alyssum maritimum*

B1 *Canna x generalis*
  2 *Heliotrope 'Marine'*
  3 *Verbena venosa*
  4 *African Marigold 'Inca Yellow'*

random within the carpet some plants which act as a foil. These are taller than the carpet and are popularly known as dot plants. Suitable subjects include the silver-leaved *Cineraria maritima* and heliotrope.

So far we do not have much height so we can include some tall plants, perhaps in the centre of the bed or give a random effect of structure to the entire bed. The ornamental maize, *Zea mays*, is especially useful and so too is the castor oil plant or *Ricinus communis*. Varieties of *Canna x generalis* are highly recommended for their bold foliage. Other tall plants include some of the nicotianas, African marigolds and standard plants (grown like small trees) or zonal geraniums and heliotrope.

The possible combinations of plants for summer bedding are virtually limitless but the accompanying illustrations give a few examples which hopefully will get you started.

HALF-HARDY ANNUAL BEDS

C1 Zea mays 'Gigantea Quadricolor'
2 Heliotrope 'Marine'
3 Begonia semperflorens
4 Ageratum

D1 Ricinus communis 'Gibsonii'
2 Pelargonium 'Orange Orbit'
3 Petunias

Spring bedding schemes Here we use hardy biennials which are mass planted in a similar way to summer bedding schemes. Again they are frequently grown in formal beds around the house or patio but the display is provided in the spring. Spring bedding plants are planted in the autumn as soon as the summer bedding plants have been cleared.

Again we plant a main carpet of plants which may be wallflowers, forget-me-nots, polyanthus or double daisies. Often we interplant with tulips which grow through the carpet and flower above it. The beds can be edged if desired with a contrasting edging plant – double daisies and forget-me-nots are often used for this purpose.

Alternatively, you could get away from these traditional arrangements and have several large informal groups or drifts of different plants such as wallflowers, polyanthus and winter-flowering pansies (which bloom also in spring).

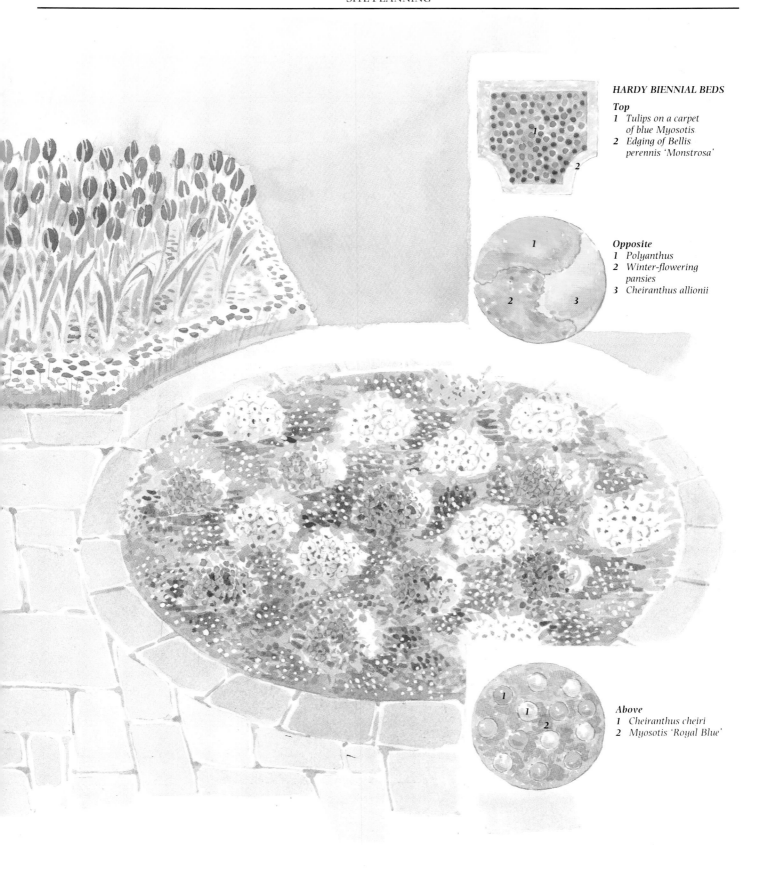

HARDY BIENNIAL BEDS

Top
1 Tulips on a carpet
   of blue Myosotis
2 Edging of Bellis
   perennis 'Monstrosa'

Opposite
1 Polyanthus
2 Winter-flowering
   pansies
3 Cheiranthus allionii

Above
1 Cheiranthus cheiri
2 Myosotis 'Royal Blue'

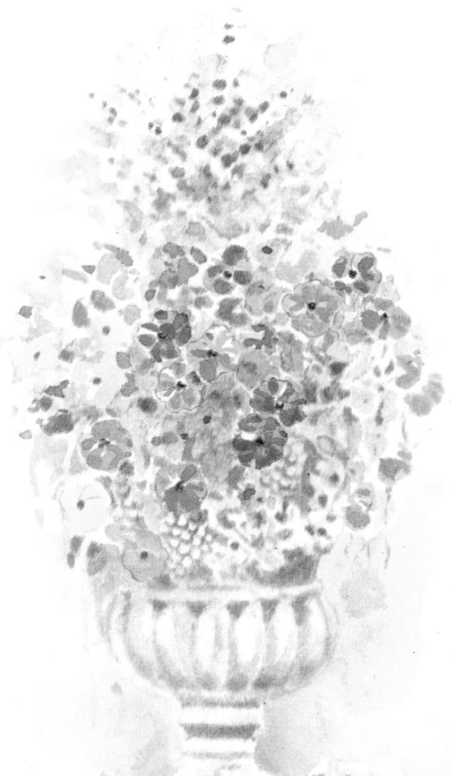

URN

1 *Cineraria maritima*
2 *Petunias*

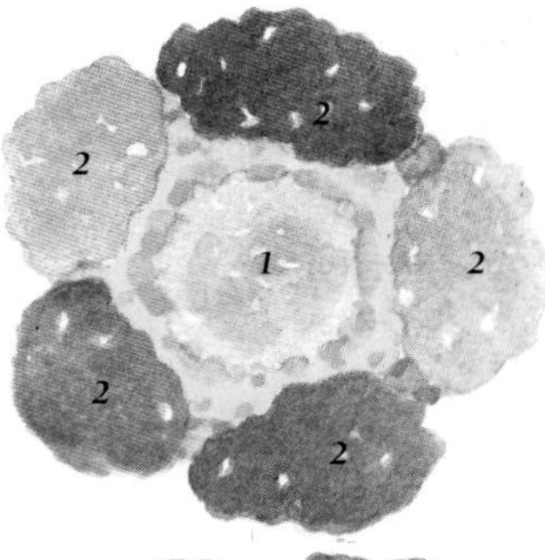

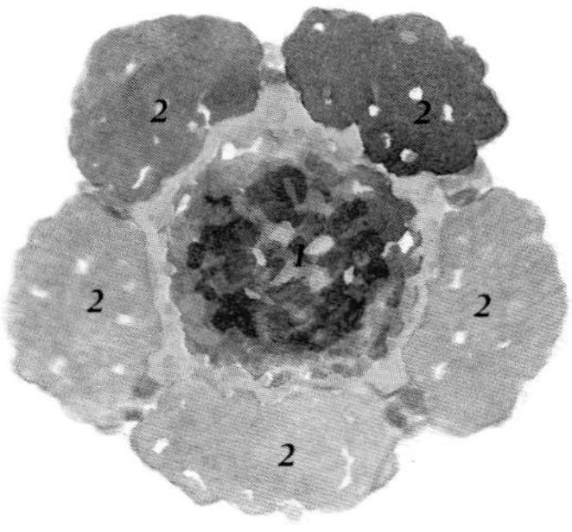

TUB

1 *Pelargonium x hortorum*
2 *Verbena x hybrida*

Containers

Growing colourful plants in ornamental containers, such as tubs and urns on patios and terraces, is very popular. Window boxes are also widely used to provide colour on a higher level. Half-hardy annuals are used for the summer display and hardy biennials for spring colour.

The usual way of arranging plants in tubs, etc, is to have tallish plants such as zonal geraniums in the centre and to plant trailing kinds such as *Verbena x hybrida*, trailing lobelia or petunias around the edge. With window boxes you can aim for a triangular shape by planting tallish plants in the middle and grading down to each end with shorter plants. Trailers can be planted to hang over the front and ends.

Some popular half-hardy annuals for containers are *Ageratum houstonianum*, *Begonia semperflorens*, *Begonia tuberosa* (Tuberous Begonia), *Gazania x hybrida*, *Heliotropium arborescens* (Heliotrope), *Impatiens wallerana* (Busy Lizzie), *Lobelia erinus*, *Mimulus x hybridus*, *Nicotiana alata* (dwarf varieties), *Pelargonium x hortorum* (Zonal Geranium), *Petunia x hybrida*, *Salvia splendens*, *Cineraria Maritina* (Silver-leaved Cineraria), *Tagetes patula* (French Marigold), *Tagetes tenuifolia* and *Verbena x hybrida*.

Hardy biennials which grow well in containers include *Bellis perennis* (Double Daisy), *Cheiranthus cheiri* (Wall-flowers), *Cheiranthus allionii* (Siberian Wallflower), *Myosotis sylvatica* (Forget-me-not), *Primula polyantha* (Polyanthus) and winter-flowering pansies or *Viola x wittrockiana*. Spring-flowering bulbs such as tulips (particularly dwarf varieties) and hyacinths can be planted among these.

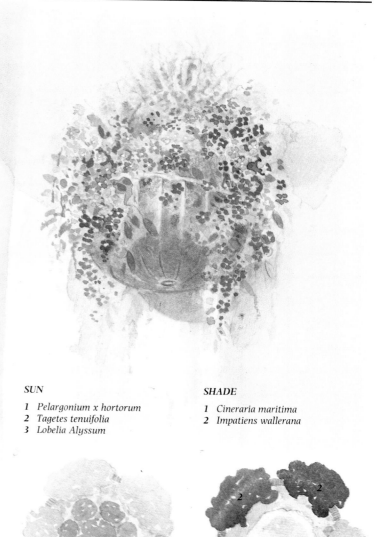

SUN

1 *Pelargonium x hortorum*
2 *Tagetes tenuifolia*
3 *Lobelia Alyssum*

SHADE

1 *Cineraria maritima*
2 *Impatiens wallerana*

Hanging Baskets

Hanging baskets are very popular for providing colour on a higher level. They can be hung on the walls of the house, particularly in the area of a patio, on garage and garden walls, and on pergolas. They do need constant care and watering to be successful, however.

For the best effect – a complete ball of colour – wire baskets are best, because plants can be inserted through the wires in the sides as well as in the top. With solid-sided baskets it is possible to plant only in the top.

Half-hardy annuals are used for baskets, and the way to arrange them is to have bushy plants in the centre to give height, some shorter plants around these if there is sufficient space, and trailing kinds around the edge and also planted through the wires.

For a sunny aspect, a basket with a red-orange zonal geranium at the centre surrounded with dwarf orange *Tagetes tenuifolia* and trailing lobelia mixed with white alyssum can make a dramatic feature; while for a position in shade try a basket of impatiens in mixed colours with a centrepiece of silvery *Cineraria maritima*.

Other trailing plants for baskets include ageratum, pendulous tuberous begonias, petunias and trailing varieties of verbena. More upright plants for the centre include tuberous and fibrous-rooted begonias, coleus, heliotrope, French marigolds and mimulus.

Rock Gardens and Paved Areas

Some of the small hardy annuals are ideal for adding colour to a rock garden during the summer, by which time most alpines have finished flowering. Small annuals can also be sown in gaps in paving, particularly in the crazy paving (random-stone paving) which is often a feature of cottage gardens.

Some recommended annuals are *Convolvulus tricolor, Dianthus chinensis, Eschscholzia californica* (Californian Poppy), *Iberis umbellata* (Candytuft), *Ionopsidium acaule, Linaria maroccana, Malcolmia maritima* (Virginia Stock), *Nemophila menziesii, Phacelia campanularia* and *Viola x wittrockiana* (viola types).

Try also the following half-hardy annuals, planting them out when danger of frost is over: *Dimorphotheca aurantiaca (Star of the Beldt), Gazania x hybrida, Lobelia erinus, Nemesia strumosa, Phlox drummondii, Portulaca grandiflora* and *Tagetes tenuifolia.*

Specimen Plants

Sometimes we need a focal point in the garden to lead the eye to a particular part – for instance, at the end of a lawn or in a corner of the garden. Tall bold plants are called for here, ideally planted in a group of maximum impact. Several of the plants described in this book are suitable for creating focal points, and use light-coloured plants such as onopordum and verbascum to create a sense of distance. And we would recommend: *Althaea rosea* (Hollyhock), *Digitalis purpurea* (Foxglove), *Helianthus annuus* (Sunflower), *Onopordum acanthium, Ricinus communis, Verbascum bombyciferum* and *Zea mays.*

Walls and Fences

There are several climbers featured in the book which are ideal for clothing walls and fences. Remember, though, that climbing annuals can also be grown up trelliswork and pillars. They can also be allowed to scramble over large shrubs or cascade down banks.

The following climbers are worth considering: *Cobaea scandens, Cucurbita pepo ovifera* (Ornamental Gourds), *Ipomoea tricolor* (Convolvulus), *Lathyrus odoratus* (Sweet Pea), *Thunbergia alata, Tropaeolum majus* (Nasturtium) (some varieties climb) and *Tropaeolum peregrinum* (Canary Creeper).

Wild Areas

Many people are devoting areas of their garden to wild flowers. Growing wild meadow flowers in grass has the advantage that the grass needs cutting only once a year so being labour-saving as well as a conservation area. A long-grass area would be suitable for a bank; or a carefully selected part of the lawn could be devoted to wild flowers, creating a nice contrast between mown and long grass. But don't plan a wild area too close to cultivated beds – seeding would be a great arrogance.

There are also wild flowers suitable for woodland conditions, so anyone with an area of woodland could devote part of it to native plants.

Seedsmen on both sides of the Atlantic supply seeds of native wild flowers, both separate and in mixtures suited to different purposes. It is also possible to buy mixtures of wild meadow flowers and grass seeds, so that you can sow both in one operation. Some wild flowers are annuals and will seed themselves every year, while others are perennial.

The best time to cut a flower meadow is in late summer or early autumn, once the wild flowers have finished blooming and the seeds have set.

Catalogue of Annuals and Biennials

This catalogue of annuals and biennials has been arranged by the predominant colour of the flowers, and this is to help you plan colour schemes for different effects in different parts of the garden. The plant descriptions and special attributes are followed by hints on cultivation and propagation.

KEY TO SYMBOLS

Spread: This is the maximum width of the plant under ideal growing conditions and is also a guide to planting or thinning distances.

Height: The maximum height under ideal growing conditions.

HA Hardy Annual

HHA Half-Hardy Annual

HB Hardy Biennial

Full sun

Partial shade

Full shade

S Scented

Climber

Trailer

Climber/Trailer

Interesting foliage

Suitable for cut flowers

Ideal for planting singly

Ideal for planting in groups

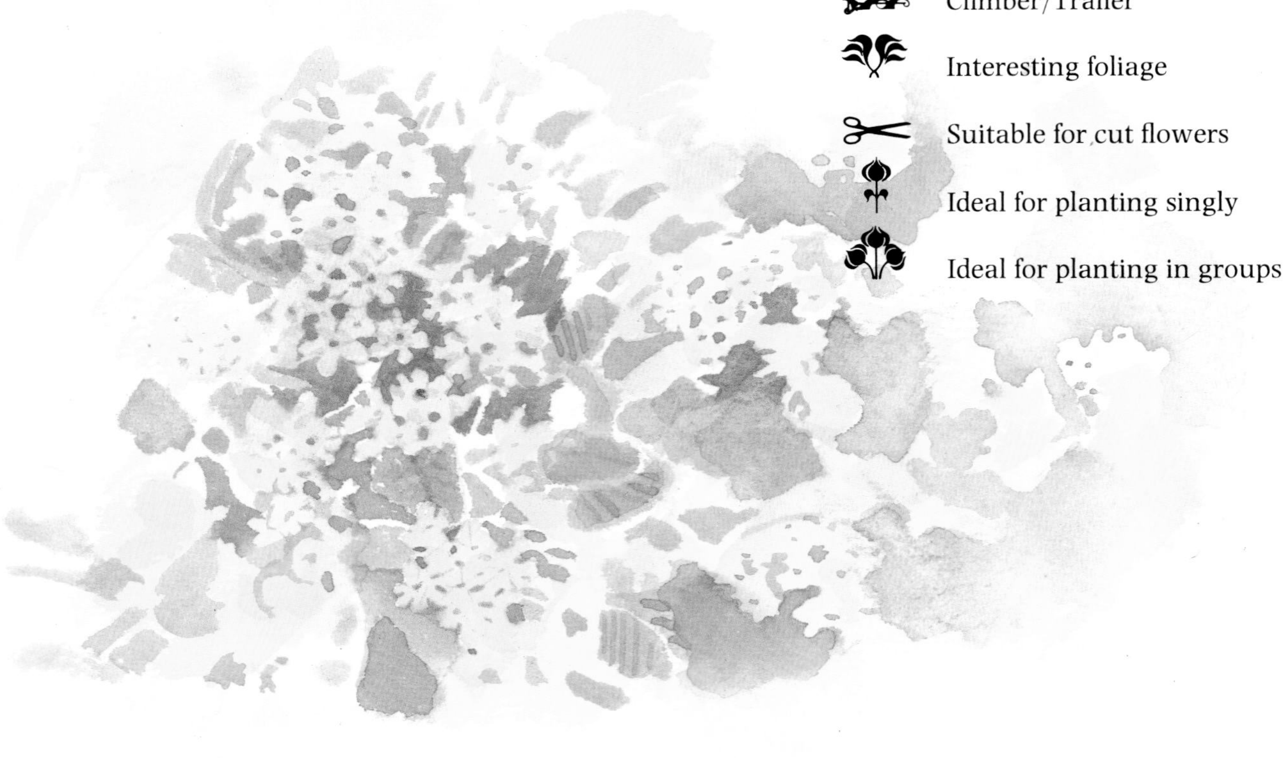

Briza maxima _____
Greater Quaking Grass

Spread 15–20cm (6–8in)
Height 60cm (24in)

HA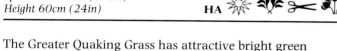

Coix lacryma-jobi _____
Job's Tears

Spread 20cm (8in)
Height 90cm (36in)

HHA

The Greater Quaking Grass has attractive bright green foliage and silvery brownish flowers, making an ideal foil for strongly coloured flowers. One of the best of the annual grasses, it may be dried and used for winter decoration if cut before the seeds heads ripen.

CULTIVATION
A position in full sun with well-drained soil will suit this grass. Make sure the soil is not too rich.

PROPAGATION
Sow seeds in early to mid-spring where the plants are to grow and thin out seedlings before they become overcrowded.

This grass has broad medium-green leaves in tufts and greyish green seeds in clusters on arching stems. The main attraction is the seed heads which unfortunately are not suitable for cutting and drying. Job's Tears makes a good foil for brightly coloured flowers and looks particulary at home in a cottage garden.

CULTIVATION
This grass must have full sun and a very well-drained soil. It will appreciate plenty of organic matter in the soil such as garden compost or peat.

PROPAGATION
Sow seeds during late winter/early spring in warmth, indoors or in a greenhouse. Prick out seedlings into 7.5cm (3in) pots and plant out when danger of frost is over. Alternatively sow outdoors in mid-spring.

31

Euphorbia marginata ———————
Snow on the Mountain

Spread 30cm (12in)
Height 60cm (24in)   **HA**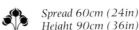

Kochia scoparia 'Trichophylla' ———————
Burning Bush

Spread 60cm (24in)
Height 90cm (36in)   **HHA**

This annual has a bushy habit of growth and white-edged bright green foliage bracts at the top of the plant. The flowers which appear in summer are insignificant. Snow on the Mountain is popular for cutting for use in flower arrangements. When cut it exudes a white sap which can be stopped by dipping the bases of the stems in hot water.

It is an especially useful annual for filling gaps in shrub borders and would also look at home in a cottage garden. It is indispensable for green and white planting schemes. There is a variety called 'White Icicle' which is faster growing than the species.

CULTIVATION
Any well-drained soil is suitable, in full sun or partial shade. In dry poor soils the foliage colour is much better.

PROPAGATION
Best treated as a half hardy annual, but also can be sown in early to mid-spring where the plants are to grow and thinning out seedlings before they become overcrowded.

For many years the Burning Bush has been popular for summer bedding schemes in which it is often used as a dot plant. It forms a conifer-like bush of feathery foliage, which at first is light green but gradually changes to deep red. There is another variety named 'Childsii' which has a neater habit and is more compact than 'Trichophylla', but does not go red in the autumn.

CULTIVATION
The ideal situation is full sun with a light well drained soil, but plants will grow in any kind of soil. If the garden is prone to wind it may be necessary to provide supports for the plants: a thin bamboo cane for each one will be sufficient, tying in with soft garden string or raffia.

PROPAGATION
Sow the seeds in heat, in a greenhouse or indoors in early spring, and prick out the seedlings individually into 7.5cm (3in) pots. Plant out when danger of frost is over. Seeds may also be sown outdoors in mid-spring.

Molucella laevis
Bells of Ireland

Spread 20cm (8in)
Height 60cm (24in)

HHA

Zea mays
Ornamental Maize

Spread 60cm (24in)
Height 1–1.8m (3–6ft)

HHA

This is a favourite cottage-garden annual and the flowers are often dried for use in winter flower arrangements. It has roundish leaves which are pale green and in summer it sends up flower spikes carrying small white blooms, each surrounded by a large light green leaf-like calyx shaped like a shell. An excellent annual for filling gaps in a shrub or mixed border and for 'cool' green and white planting schemes.

Ornamental Maize is often used to give height and contrast in summer bedding schemes. It can also be used in sub-tropical bedding schemes, in shrub or mixed borders or grown as a specimen plant to act as a focal point in the garden. It has large grassy foliage and large seed heads known as cobs. There are several varieties such as 'Gigantea Quadricolor' with leaves variegated in white, pink and light yellow; 'Japonica Multicolor' whose cobs contain red, yellow, orange and blue seeds; and 'Strawberry Corn' with strawberry shaped red cobs.

CULTIVATION
Grow in any ordinary garden soil but ideally in a light well-drained one well supplied with organic matter and fertilizer. Choose a site in full sun for best results.

PROPAGATION
Sow seeds in early spring, in a greenhouse or indoors, providing warmth for germination. Seedlings can be pricked out into trays or individual 7.5cm (3in) pots. Harden off and plant out when danger of frost is over. Alternatively sow outdoors in mid-spring where the plants are to flower.

CULTIVATION
Full sun is essential together with soil that has been well-supplied with organic matter and fertilizer. Plenty of water is needed in summer.

PROPAGATION
Sow seeds in warmth under glass or indoors in mid-spring, one per 7.5cm (3in) pot. Plant out when danger of frost is over. Alternatively sow outdoors in late spring.

Alyssum maritimum (Lobularia maritima)
Sweet Alyssum

Spread 20–30cm (8–12in)
Height 7.5–15cm (3–6in)

HA

Alyssum is in the top-ten list of summer bedding plants and rightly so because it is very easily propagated and grown and flowers profusely for months on end.

It forms a hummocky mat of growth and when in full flower the foliage is barely visible. The individual flowers are tiny but are carried in clustered heads.

The traditional colour of Sweet Alyssum is white, and popular varieties in this colour include 'Little Dorrit', with an upright habit of growth and 'Carpet of Snow', a low-growing spreading variety with masses of pure white blooms.

There are varieties with flowers in other colours and these are becoming almost as popular as the white varieties. Particularly recommended are 'Rosie O'Day' in a most attractive clear rose-pink; 'Wonderland', with beautiful rich rose-red flowers and a sweet scent, borne on compact plants; and 'Oriental Night' with intense violet-purple flowers on compact plants with a spread of 20cm (8in).

Sweet Alyssum can be used in many ways for summer colour. Probably the most popular use is as edging to beds or borders, particularly if the planting consists of strongly coloured plants such as scarlet salvias or pelargoniums. It looks good planted in a wide band – at least 30cm (12in) – rather than in a thin strip.

Drifts of white alyssum look superb among shrubs in a mixed or shrub border and it *must* be included in any green and white planting scheme. It can also be grown on a rock garden to provide colour when the spring-flowering alpines have finished their display.

Sweet Alyssum is often used with other plants, such as lobelia and petunias, in ornamental containers such as hanging baskets, window boxes, tubs and urns: it is generally planted at the edges so that it cascades over the sides of the containers. It can be planted through the wires of hanging baskets, perhaps alternatively with blue lobelia. Alyssum will look perfectly at home in a cottage-garden border.

CULTIVATION
Alyssum will grow in any ordinary well-drained soil and best results are achieved in full sun. Shade for a small part of the day would be acceptable, though. Regularly remove dead flower heads with a pair of florists' scissors.

PROPAGATION
Sow seeds under glass or indoors in late winter/early spring and germinate in gentle heat. Prick out seedlings into trays, harden off and plant out in mid- or late spring. Alternatively sow outdoors in mid-spring where the plant are to flower.

Cineraria maritima
Silver-leaved Cineraria

Spread 30cm (12in)
Height 60cm (24in)

HHA

Although perennial this popular summer bedding plant is generally treated as a half-hardy annual. It will only survive mild winters out of doors. It has lobed and deeply cut leaves which are silvery grey, and the plant makes an excellent foil for bedding plants with strongly coloured flowers, such as scarlet pelargoniums and salvias. Use it as a dot plant in summer bedding schemes; also in containers such as tubs and window boxes. An excellent plant for a pink and silver planting scheme. Good varieties include 'Cirrus' and 'Silver Dust'.

The Silver-leaved Cineraria is an excellent temporary plant, too, for the mixed border, being ideal for filling gaps at the front of the border, especially if it can be combined with brightly coloured flowers or shrubs. It can also be recommended for edging beds of roses, as the silver foliage is a marvellous foil for highly coloured rose blooms.

There is no need to throw plants away at the end of the season – lift and pot them into suitable-size pots and grow as pot plants in a cool or slightly heated greenhouse. Or even take them into a cool room indoors where the foliage can be enjoyed over the winter.

CULTIVATION
Any ordinary well-drained soil is suitable and best growth is achieved in full sun, although the plant will not mind shade for part of the day. Cut off any flowers produced as they do not enhance the plants.

PROPAGATION
Sow seeds under glass or indoors in late winter/early spring and provide warmth for germination. Prick out seedlings into trays and plant out when the danger of frost is over. Alternatively, prick out individually into small pots.

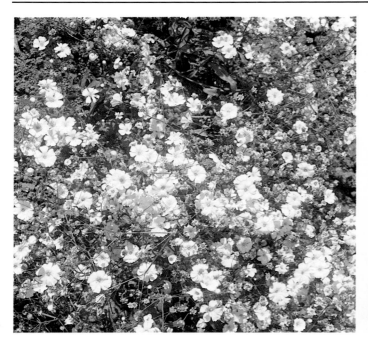

Gypsophila elegans
Baby's Breath

Spread 30cm (12in)
Height 60cm (24in) **HA**

This annual is an excellent foil for plants with strong coloured flowers and is good for separating strong or clashing colours. It is highly recommended for cutting and is often arranged with sweet peas. It looks at home in a shrub or mixed border and should be included in every green and white planting scheme.

Good varieties are 'Monarch Strain' and 'Giant White'.

CULTIVATION
Needs a well-drained soil but any type is suitable and it is particularly good on chalky soils. Provide a position in full sun for best results. Use twiggy sticks to support the thin stems.

PROPAGATION
Sow seeds in their flowering positions in early to mid-spring and thin out seedlings. Can also be sown in early autumn when flowering will be earlier the following year.

Matricaria eximea (Chrysanthemum parthenium)
Feverfew

Spread 20–45cm (8–18in)
Height 20–45cm (8–18in) **HA** **S**

Strictly speaking this is a short-lived perennial but it is generally treated as a hardy annual and discarded at the end of its flowering season. It's a bushy plant with aromatic foliage and in summer produces masses of button-like flowers. There are several varieties such as 'Snow Dwarf' ('White Stars') with double white flowers; 'Snowball', also white; and the golden-yellow 'Golden Ball'.

Feverfew is particularly useful for edging beds and borders, preferably in a wide band. It would also look good on a rock garden and is ideal for the edges of ornamental containers such as window boxes and tubs.

CULTIVATION
Any well-drained soil in full sun. Regularly remove dead flowers to encourage more to follow.

PROPAGATION
Generally raised under glass in early spring to get earlier flowers, but can also be sown outdoors in mid-spring where it is to flower.

Onopordum acanthium
Scotch Thistle

Spread 60cm (24in)
Height 1.8m (6ft)

HB

This is a really bold plant with branching winged stems and huge silvery-grey hairy leaves. During the summer the plant produces heads of purple thistle flowers. It's an extremely prickly plant so do not plant it where you are liable to brush by it!

The Scotch Thistle makes a superb specimen plant to act as a focal point in the garden. It can also be grown in a shrub or mixed border. It seeds itself so you may well find seedlings appearing around the parent plants.

CULTIVATION
Growth will be vigorous in a rich soil. Drainage must be good and a position which receives plenty of sun is needed. To prevent self-seeding remove dead flower heads. Protect plants from slugs.

PROPAGATION
Sow seeds in late spring where the plants are to grow and flower. Alternatively, sow under glass in early or mid-spring, one seed per small pot, and plant out before the seedlings become pot-bound.

The plants will flower the following year, after which they die.

Reseda odorata
Mignonette

Spread 30cm (12in)
Height 30–60cm (12–24in)

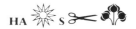

HA   S

A lovely old-fashioned annual with scented flowers. often grown in cottage gardens. It also looks at home in shrubberies or mixed borders and, of course, in annual borders. The blooms are excellent for cutting and arranging indoors. In the garden they attract bees.

The plant has an upright branching habit of growth and in summer bears off-white flowers. There are several varieties such as 'Fragrant Beauty', particularly well scented; 'Machet' with red-flushed blooms; and 'Red Monarch' which has red flowers.

CULTIVATION
An excellent annual for chalky or limy soils, although these conditions are not essential. Good drainage is, though. Be fairly generous with the fertilizer. Regularly remove dead flower heads to encourage more blooms to follow.

PROPAGATION
So seeds in early to mid-spring where the plants are to flower and thin out the resultant seedlings before they become overcrowded. Or sow under glass in early spring and plant out before plants become overcrowded in their trays. They will flower earlier. Can also be sown in early autumn to overwinter outdoors – again plants will flower earlier.

Verbascum bombyciferum (V. 'Broussa')
Mullein

Spread 60cm (24in)
Height 1.2–1.8m (4–6ft)   **HB**

Argemone mexicana
Prickly Poppy

Spread 30cm (12in)
Height 60cm (24in)   **HA**   **S**

This is a stately plant with silver hairy leaves and branching stems carrying pale yellow flowers. The flowering period is early to mid-summer.

This Mullein makes a superb specimen plant to act as a focal point in a garden. Alternatively use it at the back of a shrubbery or mixed border.

CULTIVATION
Any ordinary well-drained soil is suitable plus a position in full sun. Staking may be necessary in windy gardens, using a stout bamboo cane for each plant. Cut off the flower spikes when the blooms have faded.

PROPAGATION
Sow seeds in mid-spring and germinate in a cold frame. Prick out into nursery rows and plant in flowering positions in early autumn. Alternatively, plant direct into final positions.

This is an unusual annual and is certainly not found in all seed catalogues, but nevertheless it is easily grown and well worth garden space. The prickly deeply cut leaves are greyish green and attractively marked with white. Flowering starts in early summer and the poppy-like blooms are mainly yellow although sometimes orangy and are scented.

This is a suitable subject for a shubbery, or an annual or mixed border and is best sown in a bold group for maximum impact.

CULTIVATION
This annual revels in a light, dry, sandy soil and full sun, so plant it in those difficult 'hot spots'. Although the stems are somewhat sprawling and succulent the plants should not be provided with supports. Regular removal of dead flowers will encourage more blooms to follow.

PROPAGATION
Sow under glass or indoors during early spring, transplant seedlings into small pots, harden and plant out in late spring. Alternatively sow in the open during mid-spring where the plants are to flower.

Calceolaria integrifolia (C. rugosa)
Slipperwort, Bedding Calceolaria

Spread 30cm (12in)
Height 45–60cm (18–24in)   **HHA**

Coreopsis tinctoria
Tickseed

Spread 15–20cm (6–8in)
Height 30–90cm (12–36in)   **HA**

This is one of the bedding calceolarias and strictly speaking is a half-hardy perennial, but plants are generally discarded at the end of the flowering season. It is a bushy plant with a long succession of bright yellow pouched flowers. A popular variety, easily raised from seed, is 'Sunshine'. Also worth growing is 'Golden Bunch' (a *C. rugosa* × *C. herbeo-hybrida* variety).

An attractive annual for summer bedding, containers or rock garden.

CULTIVATION
A light well-drained soil is best plus a sunny sheltered position.

PROPAGATION
Sow seeds in early spring under glass or indoors and germinate in gentle warmth (15°C/60°F). Do not cover seeds with compost. Transplant seedlings into trays; eventually harden and plant out when the danger of frost is over.

This annual has a long succession of daisy-like flowers which are suitable for cutting and arranging indoors. The species has bright yellow flowers but mixtures are also offered with blooms in various shades. Popular are dwarf mixtures which grow to about 30cm (12in) in height. Grow Tickseed in an annual border or sow bold groups in a mixed border.

CULTIVATION
The ideal soil is light, well drained and reasonably fertile. Plenty of sun is needed for sturdy growth and flowering. Twiggy sticks will be needed to support tall plants. Remove dead flower heads to encourage more blooms to follow.

PROPAGATION
Sow seeds where the plants are to flower during early to mid-spring and thin out the seedlings before they become overcrowded, or sow in early autumn to overwinter under cloches for earlier flowers.

Helianthus annuus
Sunflower

Spread 30–45cm (12–18in)
Height 1–3m (3–10ft)

HA

Although the Sunflower is often considered a 'fun plant' and is popular with children on account of its height and huge flowers, it does, nevertheless, make a fine show at the back of a border. The blooms are like massive daisies. The main colour is yellow but mixtures are also offered with flowers in several colours. Most popular are varieties such as 'Giant Single' and 'Sunburst Mixed'. Also worth growing is *H. cucumerifolius* 'Bouquet Mixed'.

Unfortunately in Britain Sunflowers can be disappointing if the summer is wet – as it often is. The blooms appear in late summer and autumn, at which time the air can also be very damp. In wet or damp conditions the blooms may become infected by the fungal disease botrytis or grey mould, which reduces them to a soggy mess. The blooms become covered with grey fluffy fungus. There is really not a great deal one can do about this, except perhaps to spray the plants with systemic fungicide such as benomyl.

It is interesting to note that some farmers in Britain are trying to grow Sunflowers for the seeds, the oil of which is used in the manufacture of margerine. So in the future, if the trials prove successful, we may see vast fields of sunflowers in the countryside!

CULTIVATION
Plenty of sun is needed for sturdy growth and flowering, plus well-drained soil. The tall varieties will need the support of thick bamboo canes, tying in the stems with soft garden string. Remove dead flower heads to prevent self-seeding.

PROPAGATION
Sow seeds where the plants are to flower, in early or mid-spring. Place two or three seeds at each position and thin out the resultant seedlings to leave the strongest one.

Hunnemannia fumariifolia
Mexican Tulip Poppy

Spread 20cm (8in)
Height 60–90cm (24–36in)

HHA

A rather unusual annual but a most attractive one with its brilliant yellow poppy flowers in summer and lacy bluish green foliage. The flowers last well in water so are suitable for cutting. It is best to seal the ends of the stems in a flame before arranging in vases. There is a variety named 'Sunlite' which has semi-double flowers.

Grow the Mexican Tulip Poppy in an annual, mixed or shrub border in a bold group for best effect.

CULTIVATION
A hot dry spot is ideal for this annual. Remove dead flowers. A few small twiggy sticks may be needed for support.

PROPAGATION
Seeds are sown under glass or indoors in early spring, transplanting the seedlings to individual small pots. Harden and plant out when danger of frost is over. Alternatively sow the seeds in the open during mid-spring where the plants are to flower.

Mentzelia lindleyi (Bartonia aurea)
Blazing Stars

Spread 15–20cm (6–8in)
Height 45cm (18in)

HA

This is a popular hardy annual, bushy in habit, with succulent stems, coarsely toothed green foliage and shiny deep yellow cup-shaped flowers each with a central prominent tuft of stamens. The flowering period is early to mid-summer.

Blazing Stars can be most effective in mixed borders, annual borders, in cottage gardens and even on a largish rock garden.

CULTIVATION
A hot dry situation suits this annual and it will even succeed in an exposed windy garden, when it may need a few short twiggy sticks for support.

PROPAGATION
Seeds are sown where the plants are to flower, in early to mid-spring. Thin out the seedlings before they become overcrowded, but do this carefully to avoid damaging the soft succulent seedlings which are to remain.

Pyrethrum parthenium (Chrysanthemum parthenium)
Golden Feather

Spread 20cm (8in)
Height 25cm (10in)   HA

Rudbeckia hirta
Black-eyed Susan

Spread 30–45cm (12–18in)
Height 45–60cm (18–24in)   HHA

Golden Feather is a popular edging plant for summer bedding schemes and has bright yellow foliage which is finely cut. Flowers can be cut off before they open if you feel they detract from the beauty of the plants.

This annual (or strictly speaking, short-lived perennial) can also be grown in containers such as tubs and window boxes, planting it at the edges. Also use it to fill gaps on a rock garden and plant it in gaps in paving.

There are several varieties available such as 'Golden Fleece' and 'Golden Moss'.

Although this is a short-lived perennial it is grown as a half-hardy annual. The large yellow black-eyed daisy flowers are extremely showy and excellent for cutting and arranging indoors. The flowering period is late summer and autumn when many other annuals are going over.

There are several good varieties including 'Goldilocks', with double and semi-double blooms in rich golden-orange, on long stems; 'Marmalade', rich golden-orange flowers with black centres; and 'Rustic Dwarfs' in gold, bronze and mahogany shades.

CULTIVATION
Any well-drained soil is suitable plus full sun or partial shade. Too much shade will result in loss of leaf colour. If you wish, leave the plants in the ground at the end of the season – they may well overwinter successfully.

PROPAGATION
Sow seeds in early spring under glass or indoors, transplant the seedlings to trays and plant out in late spring. Can be sown out of doors if desired in mid- to late spring but this is not the normal practice.

CULTIVATION
Easily grown in any well-drained soil and full sun. May need a few short twiggy sticks for support. Stands up well to adverse weather conditions. Watch out for slugs and snails.

PROPAGATION
Sow seeds under glass or indoors in early to mid-spring, transplant seedlings to trays, harden before planting out in late spring.

Tagetes erecta
African Marigold

Spread 30–45cm (12–18in)
Height 30–90cm (12–36in)

HHA

African Marigolds are extremely popular for summer
bedding. They make an incredible show, flowering
continuously from early summer until the frosts start in
autumn.

They are often mass planted in beds, especially the dwarf
ones; the dwarfs can also be grown in tubs and window
boxes; and they can be planted in bold groups in an annual
border, particularly the tall varieties. The flowers last well
when cut and arranged indoors.

There are dozens of varieties to choose from, such as the
'Inca' series. These are dwarfs, attaining about 35cm (14in)
in height, and include 'Inca Orange' which has enormous
ball-like double flowers of bright orange; 'Inca Yellow', the
bright yellow counterpart of 'Inca Orange'; and 'Inca Gold'
in a rich golden-yellow. It is also possible to buy a mixture of
'Inca' varieties.

The 'Galore' series is popular in the USA and also available
in Britain. They have huge double flowers and grow to about
45cm (18in) in height. There's 'Gold Galore' in
golden-yellow and 'Yellow Galore', a good clear yellow.

The Jubilee series is highly recommended, with large
double flowers and growing to about 60cm (24in). They are
known in America as 'hedge marigolds' and are vigorous
bushy plants with good wind resistance. Varieties are
'Diamond Jubilee', bright yellow; 'Golden Jubilee', golden
yellow; and 'Jubilee Mixed', which includes yellow,
golden-yellow and orange.

The 'Perfection' series has double flowers and reaches
35cm (14in) in height. 'Perfection Gold' is compact,
vigorous, free-flowering and highly resistant to bad weather.

The large rounded flowers are packed with golden-yellow
petals.

The 'Climax' series is tall, up to 76cm (30in), with large
fully double flowers. Colours include yellow, gold, pale
yellow and orange.

'Toreador' grows to 76cm (30in) and carries huge double
rich orange flowers.

CULTIVATION
Marigolds grow best in a
reasonably fertile soil but will
also succeed in poor dry
conditions. Full sun is needed.
Regularly cut off dead flower
heads to encourage more
blooms to follow. Guard against
slugs and snails.

PROPAGATION
Sow seeds under glass or
indoors during early or
mid-spring. Transplant
seedlings to trays or small pots;
harden and plant out when the
danger of frost is over.

Tagetes patula
French Marigold

Spread 20–30cm (8–12in)
Height 15–30cm (6–12in)

HHA

The French Marigolds are as popular as the Africans. They are also used for summer bedding, being mass planted in beds where they make a continuous show from early summer until the frosts of autumn put a stop to the display.

They can also be used for edging beds and are ideally suited to containers such as tubs and window boxes. French Marigolds can also be planted in hanging baskets.

All varieties are dwarf and may have fully double or single flowers. The main colour is yellow but other colours are available.

'Honeycomb' grows to 25cm (10in) high and has fully double crested blooms in yellow and reddish orange – a variegated effect. The flowers really glow.

The 'Queen' series is highly recommended. These are camellia-flowered marigolds and attain a height of around 30cm (12in). 'Queen Sophia' is dark apricot-orange and red while 'Scarlet Sophia' has vermilion-red blooms. Also available is a 'Queen Mixture'.

'Yellow Jacket' is a crested marigold with large double blooms in mid-yellow and it grows to a height of 20cm (8in). 'Susie Wong' has large single flowers in deep yellow and attains about 30cm (12in) in height.

'Cinnabar' grows to 30cm (12in), has superb large single blooms in scarlet and comes into bloom early. 'Seven Star Red' is a triploid hybrid – that is, it is unable to produce seeds so it puts all its energy into flowering. It grows to 30cm (12in) in height and has beautifully ruffled, fully double, mahogany red blooms at least 7.5cm (3in) across. It is extremely early and most impressive when mass planted.

The 'Boy' series is also recommended, with double flowers, such as 'Orange Boy', 15cm (6in), deep orange, and 'Boy-O-Boy Mixed', 15cm (6in), in golden-yellow, pure yellow and mahogany/gold.

There are many others that could be recommended so have a look through the catalogues to see what takes your fancy. Look out, too, for the 'Bonanza' series.

CULTIVATION
Provide a reasonably fertile soil. although plants will succeed in poor dry conditions. Full sun is needed. Regularly cut off dead flower heads to encourage more blooms to follow. Guard against slugs and snails.

PROPAGATION
Sow seeds under glass or indoors during early or mid-spring. Transplant seedlings to trays; harden and plant out when the danger of frost is over.

Tagetes tenuifolia (T. signata)
Tagetes

Spread 20–30cm (8–12in)
Height 20–30cm (8–12in)

HHA

This is a neat bushy annual with light green feathery foliage and a long succession of small flowers, produced in such profusion that they almost obscure the foliage. It's a popular plant for summer bedding, particularly for edging beds, and for colour in tubs, window boxes and hanging baskets.

Flower colours include orange, yellow, golden-yellow and red. One can buy varieties in single colours or in mixtures. The orange, yellow or golden-yellow varieties make a particularly attractive edging for a bed or blue or purple petunias or heliotrope. They are often used, too, with the wax begonia, whose flowers are red, pink or white.

Tagetes can also be recommended for the mixed border as they are useful for filling gaps at the front. In this instance they can be planted in bold informal groups, ideally associating them with blue-flowered shrubs or perennials, or with purple-leaved shrubs. They would not look too much out of place on the larger rock garden, where they would provide much-needed colour in summer and early autumn.

Many people prefer Tagetes to French Marigolds as the foliage is sweet smelling, whereas that of marigolds is very pungent and not to everyone's liking.

It is normally the *pumila* varieties that are grown such as 'Tangerine Gem' with large flowers of intense deep orange; 'Lemon Gem', like 'Golden Gem' in habit but with larger bright lemon-yellow flowers; 'Golden Gem', bright golden-yellow flowers on compact globular plants; 'Paprika', brilliant red petals edged with gold, tiny flowers; and 'Starfire', a mixture of reds, oranges and yellows, giving overall an incredibly brilliant effect.

CULTIVATION
Ideally grown in a fertile soil in full sun, Tagetes will also tolerate poor soils and very dry conditions. Regularly remove dead flowers, and guard against slugs.

PROPAGATION
Sow seeds under glass or indoors in early to mid-spring. Transplant seedlings to trays, eventually harden and plant out when the danger of frost is over.

Thunbergia alata
Black-eyed Susan

Spread 15cm (6in)
Height 3m (10ft)   HHA

Tropaeolum peregrinum (T. canariense)
Canary Creeper

Spread 90cm (36in)
Height 3.6m (12ft)   HA

This annual can be grown up a wall or trellis or allowed to trail from a hanging basket. The flowers are about 5cm (2in) wide and yellow with a dark brown centre. The flowering period is early summer to early autumn. Best results are obtained in a warm summer. Can also be grown in pots in a greenhouse or conservatory.

'Susie Mixed' includes several colours: orange, yellow and white self-colours and the same shades with black centres. Particularly recommended for hanging baskets.

CULTIVATION
A very well-drained soil is needed and a sheltered position in full sun. If these plants are to be grown against a wall or fence give them something to grip on to such as netting or wall trellis.

PROPAGATION
Seeds are sown under glass or indoors in early spring, ideally one per 7.5cm (3in) pot. Pot on to a 10cm (4in) pot. Harden and plant out when the danger of frost is over.

This extremely vigorous plant is really a short-lived perennial but is treated as an annual. The foliage is bluish green and in summer masses of yellow flowers are produced. Flowering generally continues well into the autumn.

Grow it up a wall or fence, providing something for it to cling to such as netting or wall trellis. Or allow it to scramble through large shrubs. It can also be grown up tall twiggy sticks in a border, particularly in a shrub or mixed border.

CULTIVATION
Needs plenty of sun and a moderately fertile soil if it is to grow to its full extent. Initially support plants with short twiggy sticks.

PROPAGATION
Sow outdoors in mid-spring where the plants are to flower. Best to sow two seeds at each position; if both germinate remove the weaker seedling.

Calendula officinalis
Pot Marigold

Spread 30cm (12in)
Height 30–60cm (12–24in)

HA

The Pot Marigold is an old-fashioned hardy annual which was a familiar sight in cottage gardens of the past. It is still as popular as ever but in recent years many new and improved varieties have appeared, most being of dwarf compact habit and in a wider range of colours. The traditional colour of the daisy-like flowers is orange and the flowering season is from late spring to autumn.

One of the best orange varieties is 'Orange King' with large double flowers and growing to a height of 45-60cm (18-24in).

'Fiesta Gitana' is a mixture of colours which vary from creamy yellow to deepest orange. The flowers are double, some with yellow centres others with brown. Height is 30cm (12in).

rather like chrysanthemums in a range of bright colours. Height is 60cm (24in).

A brand new mixture is 'Touch of Class', which includes peach-pink shades. The petals are bronze on the undersides. This mixture is something quite different.

Pot Marigolds have various uses: grow them in an annual or mixed border, in a cottage garden border, or even in a row in the vegetable plot specially for cutting – the blooms last well in water.

CULTIVATION
Pot Marigolds have few demands. They will grow in the poorest soils although best results are achieved in moderately fertile soils. Drainage must be good. Full sun is recommended for sturdy growth and optimum flowering. If you are growing the plants specially for cutting the terminal buds of the young plants should be cut out to encourage branching and therefore more flowers. Regularly remove dead flower heads to encourage more blooms to follow and to prevent self-seeding – marigolds can become weeds! Guard plants against slugs and snails.

PROPAGATION
Seeds are sown where the plants are to flower in early or mid-spring. Thin out the seedlings to the recommended spacing before they become overcrowded. Alternatively sow seeds in early autumn and overwinter the seedlings in the open, or under cloches in colder areas, to obtain earlier flowers the following year.

Dimorphotheca aurantiaca
Star of the Veldt

Spread 30cm (12in)
Height 30–45cm (12–18in)

HHA

Eschscholzia californica
California Poppy

Spread 15cm (6in)
Height 30cm (12in)

HA

Strictly speaking this is a perennial but it is usually grown as a half-hardy annual. It produces quite large bright orange daisy flowers in profusion from early summer to early autumn. These open only when the weather is bright and sunny – they will not open on dull days or if the plants are grown in shade.

Most seedsmen offer mixed hybrids in a range of colours including orange shades, buff, amber, gold, salmon, etc.

Use dimorphothecas for summer bedding or for the front of an annual, mixed or shrub border. They're ideal for providing summer colour on a rock garden and suitable for tubs and window boxes.

CULTIVATION
Full sun is essential, together with well-drained soil. Regularly remove dead flower heads to encourage more blooms.

PROPAGATION
Sow seeds under glass or indoors in early spring, transplant to small pots, harden off and plant out when the danger of frost is over. Alternatively sow outdoors in late spring.

This easy annual with bright poppy-like flowers will grow even in the poorest conditions. It must have plenty of sun for the flowers to open. The species itself, with bright orange flowers, is popular but mixtures such as 'Monarch Art Shades Mixed' with semi-double flowers in many brilliant colours are also widely grown. The mixture 'Ballerina' has more double and ruffled blooms.

The flowering period is from early summer to mid-autumn.

CULTIVATION
Full sun and well-drained soil are essential. Poor soils are perfectly acceptable. Pick off dead flowers before they set seeds.

PROPAGATION
Sow seeds where they are to flower, particularly in annual borders, mixed borders and on a rock garden. Sowing time is early spring, or early autumn for earlier flowers the following year.

Tithonia rotundifolia (T. speciosa) _____
Mexican Sunflower

Spread 30cm (12in)
Height 90cm (36in)

HHA

This half-hardy annual, which is not too well-known, has attractive bright daisy flowers from mid-summer until the frosts of autumn. The colour is deep orange-red and each flower has a yellow centre. Blooms are excellent for cutting.

Good varieties are 'Goldfinger' in bright orange-scarlet and 'Torch' in the same colour.

Grow the Mexican Sunflower in an annual or mixed border, setting it fairly well back because it's a tallish plant.

CULTIVATION
The Mexican Sunflower flourishes in any soil with good drainage provided the site is in full sun. Regularly cut off dead flower heads and provide twiggy sticks for support.

PROPAGATION
Sow seeds in late winter or early spring under glass or indoors. Transplant to trays and plant out when the danger of frost is over, after hardening.

Ursinia pulchra (U. versicolor) _____
Ursinia

Spread 15cm (6in)
Height 30cm (12in)

HHA

This is a charming bushy annual with feathery deep green leaves and brilliant orange flowers, each with a purplish zone. The flowering period is from early to late summer.

Ideal for the annual or mixed border and even for the larger rock garden.

CULTIVATION
Ursinia prefers a light sandy soil and it must be given a position in full sun. Picking off the dead flower heads will encourage more blooms to follow.

PROPAGATION
Seeds are sown in early spring under glass or indoors and should be only lightly covered with compost. Transplant to trays and plant out when the danger of frost is over, after hardening.

Venidium fatuosum
Monarch of the Veldt

Spread 30cm (12in)
Height 60cm (24in)

HHA

Alonsoa warscewiczii (A. grandiflora)
Mask Flower

Spread 20cm (8in)
Height 45cm (18in)

HHA

Monarch of the Veldt has large daisy flowers in deep orange, each with a brown central zone. The flowering period is early summer to mid-autumn. The foliage is also attractive, being deeply lobed and silvery in colour.

Can be mass planted in summer bedding schemes or used to fill gaps in a mixed or shrub border. Suitable for growing in large tubs. The flowers are good for cutting.

CULTIVATION
Monarch of the Veldt prefers a light well-drained soil with organic matter added. A site in full sun is recommended. It is best to provide the plants with a few twiggy sticks for support and the dead flower heads should be removed.

PROPAGATION
Sow seeds under glass or indoors during early spring and transplant the seedlings to individual small pots. Harden off and plant out when the danger of frost is over. Alternatively sow outdoors in late spring and thin out resultant seedlings.

This is a bushy perennial but generally treated as a half-hardy annual. It has a long flowering season, from early summer until well into autumn, when the frosts put a stop to the display. Masses of flattish rounded red flowers are produced against a background of deep green toothed foliage.

Grow the Mask Flower in an annual border or in a mixed or shrub border. It is a fairly unusual annual but well worth growing for its profusion of flowers.

CULTIVATION
The Mask Flower likes a moisture-retentive yet well-drained soil in full sun. One can with advantage add organic matter such as peat to soils which are naturally very dry.

PROPAGATION
Sow seeds under glass or indoors during early spring. Transplant to trays and plant out when the danger of frost is over, after hardening the plants.

Amaranthus caudatus
Love-lies-bleeding

Spread 45cm (18in)
Height 90cm (36in)

HHA

This plant is grown for its pendulous tassels of red flowers which may be up to 45cm (18in) long. The flowering period is from mid-summer to mid-autumn.

In catalogues it is usually offered as *Amaranthus* Dark Red, with deep red blooms. Also worth growing is the variety 'Viridis' with pale green tassels, an ideal plant for a green and white planting scheme.

Love-lies-bleeding is often used in sub-tropical bedding schemes. It could also be grown in a mixed border or in large tubs.

CULTIVATION
A good deep fertile soil with manure or compost added suits this amaranthus, but reasonable results are achieved in poorer soils. Choose a position which receives plenty of sun.

PROPAGATION
Sow seeds in early spring under glass or indoors. The seedlings should be potted into individual small pots. Harden and plant out when the danger of frost is over. Alternatively sow outdoors in flowering position during mid-spring.

Amaranthus tricolor
Joseph's Coat

Spread 30–45cm (12–18in)
Height 60–90cm (24–36in)

HHA

This amaranthus is also recommended for sub-tropical bedding schemes and is grown for its brilliant foliage which is basically red although other colours are present. It would also make a good dot plant in summer bedding schemes to give height and contrast. Also suitable for growing in large tubs.

It makes a bushy plant and the large leaves are generally oval and pointed, but can vary in shape according to variety.

It is varieties that are grown rather than the species. There are several to choose from and particularly recommended is 'Joseph's Coat', an improved form of the species with scarlet, yellow and green leaves.

'Flaming Fountains' is truly spectacular, almost overpowering, with glowing flame-coloured leaves. It is a compact base-branching plant, shorter than average at only 30cm (12in) in height. 'Molten Fire' is variegated with purple, bronze and crimson-scarlet leaves and is also a most striking variety.

CULTIVATION
A good deep fertile soil with manure or compost added suits this foliage amaranthus, but reasonable results are achieved in poorer soils. Choose a position which receives plenty of sun.

PROPAGATION
Sow seeds in early spring under glass or indoors. The seedlings should be potted into individual small pots. Harden and plant out when the danger of frost is over.

Begonia semperflorens
Wax Begonia

Spread 15–20cm (6–8in)
Height 15–30cm (6–12in)   HHA

The Wax Begonia is a favourite summer bedding plant, particularly as a carpet in formal schemes, and as an edging for beds and borders. It is also good in tubs, window boxes and hanging baskets.

Flowering period from early summer until the autumn frosts, the main flower colour is red but shades of pink and white are also available, with many varieties to choose from in mixed colours.

'Cocktail' comes in a wide range of rich bright colours and the leaves are dark shining bronze. 'Orandie' mixture is similar except that the leaves are both green and bronze. Both are weather resistant, dwarf compact plants.

The 'Coco' series is highly recommended: 'Coco Ducolor' whose flowers are white edged with red, set against bronze foliage; 'Coco Pink', pink flowers and bronze foliage; 'Coco Bright Scarlet', brilliant scarlet blooms and bronze foliage; and 'Coco Mixed' with deep brown foliage and scarlet, red, white, pale and deep pink flowers.

CULTIVATION
Wax Begonias like a fertile moisture-retentive soil so work in peat or compost before planting if your soil is light and sandy. Plants grow well in sun or partial shade.

PROPAGATION
Sow seeds under glass or indoors during late winter and do not cover them with compost because they are as fine as dust. Transplant to trays and plant out when the danger of frost is over after hardening the plants.

Coleus blumei
Flame Nettle

Spread 30–45cm (12–18in)
Height 30–60cm (12–24in)   HHA

The Flame Nettle is often thought of as a greenhouse pot plant but it is also successful as a summer bedding plant.

It is perhaps most suited to sub-tropical bedding schemes but it can also be included in normal summer bedding schemes, perhaps as a dot plant to give height and contrast. Use it also in containers such as tubs, window boxes and for the centres of hanging baskets.

Flame Nettle is a foliage plant with highly coloured leaves, the basic colour being red. It does flower but blooms should be cut off.

There are many varieties, all of which range from 30–60cm (12–24in) in height, including 'Fashion Parade' in a mixture of colours and leaf forms; 'Wizard Mixed', another brightly coloured mix with uniform rounded leaf form; 'Saber', narrow leaves in many colours; 'Dragon', a brilliant mix; and 'Carefree', a mixture of oak-leaved types. One can buy separate colours: 'Scarlet Poncho', 'Rose Wizard' and 'Red Monarch' all about 30cm high.

CULTIVATION
These plants require a well-drained yet moisture-retentive soil and full sun or partial shade. Guard against slugs and snails.

PROPAGATION
Sow seeds in early spring under glass or indoors, transplant to trays and harden thoroughly before planting out when the frosts have finished.

Cosmos bipinnatus
Cosmos

Spread 60cm (24in)
Height 30–90cm (12–36in)

HHA

Glaucium corniculatum
Horned Poppy

Spread 30cm (12in)
Height 25cm (10in)

HA

A popular annual for borders and for cutting. It has finely cut foliage and large rounded flowers in shades of red and pink. Flowering period is mid- to late summer to early autumn.

Recommended varieties are 'Candytripe', 75cm (30in), white flowers striped red; and 'Sensation', 90cm (36in), a mix of red, pink and white. Also try the *C. sulphureus* varieties 'Bright Lights', 75cm (30in), a mix of gold, orange and scarlet; 'Diablo', 60cm (24in), orange-red; 'Sunny Gold', 40cm (16in), golden-yellow; and 'Sunny Red', 30cm (12in), orange vermilion.

CULTIVATION
Cosmos prefers a light well-drained poor soil and full sun and does not do so well in wet summers. Tall varieties will need supports, and remove the dead flower heads.

PROPAGATION
Sow seeds under glass or indoors in late winter/early spring; transplant seedlings to trays; harden well and plant out after frosts.

This is not one of the best-known annuals but it is well worth growing in a mixed or shrub border. It produces crimson poppy flowers in summer and has deeply cut downy foliage.

CULTIVATION
Any ordinary garden soil is suitable provided the drainage is good. An open position in full sun is needed.

PROPAGATION
Sow seeds in early to mid-spring where the plants are to flower. Thin out the seedlings before they become overcrowded. Do not attempt to transplant seedlings as they do not always re-establish – they dislike root disturbance. Seeds should have only a light covering of soil.

Impatiens wallerana (I. holstii)
Busy Lizzie

Spread 30cm (12in)
Height 15–30cm (6–12in)

HHA

The Busy Lizzie has become very popular as a summer bedding plant. Formerly it was mainly grown as a greenhouse pot plant.

Many new varieties have been produced in recent years, these being of dwarf compact habit and in a wide range of colours. The basic colour is red and impatiens comes in all shades of this. Pink shades are prominent and there are also orange shades and white.

Flowering is continuous from early summer until the autumn frosts put a stop to the display. The plants smother themselves with blooms, hiding most of the foliage.

Busy Lizzies can be mass planted in summer bedding schemes (particularly in sub-tropical schemes), grown in ornamental containers such as tubs, window boxes and hanging baskets and do not look out of place planted in bold drifts among shrubs or perennials.

There are many varieties worth growing including the 'Super Elfin' series, which includes 'Lipstick', 20cm (8in) high with large rose-red flowers. It's very early, compact and free flowering. Other varieties in this series are 'Blush', 'Orange', 'Red', 'Salmon', 'Fuchsia', 'Orchid Blue' and 'White'.

'Blitz', 15cm (6in), has extra-large orange-scarlet flowers and bronze-green foliage.

'Novette Mixed' is popular, at 10cm (4in) high. The mix includes many bright colours and the flowers are large. Separate colours are also available.

The 'Rosette Hybrids', 15cm (6in), have double and semi double flowers and colours include scarlet, rose, salmon, pink and white. 'Confection Mixed', 20cm (8in), has mainly double flowers and colours include red, orange, pink and

rose. This is a considerable improvement on the 'Rosette Hybrids'.

'Accent' is another highly recommended mix and has large flowers appearing early in the season.

CULTIVATION
A moisture-retentive soil is best so add plenty of bulky organic matter if you have a light soil which rapidly dries out. Grow in full sun, partial shade or full shade. Keep well supplied with water in summer.

PROPAGATION
Sow seeds in early spring under glass or indoors. Do not cover seeds with compost because they are as fine as dust. Transplant to trays; harden and plant out after frosts.

Linum grandiflorum
Annual Flax

Spread 15cm (6in)
Height 30–45cm (12–18in)

HA

The Annual Flax or *Linum grandiflorum* is a popular and most attractive hardy annual with several uses. It is, of course, a suitable candidate for the annual border. However, it would not look out of place in the mixed border as it associates well with hardy herbaceous perennials and with shrubs.

Try the Annual Flax, too, on the larger rock garden where it will help to provide much-needed colour during the summer, when the majority of rock plants have finished their display. As it is a fairly tall plant, do not place it at the top of a rock garden, where it would create a rather top-heavy effect, but rather on the lower levels.

The Annual Flax is a thin-stemmed plant with light green, slender pointed leaves. These make a nice foil for the small bowl-shaped rose-red flowers which are freely produced between early and late summer.

Although the species is sometimes available, the variety 'Rubrum' is usually grown and it is certainly more showy than the species. It is popularly known as the Scarlet Flax due to its brilliant scarlet flowers.

CULTIVATION
Flax is easily grown and will thrive in any ordinary garden soil provided the drainage is good. If drainage needs improving then work into the soil a liberal dressing of coarse horticultural sand or grit. This will open up the soil and allow surplus water to easily drain to lower levels.

Flax enjoys lime in the soil although this is not essential for its well-being.

Full sun, though, is necessary for optimum flowering so choose an open position which receives sun for best part of the day.

As the stems of Flax are rather thin, a few short twiggy sticks may be needed for support, particularly if the garden is prone to winds. Thin-stemmed plants are particularly prone to being flattened by wind when they are heavy with rain.

PROPAGATION
Seeds should be sown where the plants are to flower, the best time being early spring. Before the seedlings start to become overcrowded they should be thinned out.

Alternatively make a sowing in early autumn if you have a very well-drained soil and live in a comparitively mild area. The plants are overwintered out of doors, ideally with a covering of cloches, and will produce earlier blooms the following year.

Pelargonium x hortorum
Zonal Geranium

Spread 30–45cm (12–18in)
Height 30–60cm (12–24in)

HHA

The Zonal Geranium is one of the essential summer bedding plants. The modern seed-raised strains are now widely used for this purpose. Although the plants are strictly perennial they are treated as annuals and discarded in the autumn when the frosts put a stop to the display. Flowering is continuous throughout summer.

The Zonal Geranium is mass planted in formal summer bedding schemes, in tubs and window boxes and can be used as a centrepiece for hanging baskets.

The main colour is red, which comes in all shades. The flowers are brilliant and need toning down with suitable dot plants such as silver-leaved cineraria or the effect can be overpowering.

Other colours include shades of pink, orange and also white. There are one or two purplish varieties.

There's a great range of varieties available from seedsmen. Here we can only take a look at a few of the best.

The 'Video' series is early flowering with a compact habit of growth. It has dark foliage and comes in a bright mix of colours. Ideal for window boxes.

The 'Diamond' series is perfect for bedding and has extremely good weather resistance. The plants are compact, free flowering and early. There's 'Scarlet Diamond', bright scarlet; 'Cherry Diamond', luminous cherry red; and 'Rose Diamond', rose-red.

'Hollywood Star' is a striking white and rose bicolor and comes into flower early in the season.

The 'Orbit' series can be highly recommended and has distinct foliage zoning. It is available in mixtures or separate colours, including 'Orange Orbit', almost pure orange;

'Scarlet Orbit Improved', with large flowers; and 'White Orbit', pure white.

Last but not least, the 'Sprinter' series is slightly later and larger than the 'Diamond' series but very free flowering. 'Sprinter' itself is a glowing salmon-scarlet.

CULTIVATION
Choose a position in full sun with a moderately fertile soil. It is important regularly to pick off dead flower heads.

PROPAGATION
Sow seeds under glass or indoors as early as possible – in early or mid-winter. Transplant the seedlings to individual 7.5cm (3in) pots; pot on to 12.5cm (5in) pots; harden well and plant out when the danger of frost is over.

Ricinus communis
Castor Oil Plant

Spread 90cm (36in)
Height 1.2–1.5m (4–5ft)

HHA

The Castor Oil Plant is excellent for giving height to formal summer bedding schemes. There's no better foliage plant for sub-tropical schemes and it does not look out of place in a shrub or mixed border.

It has large palmate leaves, green in the species but bronzy in the several varieties. The variety 'Gibsonii' has beautiful bronze foliage and is more compact in habit than the species. 'Impala' is a newer variety, again with striking bronze leaves.
Warning: all parts of the plant (including seeds) are poisonous.

CULTIVATION
A reasonably fertile soil well enriched with organic matter such as garden compost or peat is best. Full sun is ideal but it does quite well in partial shade. Provide bamboo canes for support particularly if the garden is prone to winds.

PROPAGATION
Sow seeds in late winter or early spring, under glass or indoors. It is best to sow one seed per 7.5cm (3in) pot and later to pot on to 12.5cm (5in) pots. Harden well before planting out when the danger of frost is over.

Salvia splendens
Scarlet Sage

Spread 20–30cm (8 –12in)
Height 30cm (12in)

HHA

This is one of the most popular summer bedding plants with its brilliant scarlet blooms throughout summer.

There are many to choose from and some of the best include 'Blaze of Fire', vivid scarlet, early and compact, a most popular variety; 'Carabiniere', deep crimson blooms and dark green foliage; 'Red Riches' ('Ryco'). dazzling scarlet spikes on compact plants, dark green foliage, early flowering; 'Red Hot Sally', small plants, early flowering, brilliant scarlet, highly popular in N. America; 'Caramba', scarlet; and 'Dress Parade Mixed', an eye-catching mix of scarlet, rose, pink, purple and white, early flowering and of dwarf habit. A bright deep purple variety is 'Laser Purple' which makes a good contrast with the scarlet varieties.

CULTIVATION
Any reasonable, well-drained garden soil is suitable for salvias. A position which receives plenty of sun is recommended for optimum growth and flowering. The tips of young plants should be pinched out when they are about 7.5cm (3in) high to encourage side shoots and hence more flowers. Regularly cut off dead flowers to encourage more to follow. This is a bit tedious but well worth doing.

PROPAGATION
Sow seeds in late winter or early spring in a greenhouse or indoors. The seedlings should be transplanted to trays before they become overcrowded. Grow on the young plants in warm conditions – no lower than 10°C (50°F) and harden thoroughly before planting out when the danger of frost is over.

Agrostemma githago
Corn Cockle

Spread 20cm (8in)
Height 60–90cm (24–36in)

HA

The wild Corn Cockle is a weed in southern Europe and is not grown in gardens. There is, however, an attractive variety of the wild species which is a popular hardy annual. It is called 'Milas' and bears rose-pink flowers during the summer. These make a good show if the plants are grown in a group. It should be noted that the seeds of the Corn Cockle are poisonous.

Grow the Corn Cockle in an annual border, or sow in bold groups in a mixed border or shrubbery.

CULTIVATION
Full sun is needed for optimum growth and flowering. Any ordinary garden soil is suitable provided the drainage is good. The Corn Cockle actually prefers a limy or chalky soil but this is not essential. Provide twiggy sticks for support.

PROPAGATION
Seeds are sown where the plants are to flower during early spring. Thin out the seedlings before they become overcrowded. Alternatively make a sowing in early autumn and overwinter the seedlings under cloches in cold areas. You will then get earlier flowers.

Clarkia elegans
Clarkia

Spread 30cm (12in)
Height 30–60cm (12–24in)

HA

This is one of the most popular of the hardy annuals and is easily grown. It makes a good show from mid-summer to early autumn and can be grown in an annual or mixed border. It's excellent for cutting and for this purpose could even be grown in a row in the vegetable garden.

The double flowers are produced in spikes and the predominant colour is pink. It is generally sold as a mixture including shades of pink, red, salmon, lavender, purple, orange and white.

Also worth growing is *Clarkia pulchella*, again sold as a mix of several colours which include rose-pink, violet and white.

CULTIVATION
Clarkia thrives in a light well-drained soil, on the acid side preferably although this is not essential. Full sun is needed, and do not be too generous with the fertilizer because this can result in fewer flowers.

PROPAGATION
Sow seeds in early spring in the open where the plants are to flower. Thin out seedlings before overcrowding occurs. Alternatively sow outdoors in early autumn and overwinter under cloches in cold areas.

Cleome spinosa
Spider Flower

Spread 45cm (18in)
Height 1.2m (4ft)

HHA S

This is quite a bushy plant with spiny stems and pink and white spidery flowers from mid-summer until the frosts of autumn put a stop to the display. There is a variety named 'Rose Queen' with rose-pink flowers. 'Colour Fountains' is a mix of colours: pink, rose-pink, lilac, purple and white.

The Spider Flower can be used in formal bedding schemes as a dot plant to give height and contrast and it's an excellent subject for a mixed or shrub border.

CULTIVATION
It needs a rich well-drained soil containing plenty of humus, provided by adding garden compost or peat. It's absolutely essential to choose a position in full sun.

PROPAGATION
Seeds should be sown under glass or indoors during early spring. Transplant seedlings to individual 9cm (3½in) pots. Thoroughly harden before planting out in late spring.

Dianthus chinensis
Annual Pinks

Spread 15cm (6in)
Height 15–20cm (6–8in)

HHA  S

Pinks are favourite plants for mixed borders, for cottage gardens and for bedding out. They bloom from mid-summer until the autumn.

Recommended varieties of pinks are: 'Magic Charms', which provides sturdy plants covered with large single flowers in bright and showy colours; 'Telstar', which is very early and free flowering in a mixture of many brilliant colours; and 'Lace Mixed' with its distinctive fringed lacy flowers in several shades, including white.

The annual carnations, varieties of *Dianthus caryophyllus*, can be included here, and we recommend the 'Knight' series, extra compact, with large fully double flowers on strong stems. 'Scarlet Luminette' has well-shaped double flowers in bright scarlet and is specially good for cutting. And 'Chabaud's Giant Mixed' grows to 45cm (18in) in height and has fully double large flowers in various shades of pink and red. This is excellent for cutting.

CULTIVATION
Provide well-drained soil, and, although any type is suitable, alkaline soils are particularly relished by pinks and carnations. Full sun is needed for optimum growth and flowering.

PROPAGATION
Sow seeds in late winter or early spring under glass or indoors. When seedlings are large enough to handle pot them individually into 7.5cm (3in) pots.

Digitalis purpurea
Common Foxglove

Spread 45–60cm (18–24in)
Height 1.5m (5ft)

HB

The Foxglove is a native of Britain and in early to mid-summer produces tall spikes of pink tubular flowers. It is a woodland plant and an ideal place to grow it in the garden is in a shrub border. Strictly speaking it is a short-lived perennial. Try the 'Excelsior' strain with pink, purple, cream and white flowers, all handsomely spotted with brown.

CULTIVATION
Foxgloves will grow in any type of soil and grow best in moisture-retentive soils so add plenty of bulky organic matter if you have a light soil.

Partial shade, particularly dappled shade as cast by trees, is better than a position in full sun. Full or deep shade, however, can lead to weak growth.

PROPAGATION
Although seeds can be sown in the open it is more convenient to germinate them under glass in seed trays, for they are tiny. Make the sowing in late spring and germinate in a cool greenhouse or cold frame. It's best not to cover the seeds with compost because this can prevent germination. When the seedlings are large enough to handle easily, transplant them either to other seed trays or direct into a nursery bed in the open ground. If you have transplanted into trays, the plants still need to go eventually into the nursery bed before the young plants become overcrowded.

Set out the plants in their flowering positions in early to mid-autumn.

Godetia grandiflora
Godetia

Spread 15cm (6in)
Height 30cm (12in)

HA

These are popular bushy annuals whose bright flowers, mainly in shades of pink and which are produced from early to late summer, are excellent for cutting. They are best grown in an annual or mixed border.

Several varieties are available, some with single flowers, others double. Particularly recommended are 'Double Mixed', 'Azalea-Flowered Mixed' whose semi-double blooms are rather like those of azaleas; and 'Monarch' ('Dwarf Gem') mixture.

CULTIVATION
For best results choose a position in full sun. A light sandy soil is preferred but whatever the type it must be well drained. Ensure that the soil is not too rich or the plants will produce fewer flower and a lot of foliage.

PROPAGATION
Sow the seeds in early or mid-spring where the plants are to flower. Thin out before overcrowding occurs. Alternatively for early blooms next year make a sowing outdoors in early autumn. In cold areas the seedlings should be covered with cloches during the winter.

Helipterum roseum (Acroclinium roseum)
Australian Everlasting

Spread 15cm (6in)
Height 45cm (18in)

HA

The Australian Everlasting has strawy, daisy-like flowers in rose-pink between early and late summer. Most people grow this purely for cutting, in which case it could be given a row in the vegetable plot, but it also makes a good show in an annual or mixed border.

CULTIVATION
Good results are obtained on poor dry soils and a position in full sun. In any event the plant should not be given too rich a soil so do not worry about applying fertilizer before sowing.

The flowers are particularly suitable for drying and using in winter arrangements, and they should be cut before they have fully opened. Bundle the flowers loosely and hang them upside down for a few weeks in a cool dry airy place to thoroughly dry them.

PROPAGATION
Sow the seeds in mid-spring where the plants are to flower. Before the seedlings become overcrowded thin them out to the correct distance apart.

Iberis umbellata
Candytuft

Spread 20cm (8in)
Height 15–30cm (6–12in)

HA

This is a popular hardy annual which is easily grown. The clusters of flowers come mainly in shades of pink but there are other colours too, such as shades or red, purple and also white. Generally Candytuft is offered in mixes of colours.

The following varieties are recommended: 'Fairy Maid', height 20cm (8in), with flowers in various colours; and 'White Pinnacle' which is popular for cut flowers.

Candytuft is an excellent choice for the front of an annual border, and for filling gaps in the front of mixed borders. Some people grow Candytuft in rock gardens where it will provide much-needed colour from early summer to early autumn.

Candytuft is also a good choice for ornamental containers such as tubs and window boxes and is often grown with other small hardy annuals.

CULTIVATION
Candytuft grows in virtually any kind of soil but as with all annuals the drainage must be good. If you have a poor-quality soil do not worry – Candytuft will still thrive. A position in full sun will ensure plenty of flowers.

PROPAGATION
Sow seeds where they are to flower in early spring and thin out the seedlings before they become overcrowded. To maintain a succession of flowers make further sowings in mid- and late spring. To provide early flowers make a sowing in early autumn and overwinter the young plants under cloches if you live in a cold area.

Lavatera trimestris (L. rosea)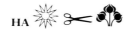
Annual Mallow

Spread 45cm (18in)
Height 60–90cm (24–36in)   HA

Malcolmia maritima
Virginian Stock

Spread 15cm (6in)
Height 15cm (6in)   HA   S

This is an easy and showy hardy annual suitable for growing in the annual or mixed border.

There are several excellent varieties including 'Silver Cup' which grows to 90cm (36in) in height. Like all Annual Mallows it flowers from mid-summer to early autumn. By mid-summer the substantial bushy plants are a mass of glowing deep rose-pink flowers, each bloom beautifully veined with a deeper shade. It's one of the best for cut flowers, and it's little wonder that this superb variety has gained an award in European flower trials. Another excellent variety that has also fared well in European trials is 'Mont Blanc'; This grows to about 60cm (24in) in height and is a glistening pure white companion to 'Silver Cup'.

This is one of the easiest and best-known of all the hardy annuals. It's an ideal subject for the front of borders (annual or mixed) where it is best sown in bold groups or drifts for maximum impact.

Available in a mixture of colours, mainly shades of pink but including lilac, red and white shades and creamy yellow. The flowers are small, only about 12mm ($\frac{1}{2}$in) in diameter and are carried on thin stems in summer. The flowers start to appear about one month after sowing and the flowering period lasts for approximately two months. This is an ideal annual for impatient children to grow because it matures so quickly.

CULTIVATION
Any ordinary garden soil is suitable for the Annual Mallows provided it is well drained. Too rich a soil can lead to excess foliage at the expense of flowers. So do not add fertilizer before sowing or farmyard manure, or garden compost.

A position in full sun is essential for optimum flowering and the site should be sheltered from winds.

PROPAGATION
Sow the seeds in mid-spring where the plants are to flower, and cover very lightly with fine soil. As soon as the seedlings are large enough to handle thin them out. Alternatively, for early flowers the following year make a sowing in early autumn.

CULTIVATION
Any ordinary garden soil is suitable for the Virginian Stock provided it drains well. A sunny site is best although good results are possible in partial shade. The plants self-sow themselves quite freely.

PROPAGATION
The seeds are sown where the plants are to flower. Make a sowing in early spring and further sowings up to mid-summer to ensure a succession of flowers. Another sowing could be made in early autumn to provide early flowers the following year. Only lightly cover the seeds with fine soil.

Silene pendula
Nodding Catchfly

Spread 15cm (6in)
Height 15–20cm (6–8in)

HA

A useful hardy annual for borders, particularly for filling gaps at the front of mixed borders. It is a neat compact grower with small star-shaped flowers in pale pink produced between late spring and early autumn, the exact period depending on when the seeds are sown.

This is also a suitable annual for sowing on rock gardens to fill any gaps and it looks good, too, growing in gaps in paving, particularly in a cottage garden

CULTIVATION
The Nodding Catchfly will grow in any ordinary garden soil provided it drains well. Best results are achieved in a sunny position but plants also do reasonably well in partial shade.

PROPAGATION
Seeds are sown where they are to flower in early or mid-spring. Thin out the seedlings before they become overcrowded. Also make another sowing in early autumn if you want early blooms the following year, but in cold areas overwinter under cloches.

Brachycome iberidifolium
Swan River Daisy

Spread 30cm (12in)
Height 30–45cm (12–18in)

HHA   S

This is a charming little plant for the front of annual or mixed borders. It also makes a good cut flower and has daisy-shaped blooms. Often the variety 'Purple Splendour' is grown which has purple-blue flowers. There is also a mixture with flowers in purple, blue, mauve and white.

Try growing the Swan River Daisy on the rock garden. The flowering period is early summer to early autumn.

CULTIVATION
Provide a sheltered spot in full sun. A fairly fertile soil gives the best results although the plants will grow in any ordinary well-drained garden soil. The growing tips of young plants should be cut out to encourage a bushy habit. Short twiggy sticks will be needed to support the plants, which have thin stems.

PROPAGATION
Seeds are sown under glass or indoors during early spring, being covered only lightly with fine compost. Transplant to trays and after hardening plant out when the danger of frost is over. Alternatively sow outdoors in mid-spring where the plants are to flower and thin out the seedlings before they become overcrowded.

Cobaea scandens _____
Cup and Saucer Vine

Spread 60cm (24in)
Height 3m (10ft)   **HHA**

Lunaria annua (L. biennis) _____
Honesty

Spread 30cm (12in)
Height 75–90cm (30–36in)   **HB**

Although this is a tender perennial it is generally grown as an annual. It is a vigorous climber with large bell-shaped purple flowers from early summer to early autumn.

Grow the Cup and Saucer Vine up walls, fences, trellis or pergolas where it will attach itself by means of tendrils. It is also a useful climber for a large conservatory where it can be grown as a perennial.

CULTIVATION
The Cup and Saucer Vine needs a sunny sheltered position and well-drained soil. Avoid too rich a soil as this leads to vigorous lush leafy growth at the expense of flowers. Water the plant well in dry weather. If growing it on a wall or fence provide something for the tendrils to cling to such as trellis panels or netting.

PROPAGATION
Sow seeds under glass or indoors in early or mid-spring, one seed per 7.5cm (3in) pot. Use soil-based potting compost. Pot on to a 12.5cm (5in) pot; harden thoroughly and plant out in early summer when all danger of frost is over.

Honesty is a popular biennial and a typical cottage-garden plant. It also looks good in a mixed or shrub border. The purple flowers are scented, produced in the period mid-spring to early summer and are followed by round flat silvery seed pods which are often cut and dried for use in winter flower arrangements. There is a variety called 'Munstead Purple' which has large rosy purple blooms.

CULTIVATION
Partial shade is recommended. The seed heads, if required for drying, should be cut in late summer before they become damaged by inclement weather.

PROPAGATION
Sow the seeds outdoors in a spare piece of ground during late spring or early summer. The seedlings then should be transplanted to another plot before they become overcrowded, spacing them 15cm (6in) apart in a row. The young plants are finally set out in their flowering positions in early autumn.

Malope trifida 'Grandiflora' _____
Mallow-wort

Spread 25cm (10in)
Height 90cm (36in)

HA

Nierembergia caerulea (N. hippomanica) _____
Cup Flower

Spread 15–20cm (6–8in)
Height 15–20cm (6-8in)

HHA

This hardy annual is of upright bushy habit and produces rose-purple trumpet-shaped blooms during early summer to early autumn. The blooms are excellent for cutting and last well in water if gathered just as they open.

This a colourful plant for borders, whether annual or mixed.

CULTIVATION
The Mallow-wort should be grown in a position in full sun. Any ordinary garden soil is suitable but a light soil is preferred, and certainly should have good drainage. If necessary, provide twiggy sticks for support.

PROPAGATION
Early or mid-spring is the sowing period. And the seeds should be sown outdoors where the plants are to flower. Cover the seeds only lightly with fine soil. Before overcrowding occurs thin out the seedlings to the recommended spacing.

Strictly speaking this is a tender perennial but it is normally grown as a half-hardy annual. It is a charming little plant with a profusion of funnel-shaped mauve flowers from early summer to early autumn. Usually the variety 'Purple Robe' is grown, which has brilliant purplish-violet blooms.

Grow it as an edging in a mixed or annual border or in a summer bedding scheme. It is also good for filling any gaps on rock gardens.

CULTIVATION
Choose a spot in full sun and sheltered from wind because these plants are easily damaged. Any ordinary garden soil is suitable, and the plant likes moisture.

PROPAGATION
Sow under glass in late winter or early spring and transplant the seedlings to trays. Before planting outdoors, when the danger of frost is over, thoroughly harden the plants. This plant can also be propagated from soft, 5cm (2in) long cuttings taken in summer and rooted in pots of cutting compost in a cold frame. Pot on when well rooted into 7.5cm (3in) pots of soil-based potting compost and overwinter in a cold frame or indoors. Pinch out growing tips of young plants to encourage bushy growth.

Ageratum houstonianum
Floss Flower

Spread 15–30cm (6–12in)
Height 15–30cm (6–12in)

HHA

The Floss Flower is as popular as Zonal Geraniums, Scarlet Salvias and Wax Begonias and is often grown with these plants.

It is an admirable plant for the main carpet in a planned bed, mixed with other dwarf plants such as Wax Begonias and Salvias. Alternatively it can be used to edge a bed and looks best if planted in a wide band, at least 10cm (12in) across, rather than in a thin strip.

The Floss Flower combines well with other summer bedding plants in tubs, window boxes and hanging baskets. A bold drift in a shrub border is also most effective. The taller varieties are suitable for cutting because the blooms last well in water, and they are often used in miniature or small arrangements.

Ageratum is a dwarf compact plant with mounds of fluffy flowers from early summer until the frosts put a stop to the display. Once started, the plants are never out of flower. Blue is the main colour but there are other colours such as mauve, purple, pink and white.

Good varieties include 'Blue Mink', 25cm (9in) high, with large trusses of powder-blue flowers on upright compact plants; 'Ocean', 20cm (8in) high, light blue, early and extremely free flowering; 'Summer Snow', 15cm (6in), pure white flowers covering uniform plants; 'Blue Danube', 15–20cm (6–8in) high, early lavender-blue flowers on uniform plants; and 'North Sea', 20cm (8in) high, deep violet-blue flowers freely produced.

CULTIVATION
The Floss Flower should be grown in full sun and appreciates some shelter from the wind. The soil should be capable of retaining moisture during drought periods because dry conditions can lead to poor growth and flowering, and a shorter flowering period. Therefore, when preparing or digging beds, add plenty of bulky organic matter such as garden compost, peat or pulverized bark, especially if your soil is on the light side and prone to drying out. Apply a general-purpose or flower-garden fertilizer before planting to ensure fertile conditions, which result in better growth.

To encourage continuous flowering it is advisable to cut off dead flower heads regularly, using a pair of gardening scissors. Do not try to pull them off or you will uproot the plants.

Keep the plants well watered in dry periods if the soil starts to dry out.

PROPAGATION
Sow seeds under glass or indoors during early or mid-spring. Transplant to trays and plant out when the danger of frost is over, and the plants have been well hardened.

Anchusa capensis
Summer Forget-me-not

Spread 15–20cm (6–8in)
Height 25–45cm (10–18in)   **HA HB**

Centaurea cyanus
Cornflower

Spread 20–30cm (8–12in)
Height 45–90cm (18–36in)   **HA**

This is a biennial which is normally grown as a hardy annual. It has a bushy habit up to 45cm (18in) in height and bears blue flowers from mid-summer to late summer. There is a good variety named 'Blue Angel' which grows to only 25cm (10in) in height, whose flowers are also in a beautiful shade of blue.

The species makes a fine show in an annual or mixed border while the dwarf variety can be used as an edging and, combined with other plants, it does well in tubs and window boxes.

The Cornflower is a real favourite; it is easily grown, it makes a fine show from early summer to early autumn and its flowers are good for cutting. Often grown in an annual border it is also effective in a mixed border of perennials and shrubs.

The daisy-like double flowers are commonly blue but other colours are available including shades of red, pink purple and white.

Good varieties include 'Blue Diadem', 60cm (24in) high, with large double flowers of the richest blue; 'Jubilee Gem', 45cm (18in) high, with deep blue double flowers on bushy plants, ideal for mass planting in bold groups; and 'Polka Dot Mixed', 38cm (15in) high, with double flowers in shades of blue, red, pink and white.

CULTIVATION
Any ordinary garden soil suits anchusa provided the drainage is good; and it needs a position in full sun.

PROPAGATION
Sow seeds where the plants are to flower during mid-spring, then thin out the resultant seedlings to the recommended spacing. If you grow the plant as a biennial sow outdoors in late summer, thin out the seedlings, and overwinter the young plants under cloches.

CULTIVATION
Cornflowers require a fertile soil to reach their maximum potential. So, add well-rotted farmyard manure or garden compost to the soil while preparing it and rake in a dressing of general purpose or flower-garden fertilizer before sowing. A position in full sun is essential for optimum flowering.

Provide the plants with twiggy sticks for support, particularly the taller varieties, or they may be flattened by wind and rain.

PROPAGATION
Sow seeds during early or mid-spring where the plants are to flower and thin out the seedlings to the recommended spacing before they start to become overcrowded.

Alternatively, make a sowing in early autumn to provide earlier flowers in the following year. In cold areas the plants should be overwintered under cloches.

Convolvulus tricolor (C. minor)
Dwarf Morning Glory

Spread 15–20cm (6–8in)
Height 30cm (12in)

HA

A low bushy annual with large wide trumpet-shaped flowers from mid-summer to early autumn, which are a brilliant blue with a white centre. Although each flower does not last for more than a day, plenty more follow, so flowering is continuous.

Good varieties include 'Blue Flash', 20cm (8in) high, a beautiful shade of blue with white centres; and 'Royal Ensign', 30cm (12in) high, deep bright ultramarine blue, extremely free flowering. There are also mixtures of colours available which include shades of pink, red and blue.

Ideal for mass planting in beds, it is also suitable for use as edging or for filling gaps on a rock garden.

It is also a good annual for ornamental containers where it will partially spill over the edges. If you have a steep sunny bank try mass planting the Dwarf Morning Glory on it where it will make a stunning display. The warmth, coupled with well-drained conditions, will be very much to its liking and it should romp away, producing a beautiful blue 'waterful'.

In ideal conditions the Dwarf Morning Glory can self-sow itself, so if your garden is in a mild or hot climate you may well never be without plants once you have made the first sowing.

The Dwarf Morning Glory also makes an excellent pot plant for the conservatory provided it receives enough sun. It will enjoy the extra warmth and will flower throughout summer and well into the autumn.

CULTIVATION
Provided the drainage is good any ordinary garden soil is suitable for the Dwarf Morning Glory. Full sun, however, is needed for optimum flowering.

To encourage more blooms pick off the dead flower heads regularly.

PROPAGATION
Seeds can be sown under glass or indoors during early spring and young plants set out in late spring after thorough hardening; alternatively, make a sowing in mid-spring where the plants are to flower; it can also be sown in early autumn and overwintered under cloches.

Didiscus caerulea _____
Blue Lace Flower

Spread 20cm (8in)
Height 45cm (18in)

HHA  S

This is an upright annual, useful both for annual or mixed borders and for growing specially for cutting. It has deeply cut foliage and between mid- and late summer produces rounded heads of lavender blue flowers, similar to those of scabious.

CULTIVATION
The Blue Lace Flower is an undemanding plant, but prefers a position in full sun and a well-drained soil that is reasonably fertile. Try to provide a sheltered spot and support the stems with twiggy sticks.

PROPAGATION
Seeds should be sown in early spring under glass or indoors and covered only lightly with fine compost. Transplant to 7.5cm (3in) pots (or trays if preferred), harden thoroughly and plant out when the danger of frost is over.

Felicia bergerana _____
Kingfisher Daisy

Spread 15cm (6in)
Height 15cm (6in)

HHA

This is a charming little annual with blue daisy flowers from early summer to early autumn. It looks good mass planted as the main carpet in a formal design, and makes a change from such plants as Ageratum and Begonias. Use it also for edging beds and borders or plant a drift at the front of a mixed or shrub border. It is suitable, too, for the rock garden and for containers such as window boxes and urns. The blooms open fully only in the sun – they remain closed during dull weather.

CULTIVATION
Full sun is essential together with well-drained soil. Any type of soil is, however, suitable. Remove dead flower heads regularly.

PROPAGATION
Sow seeds under glass or indoors in late winter or early spring. Transplant the seedlings to individual small pots or into trays. Harden thoroughly before planting out when the danger of frost is over.

Gilia capitata
Blue Thimble Flower

Spread 20cm (8in)
Height 45cm (18in)

HA

The Blue Thimble Flower has ferny green foliage and lavender-blue globular flowers from early summer to early autumn. The blooms are especially good for cutting as they last well in water. Grow it in a bold group in an annual or mixed border.

CULTIVATION
If the plants are to grow and flower well they must be given a position in full sun. Although any well-drained garden soil is suitable for gilias, they do prefer a light sandy type. It is advisable to provide twiggy sticks for support otherwise rain and winds may flatten the plants.

PROPAGATION
Sow seeds in early spring where the plants are to flower and thin out the resultant seedlings to the recommended spacing before they start to become overcrowded. Alternatively make a sowing in early autumn for early blooms the following year. It's best to protect these young plants with cloches through the winter months.

Heliotropium arborescens (H. peruvianum)
Heliotrope

Spread 30–38cm (12–15in)
Height 45–60cm (18–24in)

HHA

Although this is a bushy perennial it is grown as a half-hardy annual for summer bedding schemes. It has flowers in various shades of blue and one of the most popular varieties is 'Marine' which attains a height of 60cm (24in) and has extremely large heads of deep violet flowers on compact dark-leaved plants.

Heliotrope is as popular as Zonal Geraniums, Scarlet Salvias, Petunias, and Marigolds for summer bedding and is usually combined with these plants in formal schemes. It can be used as a dot plant in a carpet of plants, and also as a useful foil for those bedding plants that have strongly coloured flowers of scarlet, crimson or brilliant orange.

The flowering period of Heliotrope is late spring to mid-autumn.

CULTIVATION
Full sun is needed for best growth and flowering as is a well-drained, fertile soil. It pays to improve the soil, particularly poor light kinds, by adding bulky organic matter such as well-rotted farmyard manure, garden compost, peat or pulverized bark. Then before planting, fork into the soil a base dressing of general purpose or flower garden fertilizer. Keep well watered in dry weather and regularly pick off dead flower heads.

PROPAGATION
Sow seeds in late winter under glass. Pinch out growing tips of transplants to encourage bushy growth, and harden well before planting out after frosts are over.

Heliotrope can also be increased from cuttings taken in late summer or early autumn and rooted in heat. The young cuttings must overwinter in a frost-free greenhouse.

Ionopsidium acaule
Violet Cress

Spread 10cm (4in)
Height 5–7.5cm (2–3in)   HA

This little annual is not too well known but is a good choice for sowing on the rock garden or in gaps in paving. It has a tufted habit and pale blue flowers from early summer to early autumn. The blooms are very tiny, about 6mm ($\frac{1}{4}$in) across.

CULTIVATION
Partial shade is recommended because very hot conditions can result in the little plants being scorched. Also a moist soil is necessary – one that is not prone to rapid drying out in the summer.

PROPAGATION
Sow the seeds in mid-spring and in succession, if desired, up until mid-summer. If you sow thinly you will not need to thin out the seedlings, which can be a bit tedious. Cover the seeds lightly with fine soil. If your garden is in a mild area it may be possible to overwinter young plants under cloches from an early autumn sowing. This will give you earlier flowers the following year.

Ipomoea tricolor (I. rubrocoerulea)
Morning Glory

Spread 30cm (12in)
Height 2.4m (8ft)   HHA

This is one of the few annual climbers (or strictly speaking a tender perennial grown as an annual). The thin stems twine around supports such as pergolas or trellis and from mid-summer to early autumn bear large saucer-shaped blooms each of which lasts for only one day. But plenty more follow!

Two varieties are commonly grown; 'Flying Saucers' with 10cm (4in) wide flowers striped bright blue and white; and 'Heavenly Blue' with beautiful sky-blue flowers.

CULTIVATION
Morning Glory needs a warm sunny sheltered position to succeed outdoors in temperate climates. Provide also a well-drained, fertile soil and a fence or trellis to climb over. A light sandy soil is ideal, and cut off the dead flowers to ensure that more follow.

PROPAGATION
First soak seeds in water for a day to soften the hard seed coat, then sow under glass or indoors during early to mid-spring, one per 7.5cm (3in) pot. Pot on to 12.5cm (5in) pots, harden and plant out when the danger of frost is over.

Lobelia erinus
Lobelia

Spread 10cm (4in)
Height 10–20cm (4–8in)

HHA

In Britain Lobelia is in the top-ten list of summer bedding plants, and is widely used in formal bedding, and in containers and hanging baskets. The summers in North American tend to be rather too hot for it to succeed as well.

Lobelia is used as an edging for beds or containers and it goes will with all other summer bedding plants. It is very effective when combined with white Alyssum around the edges of hanging baskets, or planted through the wires. The trailing varieties are best for baskets and edges of other containers.

Lobelia varieties are split into two groups: the compact and the trailing. The main flower colour is blue although there are Lobelias in shades of pink, red and also white. The flowering period is from late spring until the frosts of autumn put a stop to the display. Flowering is continuous and prolific.

Good varieties are 'Blue Stone', a clear blue without a white 'eye', compact habit; 'Cambridge Blue', a true Cambridge blue, compact habit, an extremely popular variety; 'Crystal Palace Compacta', deep blue flowers set against attractive bronze foliage; 'Blue Cascade', trailing variety with Cambridge blue flowers which continue well into the autumn; 'Sapphire', trailing, sapphire-blue flowers each with a white eye; 'String of Pearls', compact variety, includes all the Lobelia colours of blue, violet, rose and white; and 'Colour Cascade', trailing, in a mix which includes blues, reds, mauve, rose-red and white.

CULTIVATION
Lobelia is an adaptable plant and will grow in any type of well-drained soil but it is best in soil which does not dry out excessively in summer, so keep the plants well watered if the soil becomes dry. The best position is in sun although shade for part of the day will not adversely affect growth and flowering.

PROPAGATION
The seeds of Lobelia are as fine as dust and the seedlings tiny, which makes transplanting fiddly. Seeds should be sown under glass or indoors in late winter. Do not cover them with compost. Transplant the seedlings to trays, moving them in batches of three or four, which makes handling so much easier than trying to transplant single seedlings. Grow on in warmth and then harden thoroughly before planting out, which should be done when all danger of frost is over.

Lupinus texensis
Texas Blue Bonnet

Spread 30cm (12in)
Height 30–45cm (12–18in)

HA

This annual Lupin has spikes of blue flowers, marked with white, in summer and hand-shaped leaves. It is a worthwhile addition to all types of borders and is probably more popular in North America, from where it originates, than in Britain, but it is listed in some British seed catalogues and is worth searching out.

CULTIVATION
A well-drained soil in full sun is needed. Cut off the dead flower heads and watch out for slugs and snails which are partial to the succulent young shoots and leaves.

PROPAGATION
Sow seeds during early spring where the plants are to flower. To aid germination soak the seeds in water for a day before sowing to soften the hard seed coats. The seeds are large enough to sow thinly so, if sown to the correct spacing, there should be no need for subsequent thinning of seedlings.

Myosotis sylvatica (M. oblongata)
Forget-me-not

Spread 15cm (6in)
Height 15–30cm (6–12in)

HB

The Forget-me-not is one of the major subjects for spring bedding schemes and is often planted as a carpet over an entire bed to act as a hazy blue background for tulips. It also combines well with many other spring bedding plants such as Wallflowers, Polyanthus and Winter-flowering Pansies.

It makes a pleasant edging, and is also used in tubs and window boxes, for a spring display with tulips or other spring bulbs.

Varieties of Foreget-me-not include 'Marine', 15cm (6in) high, dwarf and compact with bright mid-blue flowers; 'Royal Blue', 30cm (12in) high, early, with deep indigo-blue flowers; 'Blue Cloud', 30cm (12in) high with true-blue flowers, a less-compact variety ideal for informal planting in a cottage garden; and 'Blue Bird', 30cm (12in) or more in height with long sprays of blue flowers.

The main flowering period is mid-spring to early summer.

CULTIVATION
Forget-me-nots will grow in full sun but they really prefer a position in partial sun – dappled shade cast by trees is ideal. A fertile soil that retains moisture is ideal but it must be well drained. Add bulky organic matter when preparing a bed for For-get-me-nots. Also apply a base dressing of general-purpose fertilizer.

PROPAGATION
Sow seeds in an outdoor seed bed in a spare part of the garden during late spring or early summer. When the seedlings are large enough to handle transplant to nursery rows, spacing them about 15cm (6in) apart each way. Then in early or mid-autumn plant out in their flowering positions.

Nemophila menziesii (N. insignis)
Baby Blue Eyes

Spread 15cm (6in)
Height 15–20cm (6–8in)

HA

A charming diminutive hardy annual for the front of borders or for the rock garden. Also try it in gaps in paving, particularly if you have a cottage garden.

The light green feathery foliage makes a nice foil for the small blue, white-eyed bowl-shaped flowers which are produced freely between early and late summer.

CULTIVATION
Any ordinary garden soil is suitable for Baby Blue Eyes provided it drains well. The ideal is a light but moisture-retentive soil to which has been added plenty of compost, peat or leafmould. It will succeed in full sun or partial shade.

PROPAGATION
Seeds are sown in early spring where the plants are to flower and the seedlings thinned out to the recommended distance before they become overcrowded. Alternatively, make a sowing in early autumn for earlier flowering the following year but only if your soil is very well drained.

Nicandra physalodes
Apple of Peru

Spread 30cm (12in)
Height 90cm (36in)

HA

An unusual hardy annual for any type of border. All its parts are attractive – the leaves, blooms and fruits. It has a branching habit and large wavy-edged leaves. The blooms, which appear between mid-summer and early autumn, are bell-shaped and a pale shade of violet, each having a white throat. Each bloom lasts for only one day. The large inedible fruits which follow are globe-shaped and encased in calyces which are bright green and purple.

CULTIVATION
Full sun is needed for optimum growth together with highly fertile moisture-retentive soil.

PROPAGATION
Although a hardy annual, seeds are best sown under glass or indoors in early spring. Transplant the seedlings to individual 9cm (3½in) pots, and harden well before planting out in late spring.

Nigella damascena
Love-in-a-mist

Spread 20cm (8in)
Height 45–60cm (18–24in)

HA

Phacelia campanularia
Californian Bluebell

Spread 15cm (6in)
Height 22cm (9in)

HA

This is one of the most popular hardy annuals because it's easily grown and makes an excellent show from early to late summer. The bright green feathery foliage makes a nice foil for the blue flowers which are excellent for cutting and arranging indoors. The blooms are followed by large inflated seed pods which are quite attractive and these can be cut and dried for winter flower arrangements. Hang them up for a few weeks in a cool dry airy place. Grow Love-in-a-mist preferably in the annual or mixed border, but it does not look out of place grouped around shrubs. Good varieties are 'Miss Jekyll' with deep sky blue flowers; and 'Persian Jewels' which comes in a mix of colours including light and dark blue, pink and white.

CULTIVATION
Provide a reasonably fertile, well-drained soil in a position which receives plenty of sunshine. Remove the dead flowers to encourage more to follow unless you want to save the seed heads for drying.

PROPAGATION
Sow the seeds in early spring where the plants are to flower and, before the seedlings become overcrowded, thin them to the recommended spacing. In mild areas with well-drained soil, a sowing can be made in early autumn to provide earlier blooms the following year, and it is sensible to overwinter the young plants under cloches.

This easily grown and free-flowering annual is recommended for the front of borders, including shrub and mixed borders. It should be sown in bold groups or it can be selectively sown on rock gardens and in gaps in paving.

The first rich true-blue bell-shaped flowers are produced very soon after germination.

CULTIVATION
Best results are obtained in a sunny spot and a light sandy soil with good drainage. Protect plants from slugs and snails.

PROPAGATION
Sow seeds in early or mid-spring where the plants are to flower and only lightly cover them with fine soil. Before the seedlings become overcrowded, thin them to the recommended spacing. If your garden is in a mild area and the soil drainage is good, a sowing could be made in early autumn. The young plants should be protected during the winter to come earlier into flower the following year.

Salvia farinacea 'Victoria'
Sage

Spread 20–30cm (8–12in)
Height 45cm (18in)

HHA

Trachelium caeruleum
Throatwort

Spread 30cm (12in)
Height 60–90cm (24–36in)

HHA

This is an almost hardy perennial but is generally grown as a half-hardy annual. It is a very different type of salvia from *S. splendens,* the Scarlet Sage, and is considered to be one of the finest blue summer bedding plants. Long slender spikes of violet-blue flowers are produced throughout summer until the autumn frosts. This Sage is especially good as a dot plant in summer bedding schemes, especially when combined with plants which have strong colours. It can be used for cutting, and the flowers may be dried for winter decoration if cut as soon as they have opened.

This is a half-hardy perennial which is generally treated as an annual. It should be grown in a sunny warm border to give blue flowers, which are good for cutting, between early and late summer.

CULTIVATION
Any ordinary soil is suitable as long as the drainage is good and the plant revels in full sun. Cut off dead blooms regularly to encourage more to follow.

PROPAGATION
Sow seeds under glass or indoors during late winter or early spring and transplant seedlings to trays. Harden well and plant out when the danger of frost is over.

CULTIVATION
It needs a warm, sheltered position in full sun and a light, sandy, well-drained soil. If you do not have the right conditions, you might consider growing it as a pot plant. Cut off the dead flowers, regularly.

PROPAGATION
Sow seeds in early or mid-spring under glass or indoors. Transplant to seed trays, harden well and plant out when the danger of frost is over.

Althaea rosea (A. chinensis)
Annual Hollyhock

Spread 45cm (18in)
Height 60cm–1.8m (2–6ft)

HHA

Hollyhocks are favourite cottage-garden plants flowering from mid-summer to early autumn. They vary from dwarf to typically tall plants and bear their double rounded rosette-like flowers in spikes. The tall varieties are ideal for the back of shrub or mixed borders, and all look good grown against walls or fences. Either side of the front door of a country cottage is still a popular place for these flowers.

Although Hollyhocks are hardy, the annual varieties are given the half-hardy treatment to encourage the plants to flower reasonably early. Varieties include the 60cm (24in) high 'Majorette' which comes in a wide range of colours; and the 1.5–1.8m (5–6ft) high 'Summer Carnival', also in a wide range of colours.

CULTIVATION
Choose a sunny sheltered site. Hollyhocks are not fussy, though they prefer a heavy soil, but high fertility is desirable. Provide supports for tall varieties in exposed gardens, and water freely during dry spells.

PROPAGATION
Sow seeds in late winter under glass or indoors. Transplant to small pots, harden well and plant out in mid-spring. Alternatively sow direct in the flowering site when weather and soil have warmed up sufficiently.

Antirrhinum majus
Snapdragon

Spread 20–45cm (8–18in)
Height 30–90cm (12–36in)

HHA 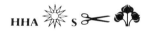 S

Snapdragons give a superb show from mid-summer on when mass planted. They vary in height from 30cm to 90cm (12–36in) and the dwarf kinds are ideal for planting in large tubs or window boxes.

There are literally dozens of varieties available, with mixtures the most popular though separate colours are available for a colour scheme.

A good tall variety is 'Double Madame Butterfly', 60–75cm (24–30in), with large double blooms in shades of red, pink and yellow. In the intermediate size range – about 45cm (18in) in height – are: 'Coronette' in an excellent mix of colours: and the 'Monarch' series.

An excellent dwarf variety is 'Little Darling', 30cm (12in) high, with open trumpet-shaped flowers in a wide colour range.

CULTIVATION
Snapdragons make few demands: an open, sunny site with reasonably fertile, well-drained soil will suit well. Add bulky organic matter when preparing the soil, and before planting apply a base dressing of general purpose or flower-garden fertilizer.

PROPAGATION
Sow seeds under glass or indoors during late winter or early spring, and cover them only very lightly with fine compost. When seedlings are big enough to handle, transplant to trays and thoroughly harden before planting out in late spring.

Arctotis x hybrida
African Daisy

Spread 30cm (12in)
Height 30–60cm (12–24in)

HHA

Begonia × tuberhybrida
Tuberous Begonia

Spread 30–38cm (12–15in)
Height 30cm (12in)

HHA

The African Daisy has large daisy-like flowers in many colours from mid-summer until the autumn frosts put a stop to the display. Mass plant them at the front of mixed borders or in formal summer bedding schemes. They are also suitable plants for tubs and window boxes. The blooms are good for cutting and come in many colours: shades of yellow, orange, red, cream and white. Often the blooms are zoned with a contrasting colour. These seeds are only available as large-flowered hybrids.

The Tuberous Begonias have long been popular for summer bedding and for containers such as tubs and window boxes and were traditionally grown from tubers. Now it's possible to raise them from seeds. Good seed strains include 'Nonstop', 30cm (12in) high, the best for summer bedding with fully double flowers up to 7.5cm (3in) in diameter which are produced non-stop all summer until the autumn frosts. Colours include shades of red, yellow, pink and also white. 'Clips', 25cm (10in) in height, is new and early flowering, with double blooms in shades of orange, yellow, scarlet and white. Compact and flowering over a long period, 'Clips' is specially recommended for containers such as tubs and window boxes.

CULTIVATION
Full sun is needed for optimum flowering together with a well-drained, light soil. Pinch out the tips of young plants when they are about 10cm (4in) high to ensure a bushy habit. Regularly remove dead flowers to encourage more to follow.

PROPAGATION
Sow seeds under glass or indoors during early spring and transplant seedlings to individual 7.5cm (3in) pots. Prererably use a soil-based seed and potting compost. Harden well and plant out when danger of frost is over.

CULTIVATION
Grow in full or partial sun in well-drained humus-rich soil. In beds add plenty of peat or leafmould before planting. Regularly cut off dead blooms.

PROPAGATION
Sow seeds under glass or indoors in late winter and do not cover with compost because they are as fine as dust. Transplant to seed trays and grow on in warmth. Before planting out, when all danger of frost is over, harden the plants thoroughly.

Bellis perennis
Double Daisy

Spread 15–20cm (6–8in)
Height 15cm (6in)

HB

Brassica oleracea capitata
Ornamental Cabbage

Spread 30–45cm (12–18in)
Height 30–45cm (12–18in)

HA HHA

The varieties of Double Daisies are far superior to the common European daisy, having large fully double flowers in shades of red, pink and white. They are good for spring bedding schemes and achieve a good effect when mass planted. They are also good as a carpet beneath spring tulips or hyacinths. Double Daisies make a fine edging display and again with spring bulbs such as dwarf tulips and hyacinths work well in tubs and window boxes.

The main flowering period is short – mid-spring to early summer, but there are numerous varieties to choose from including the excellent larger flowered 'Goliath' which comes in a mixture of colours; and 'Pomponette' which is also a mixture and produces a profusion of intensely double flowers in rose-pink and white.

CULTIVATION
Double Daisies will thrive in full or partial sun. They like a fertile garden soil, although any type is suitable provided the drainage is good.

PROPAGATION
Sow the seeds in an outdoor seed bed, in a spare part of the garden, in early summer. Sow in shallow furrows and cover the seeds lightly with fine compost. When the seedlings are large enough to handle transplant them to a nursery bed to grow on. Keep weeded and well watered during the summer. By early or mid-autumn the young plants will be large enough to set out in their flowering positions. Lift carefully and try to retain some soil around the roots.

How does one incorporate Ornamental Cabbages into flower displays? It is best to use them as dot plants in formal bedding schemes to create extra height and, more importantly, contrast in colour and shape.

Ornamental Cabbages are a good choice for sub-tropical bedding schemes in which they are best planted in bold groups.

Particularly attractive is 'Coral Queen' whose foliage is finely cut and fringed. The centre of the plant becomes red as autumn advances. 'Coral Prince' is the counterpart of 'Coral Queen' but the outer leaves are a lighter green and the centres lemony cream. 'Osaka Red' has brilliant deep mauve-pink heads and the other leaves are dark green. It is also possible to buy Ornamental Cabbages in mixed colours. Also worth growing is Ornamental Kale in mixed colours.

CULTIVATION
All cabbages like an open sunny position and well-drained fertile soil. So, prepare the ground well by adding plenty of well-rotted manure or compost. Then, before planting, give a dressing of general fertilizer. Chalky or limy soils are generally free or less prone to the cabbage disease, club-root, but it is advisable to treat transplants with club-root dip if your soil is acid.

PROPAGATION
Ornamental Cabbages can be grown as half-hardy or hardy annuals. In the former instance sow under glass or indoors during early spring. Transplant seedlings to individeual 9cm (3½in) pots. Harden off and plant out in late spring.

Alternatively sow outdoors in mid-spring where the plants are to grow or in a nursery bed.

Callistephus chinensis
China Aster

Spread 30cm (12in)
Height 15–90cm (6–36in)

HHA

China Asters are popular for summer colour in mixed borders and for cutting. They have large daisy-like flowers, mostly double, in shades of red, pink, blue, purple and white. Asters are most usually sold as mixtures but separate colours are available. The flowering period is from mid-summer until the autumn frosts arrive. The China Aster is prone to wilt disease so wherever possible buy wilt-resistant varieties and avoid growing the plants in exactly the same spot from year to year.

Recommended varieties include 'Duchess Mixed', 60cm (24in) in height, vigorous well-branched plants with strong stems carrying large double chrysanthemum-like flowers in all the aster colours, which are excellent for cutting. 'Ostrich Feather Mixed' is also highly popular and attains a height of 45cm (18in). The huge fully double blooms have long feathery recurving petals and come in all the usual colours. This variety comes into flower earlier than many.

'Thousand Wonders Mixed' reaches only 15cm (6in) in height and is of bushy habit carrying large double flowers in shades of pink, blue, red and white. 'Thousand Wonders Rose' is the same bushy size and is worth growing for its deep rose-pink blooms.

'Milady Super Mixed' grows to 25cm (10in) and has fully double globular blooms on vigorous sturdy plants in the usual aster colours. If you prefer separate colours try 'Milady Scarlet', 'Milady Rose', 'Milady Blue' and 'Milady White'.

'Powderpuffs' grows to 45–60cm (18–24in) high and has a compact habit of growth. It has large tight double flowers which all open at the same time so the whole plant can be cut if desired and placed in water. Colours in this mix include shades of scarlet, rose, pink, blue, purple and white.

'Totem Pole' is also a mixture of shades and has huge heads of long shaggy petals. Height is 60cm (24in) and is highly recommended for cutting.

CULTIVATION
Grow asters in full sun and fertile soil. Try to find a spot that is sheltered from the wind, especially if growing the taller large-flowered varieties. These may need supporting with short thin canes in windy gardens. Regularly cut off dead flower heads.

PROPAGATION
Sow the seeds under glass or indoors during early spring. Transplant to trays, and thoroughly harden before planting out when the danger of frost is over. Alternatively, seeds can be sown where they are to flower, in mid-spring, and the seedlings thinned to the recommended spacing.

Campanula medium
Canterbury Bells

Spread 30cm (12in)
Height 45–90cm (18–36in)

HB

Canna × generalis
Indian Shot

Spread 30–45cm (12–18in)
Height 60–1205cm (2–4ft)

HHA

Canterbury Bells are delightful old-fashioned plants and a familiar sight in modern as well as cottage gardens, where they are best grown in a mixed border.

Canterbury Bells are sturdy, stong-growing plants flowering between late spring and mid-summer. Popular varieties include 'Cup and Saucer Mixed' which grows to a height of 90cm (36in). The flowers of this mixture do in fact resemble a cup sitting on a saucer. 'Bells of Holland' is a more recent variety and attains a height of 45cm (18in). It's a delightful mixture of pink, blue, mauve and white shades.

Cannas are tender perennials but can be grown from seeds and indeed kept from year to year. The plants have large dramatic foliage in green or purple and exotic-looking flowers in shades of red, orange or yellow. The flowering period is summer. Cannas are often used as dot plants in formal bedding schemes, as centrepieces for large containers and for sub-tropical bedding schemes. Indeed some gardeners regard them as essential plants for the latter. Varieties include 'Giant Hybrids', 60–120cm (2–4ft) and 'Seven Dwarfs', 45cm (18in).

CULTIVATION
Canterbury Bells thrive in full or partial sun and in any ordinary garden soil, provided it is reasonably fertile. It must be well drained, though. Prepare the ground for planting by adding plenty of well-rotted manure or garden compost, and then before planting out apply a base dressing of general purpose or flower garden fertilizer. Guard the plants continuously against slugs and snails, and after the flowers are over the plants can be discarded.

PROPAGATION
Seeds should be sown in mid- to late spring. It is usually best to sow them in a seed tray. Germinate them in a cool greenhouse, cold frame or on a windowsill in a cool room. Transplant the seedlings to trays and, before they become overcrowded, transfer them to a nursery bed in the open, after hardening them. Space them about 15cm (6in) apart in rows. Set out in their flowering positions in early or mid autumn.

CULTIVATION
Cannas grow in any well-drained soil and need a sheltered position in full sun. If you want to keep the plants, lift and dry them off before the frosts start, and overwinter the fleshy rhizomes in a cool but frost-free place.

PROPAGATION
Sow seeds early in the year – before the end of winter. First soak them in water for a day to soften the hard coats and speed up germination. Sow one seed per 7.5cm (3in) pot using peat-based potting compost and germinate in a temperature of 27°C/80°F. Pot on to a 10cm (4in) pot, and thoroughly harden the plants before setting out when the danger of frost is over.

Celosia plumosa
Prince of Wales' Feathers

Spread 20–30cm (8–12in)
Height 30–45cm (12–18in)

HHA

Centaurea moschata
Sweet Sultan

Spread 20cm (8in)
Height 45–60cm (18–24in)

HA

In Britain this is generally thought of as a greenhouse pot plant but it can be used for bedding out and is an excellent choice for sub-tropical bedding schemes with its feathery plumes of flowers in shades of mainly red or yellow. It can also be shown effectively in tubs and window boxes.

Good varieties include 'Fairy Fountains', 30cm (12in) high, whose colours include pink, light orange, rich gold and brilliant orange-scarlet. 'Century Mixed', 60cm (24in) high, comes in shades of red and yellow – a really bright mix. 'Apricot Brandy' grows to about 45cm (18in) in height and has beautiful deep bright orange flowers – an unusual colour for celosias.

CULTIVATION
A sheltered spot in full sun is necessary, together with a well-drained soil. Light soil is best but not essential.

PROPAGATION
Sow seeds under glass or indoors during late winter and transplant the seedlings to individual 7.5cm (3in) pots. Pot on to 10–12.5cm (4–5in) pots. Harden thoroughly and plant out when the danger of frost is over.

A delightful old-fashioned annual for mixed borders in cottage, country or even modern town gardens. The large cornflower-shaped flowers are produced from early summer to early autumn and are excellent for cutting. Indeed a row in the vegetable garden specially for this purpose is highly recommended.

Sweet Sultan is sold in a mixture of colours which includes shades of pink, purple and white, and sometimes creamy yellow. 'Giant Imperial Mixed', particularly recommended, grows to a height of 45cm (18in). It has big double flowers in a charming combination of colours.

CULTIVATION
Choose a sunny sheltered position and sow in a fertile well-drained soil. The dead flower heads should be cut off to ensure continuous flowering.

PROPAGATION
Sow seeds where the plants are to flower in early or mid-spring and thin seedlings to the recommended spacing. Further sowings can be made until early summer if desired to ensure a longer flowering season. Also make a sowing in early autumn if you live in a mild area and your soil has impeccable drainage.

Cheiranthus cheiri _____
Wallflower

Spread 30cm (12in)
Height 30–60cm (12–24in)

In the autumn virtually every garden centre in Britain is stocked with wallflowers, such is the popularity of these spring bedding plants. They are not so widely planted in America because the winters are generally too cold for them. Indeed, a severe winter in the UK can result in considerable losses, so be prepared for this. Nevertheless this does not deter gardeners from planting wallfowers in their millions.

Certainly they make a marvellous show in the period from early spring to early summer. Flowers come in a wide range of colours – shades of red, scarlet, crimson, purple, pink, yellow, orange, cream, white, etc. Most popular are the mixtures of colours, but separate colours are also available.

Wallflowers are generally mass planted in formal beds, or bold groups planted at the front of mixed borders, often with tall tulips growing through them. They associate well with other spring bedding plants such as Forget-me-nots, Polyanthus, Double Daisies and Winter-flowering Pansies.

Among the many varieties that can be recommended is 'Fair Lady Mixed', 50cm (20in) high, which has a compact habit and all the usual wallflower colours, plus pastel shades.

The 'Bedder' series is highly recommended. The plants are dwarf, about 30cm (12in) in height, and ideal for mass planting in formal beds. You can buy a mixture, or separate colours: 'Orange Bedder', rich orange and apricot; 'Scarlet Bedder', deep, bright, rich scarlet; 'Golden Bedder', large early golden-yellow blooms; and 'Primrose bedder', primrose-yellow.

Try also the Siberian Wallflower, *Cheiranthus allionii*. It is dwarf, at 30cm (12in) high, compact, free flowering and has bright orange blooms. Varieties are 'Orange Bedder', bright orange; 'Golden Bedder', golden-yellow; and 'Yellow Bedder', pure yellow.

CULTIVATION
The soil must be well drained because if it lies wet over winter the plants are liable to die. However, any soil type is suitable for Wallflowers and they do particularly well on chalky or limy soils. Apply lime to acid soils. Full sun is needed, and shelter from cold winter winds. Sometimes hard frosts partially lift the plants out of the ground and if this happens they must be refirmed immediately or again they could die. For the sake of

PROPAGATION
Sow seeds in an outdoor seed bed during late spring or early summer. Then transplant the seedlings to a nursery bed, spacing them about 20cm (8in) apart each way. Keep weeded and water well during dry spells. It pays to treat roots of wallflowers with a proprietary clubroot dip to prevent this serious disease from crippling the plants. Wallflowers are planted in their flowering positions during mid-autumn – lift them with some soil around the roots if possible because then they re-establish more quickly.

Chrysanthemum carinatum (C. tricolor)
Annual Chrysanthemum

Spread 30cm (12in)
Height 60cm (24in)

HA

An easily grown and popular hardy annual, especially good for cutting because the blooms last well in water. The large daisy flowers are produced from early summer to early autumn. Sold in a mix of colours which includes shades of orange, yellow, red and also white. The flowers are zoned with a contrasting colour.

Also recommended is *C. multicaule* 'Gold Plate', a low grower at 15cm (6in) high, with a spreading habit and golden-yellow flowers – ideal for containers such as tubs and window boxes. Try also *C. paludosum*, 30cm (12in) high, with masses of small white and yellow flowers with yellow centres all summer, useful for containers and for edging beds.

CULTIVATION
Well-drained soil in full sun is needed for best results. Regularly remove dead flowers to ensure more to follow. Tall kinds may need twiggy sticks for support in windy gardens.

PROPAGATION
Sow seeds in early or mid-spring where the plants are to flower and thin out the seedlings to the recommended spacing. Or make a sowing in early autumn if you have well-drained soil and live in a mild area. Cover plants with cloches for the winter.

Cucurbita pepo ovifera
Ornamental Gourd

Spread 90cm (36in)
Height up to 3m (10ft)

HHA

Ornamental Gourds are grown for their fruits, which vary tremendously in shape, size and colours. The fruits are dried and used for winter decoration indoors.

There are several varieties including 'Small Fruited Mixed' with fruits in all shapes and colours.

CULTIVATION
Gourds are climbers and should be trained up suitable supports such as walls or fences equipped with trellis panels. Or grow the plants up a tripod of canes or sticks. The plants need full sun, a sheltered spot and a well-drained soil.

The fruits are cut in the autumn and kept for a few weeks in a warm dry place to allow them to dry out. They they can be varnished to give them a shine.

PROPAGATION
Sow seeds under glass or indoors during late spring, one seed per 9cm (3½in) pot. Harden thoroughly and plant out when the danger of frost is over.

Dahlia variabilis
Dahlia

Spread 30–60cm (12–24in)
Height 30–60cm (12–24in)

HHA

Dwarf Bedding Dahlias are easily raised from seeds and make a superb show from early or mid-summer until the frosts put a stop to the display. Flowering is continuous throughout the season.

Dahlias are stricly tender perennials but the bedding kinds are generally treated as half-hardy annuals. The flowers come in a wide range of colours and are excellent for cutting.

Dahlias can be used in various ways: they can be mass planted in beds, planted in bold groups in mixed borders, used as dot plants in formal bedding schemes, included in sub-tropical bedding schemes and planted in tubs or window boxes.

There are lots of dwarf varieties available including 'Unwins Dwarf Hybrids', 45–60cm (18–24in) in height, highly popular on both sides of the Atlantic, with semi-double blooms in a vast range of colours. Flowers are freely produced on bushy plants. Plants will start flowering in three months from sowing.

'Coltness Hybrids', 45cm (18in) high, are also well-known, having single flowers in a wide range of colours, freely produced on compact plants.

'Redskin', 30cm (12in) high, has gained many awards in trials, has double flowers in a range of colours, and bronze-green to maroon foliage. 'Rigoletto', 30cm (12in) high, comes into flower early, the compact plants carrying masses of double blooms in a wide range of colours. One of the best for mass bedding.

CULTIVATION
Full sun is essential for optimum flowering. Provide, too, a fertile soil although any soil is suitable. Prepare it by adding plenty of bulky organic matter such as well-rotted farmyard manure or garden compost. Apply a base dressing of general-purpose or flower-garden fertilizer before planting. Protect plants from slugs and snails by using slug pellets. Water well during dry periods in summer and give a liquid feed monthly to established plants. Regularly cut off dead flowers to ensure that plenty more follow.

PROPAGATION
Sow seeds under glass or indoors during late winter. Transplant seedlings to individual 9cm (3½in) pots. Harden thoroughly and plant out when the danger of frost is over.

Delphinium consolida
Larkspur

Spread 30cm (12in)
Height 30–120cm (12–48in)

HA 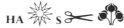 S ✂ 🌸

Dianthus barbatus
Sweet William

Spread 20cm (8in)
Height 30–60cm (12–24in)

HB  ✂ 🌸

A highly popular and easily grown hardy annual that makes a fine show in annual or mixed borders between early and late summer. Makes an ideal cut-flower, too. Flowers come in various colours: pink, red, purple, blue and white. Sold as mixtures such as 'Giant Imperial', up to 120cm (48in) in height, with a branching habit and long spikes of double blooms in pink, blue and white. 'Dwarf Hyacinth-Flowered' Double Mixed' grows to only 30cm (12in) in height and the compact plants have blooms in shades of pink, blue and white.

Also worth growing is another annual delphinium, *D. chinensis* 'Blue Mirror', 30cm (12in) in height with large gentian-blue flowers. It's best grown as a half-hardy annual.

No self-respecting cottage garden should be without Sweet Williams. They were seen in most cottage gardens of the past and are still as popular as ever. In modern gardens they fit into the mixed border, associating well with herbaceous perennials, especially early-summer flowering kinds such as lupins, irises, peonies and Oriental poppies.

The flowering period of Sweet Williams is early to mid-summer. Colours include shades of red, pink and also white. Sweet Williams are generally sold in mixtures of colours, such as 'Extra Dwarf Double Mixed', 30cm (12in) high compact plants with mainly double flowers in bright and cheerful colours. 'Auricula-eyed Mixed' is the old-fashioned sort, each flower having a contrasting centre.

CULTIVATION
Larkspur grows in any ordinary well-drained soil and full sun. The tall varieties will need twiggy sticks to support the slender stems.

PROPAGATION
Sow sees where the plants are to flower, in early or mid-spring and thin out the seedlings before they become overcrowded. Alternatively make a sowing in early autumn if you live in a mild area and have well-drained soil. Cover young plants with cloches for the winter, if available. Guard against slugs and snails.

CULTIVATION
Sweet Williams need full sun for optimum flowering, and a well-drained soil, which must be well prepared before planting by adding bulky organic matter. Apply a base dressing of general purpose fertilizer before planting, and guard the plants against slugs and snails.

PROPAGATION
Seeds are sown in early summer in a well-prepared seed bed in a spare part of the garden. As soon as the seedlings are large enough to handle they should be transplanted to a nursery bed to grow on. Space them about 20cm (8in) apart each way. The young plants are set out in their flowering positions in early or mid-autumn, and they should be lifted with some soil around the roots if possible to ensure that they re-establish quickly.

Echium plantagineum (E. lycopsis) _____
Viper's Bugloss

Spread 45cm (18in)
Height 30–90cm (12–36in)   **HA**

Gaillardia pulchella _____
Blanket Flower

Spread 30cm (12in)
Height 45–60cm (18–24in)   **HA**

A good but possibly not too well-known hardy annual for the annual or mixed border. It's a bushy plant up to 90cm (36in) high in the species with bluish or purplish flowers carried in spikes during early to late summer. However, hybrids are normally grown which come in mixtures of colours: 'Dwarf Hybrids' are especially recommended, growing to about 30cm (12in) in height, in a mix of colours that includes blue and pink shades, mauve and white. The dwarf ones would also be suitable for growing in tubs and window boxes.

Colourful daisy-flowered annual which makes a brilliant show between mid-summer and mid-autumn. The blooms are large and excellent for cutting. There are several varieties but 'Double Mixed' is popular, with double blooms in a range of colours that includes red, gold, cream and bi-colours.

Grow Gaillardias in the annual or mixed border.

CULTIVATION
Any ordinary garden soil is suitable for the Viper's Bugloss provided it is well drained. The plant actually prefers a dry light soil. Full sun is necessary for optimum flowering.

PROPAGATION
Seeds are sown where they are to flower in early spring and the seedlings thinned to the recommended spacing. Alternatively, if your soil is very light and well drained make a sowing in early autumn and overwinter the young plants under cloches. You will then get earlier blooms the following year.

CULTIVATION
A sunny site is needed but any well-drained soil is suitable. A light sandy soil is preferred but is not essential. A few twiggy sticks may be needed for support. Regularly cut off dead flower heads, when more blooms will follow.

PROPAGATION
Sow seeds where the plants are to flower, in mid-spring, and thin out the seedlings to the recommended distance. Alternatively, if you want earlier blooms, make a sowing under glass or indoors during late winter or early spring, transplant seedlings to trays, harden thoroughly and plant out in late spring.

Gazania × hybrida _____
Treasure Flower

Spread 30cm (12in)
Height 20–30cm (8–12in)   HHA

The low-growing Treasure Flowers are sun-worshippers and recommended for a hot dry site. Most have deep green or greyish foliage and large daisy flowers in shades of yellow, orange, mahogany, red, pink and cream, which usually open only in bright weather. Mainly used for edging, planted in bold drifts and to fill tubs and window boxes, they will also provide colour on the rock garden. They flower from mid-summer until the first frosts.

Latest varieties include 'Mini-star Tangerine' and 'Mini-star Yellow' with flowers more inclined to stay open in dull weather; 'Mini-star Mixed' contains a wide range of colours; 'Sundance' has exceptionally large flowers in a mixture of colours that includes red and yellow stripes, crimson, purple, orange, yellow and cream; and 'Daybreak' flowers stay open even longer in dull weather.

CULTIVATION
A position in full sun is essential together with a well-drained soil. Any soil type is, however, suitable.

If in a wet summer any blooms are affected by grey mould fungus (botrytis) cut these off to prevent the disease from spreading.

PROPAGATION
Sow seeds under glass or indoors during late winter. Transplant seedlings to individual 7.5cm (3in) pots and make sure they are well hardened before planting out, which should be done when the danger of frost is over.

Helichrysum bracteatum _____
Strawflower

Spread 30cm (12in)
Height 30–90cm (12–36in)   HHA

The Strawflower has double daisy-like flowers with a straw-like texture in shades of red, pink, yellow, orange and white. It is grown mainly for cutting and drying for winter decoration although the plants make an attractive show in the annual or mixed border.

The Strawflower is available as mixtures including 'Double Mixed', 90cm (36in) high; 'Bright Bikinis', 30–38cm (12–15in) high, in a wide range of bright colours; and 'Hot Bikini', 30–38cm (12–15in) high, with rich red flowers.

CULTIVATION
Provide a spot in full sun and a very well drained soil. Strawflowers do not mind light poor soils and indeed in such conditions the flower colour is more intense. Flowers for drying should be cut before they are completely open (before the disc in the centre shows), loosely bundled and hung upside down in a cool dry airy place away from direct sun. They will be thoroughly dry in a few weeks.

PROPAGATION
Sow seeds under glass or indoors during late winter/early spring. Transplant to trays, harden thoroughly and plant out in late spring when the danger of frost is over.

Lathyrus odoratus
Sweet Pea

Spread 15–20cm (6–8in)
Height 30cm (12in) to 3m (10ft)   HA

Sweet Peas are highly popular in Britain but of only minor interest in the USA. Many varieties have highly fragrant flowers and are excellent for cutting. They make a good show in annual or mixed borders. Some are dwarf bushy plants, others tall, ideal for growing up trellis, walls, fences and wigwams of tall twiggy sticks or bamboo canes.

There is an enormously wide range of varieties to choose from and the flowers come in virtually every colour. Mixtures as well as separate colours are available.

All we can do here is to describe a representative selection of varieties, both tall and dwarf.

'Early Mammoth Mixed' is a tall multiflora type that is noted for early flowering, large, long-stemmed blooms and fragrance. 'Early Wonder Mixed' is also a tall climber that comes into bloom early and has good fragrance. 'Galaxy Mixed', tall, comes in a wide range of beautiful colours and has many flowers on each stem. Probably better known in Britain than in North America are the Spencer varieties, which are tall climbers and popular for cutting. There are dozens of named varieties in separate colours.

Among the dwarf varieties, highly recommended is 'Jet Set Mixed', about 90cm (36in) in height, with large flowers on long stems and up to seven blooms per stem. 'Knee-Hi' mixed is virtually identical.

'Snoopea Mixed' does not have tendrils on the leaves. It cannot climb, so it forms a sort of annual ground cover about 30cm (12in) in height and freely produces normal-sized blooms on long stems. 'Supersnoop Mixed' is really an improved 'Snoopea' but it comes into flower up to 10 days earlier. The flower stems are longer and there is a wider range of colours. Last but not least is 'Bijou Mixed',

which grows only 30–38cm (12–15in) high and wide. Despite its diminutive size the blooms are large and each stem carries up to five flowers.

The flowering period of Sweet Peas is early summer to early autumn.

CULTIVATION
An open sunny site is needed with a well-drained fertile soil, well-enriched with manure or compost and fertilizer. Water well in summer, liquid feed fortnightly and remove dead flowers. Pinch out growing tips of seedlings when 10cm (4in) high. Protect from slugs and snails.

PROPAGATION
Soak seeds in water for half a day before sowing. Sow in early or mid-spring in trays and germinate in a cold frame or indoors in a cool room. Do not allow them to become too damp during germination. Plant out in late spring. Alternatively sow seeds where they are to flower during early or mid-spring.

Limonium sinuatum (Statice sinuata) _____
Sea Lavender

Spread 30cm (12in)
Height 45cm (18in)   **HHA**

Linaria maroccana _____
Toadflax

Spread 15cm (6in)
Height 20–30cm (8–12in)   **HA**

Sea Lavender is grown mainly for cutting and drying for winter flower arrangements but the sprays of flowers also make a fine show in the annual or mixed border.

Usually available in mixtures of colours including shades of blue, red, pink, yellow, etc. 'Mixed Hybrids' is a good mix of pastel colours. 'Blue River' is compact and has blue flowers. The flowering period is mid-summer to early autumn.

Popular and easily grown hardy annual used for edging beds and borders, for sowing in gaps in paving and for providing colour on the rock garden. Every cottage garden should have some!

The little antirrhinum-like flowers come in a wide range of colours and the flowering period is early and mid-summer.

Sold as mixtures, particularly recommended is 'Fairy Bouquet' in a wide range of colours and attaining about 20cm (8in) in height.

CULTIVATION
An open position in full sun is recommended. Any well-drained soil is suitable. Flowers should be cut for drying just before they are completely open. Bundle loosely and hang them upside down for a few weeks in a cool dry airy place out of direct sun.

PROPAGATION
Sow seeds under glass or indoors during late winter/early spring. Transplant the seedlings to trays, harden thoroughly and plant out in late spring.

CULTIVATION
For best results grow Toadflax in full sun and well-drained soil.

PROPAGATION
Sow the seeds during early or mid-spring where the plants are to flower, and before overcrowding occurs thin the seedlings to the recommended spacing. A sowing can also be made outdoors in early autumn to provide earlier blooms the following year. Only suitable for well-drained soils. Cover with cloches over winter if you live in a cold area.

Matthiola incana
Stock

Spread 30cm (12in)
Height 30–60cm (12–24in) **HA HHA HB**

Stocks, annual and biennial, are best loved for their scented flowers.

Among the annual stocks are the selectable 'Park Stocks' (HHA) 30cm (12in) in a mix of colours. To ensure you get double-flowers, grow seedlings at 5–7°C (40–45°F) for several days and then select only light green ones (double-flowered). 'Large Flowering Ten Week Mixed' (HHA) 30cm (12in) has a fine range of colours and compact habit. 'Giant Excelsior' column stocks (HHA) reach 60cm (24in), and are fine for cutting. *Matthiola bicornis*, the Night-scented Stock (HA) reaches 30cm (12in) with pale lilac flowers.

The Brompton Stocks are hardy biennials 60cm (24in) and give fine spring colour.

CULTIVATION
Stocks will thrive in full or partial sun but need a well-drained fertile soil.

PROPAGATION
Sow hardy annual kinds during early to mid-spring where the plants are to flower and thin to the recommended spacing. Those treated as half-hardy annuals are sown under glass or indoors during late winter/early spring. Sow biennial stocks in an outdoor seed bed during late spring/early summer. Transplant seedlings to a nursery bed and plant out young plants in their flowering positions during mid-autumn. Protect with cloches over winter in windy gardens.

Mesembryanthemum criniflorum
Livingstone Daisy

Spread 30cm (12in)
Height 15cm (6in) **HHA**

A popular little annual with masses of daisy flowers in a wide range of bright colours. These open only when the sun is shining or during bright weather. They are ideal for hot dry places such as banks, the rock garden and for gaps in paving. The flowering period is early to late summer.

Another Livingstone Daisy worth growing is *M. oculatum* 'Yellow Lunette', with early bright yellow flowers which open in duller conditions.

CULTIVATION
A hot dry spot is essential for success. Light poor sandy soils are ideal. Watch out for slugs and snails because they are partial to the soft succulent leaves and stems.

PROPAGATION
Seeds are sown under glass or indoors during early spring and the seedlings transplanted to trays. Harden thoroughly and plant out when the danger of frost is over. Alternatively, a sowing can be made during mid-spring where the plants are to flower and the resultant seedlings thinned to the recommended spacing.

Mimulus × hybridus
Monkey Flower

Spread 20–30cm (8–12in)
Height 15–20cm (6–8in)

HHA

Mirabilis jalapa
Four O'Clock Plant

Spread 30cm (12in)
Height 60cm (24in)

HHA S

In recent years mimulus have become popular for bedding out. Possibly this is because some exciting new hybrids such as 'Calypso' have been introduced with flowers in shades of red, pink, orange and yellow, some being bi-coloured; and 'Malibu' with rich deep orange blooms.

Mimulus can be mass planted in beds and are excellent for containers such as tubs, window boxes and hanging baskets. They have numerous flushes of blooms throughout the summer and can start flowering in as little as seven or eight weeks from sowing.

The Four O'Clock Plant is a colourful perennial which is grown as an annual in the annual or mixed border. The scented blooms are trumpet-shaped and come in various shades including red, pink, yellow and white. They open in late afternoon, hence the common name, and by the following morning are over, but plenty more follow – indeed this is a free-flowering annual. The blooms may open earlier in the day during dull or cool weather. The Four O'Clock Plant flowers from mid-summer to early autumn.

CULTIVATION
In temperate climates mimulus will succeed in full sun, and in partial shade. In hot climates, though, plant them in shade. The soil must be able to retain moisture during the summer because mimulus thrive in moist conditions. Add plenty of bulky organic matter especially if the soil is light and sandy.

Cut off dead flower heads to encourage more blooms to follow, and guard against slugs and snails especially after planting.

PROPAGATION
Sow seeds under glass or indoors during early or mid-spring and transplant the resultant seedlings to trays. Make sure you don't allow the compost to dry out at any time. Harden thoroughly before planting out in late spring. The plants are short-lived perennials but are normally treated as annuals and discarded at the end of the season.

CULTIVATION
Provide a spot in full sun and sheltered from winds. The plant prefers a light soil but whichever type you have it should be moderately fertile for best growth and flowering. In windy gardens twiggy sticks may have to be provided to support the plants.

PROPAGATION
Sow the seeds under glass or indoors during late winter or early spring. The seedlings are transplanted to trays, thoroughly hardened and planted out when the danger of frost is over.

Nemesia strumosa _____
Nemesia

Spread 10–15cm (4–6in)
Height 20–45cm (8–18in)   **HHA**

A popular half-hardy annual suitable for bedding out in formal beds, for planting in bold groups at the front of a mixed border and for growing specially for cutting.

It's a bushy upright plant producing tubular flowers from early to late summer. Varieties come in mixtures of colours including shades of red, pink, orange, yellow and cream. Good varieties are 'Carnival Mixed', 20–30cm (8–12in) high; 'Funfair', 20cm (8in), an exceedingly bright and warm mix of colours; and 'Triumph Mixed' ('Dwarf Compact Hybrids'), 20cm (8in), with bright showy colours and a compact habit.

CULTIVATION
Grow in full or partial sun and any ordinary soil well supplied with bulky organic matter. The plant actually prefers a light sandy acid or lime-free soil but these conditions are not essential. Keep well watered in dry weather because dry conditions lead to poor growth and flowering. Cut off dead flowers to ensure that more follow.

PROPAGATION
Sow seeds under glass or indoors during early spring, transplant seedlings to trays, harden thoroughly and plant out when the danger of frost is over.

Nicotiana alata (N. affinis) _____
Ornamental Tobacco

Spread 30cm (12in)
Height 30–90cm (12–36in)   **HHA**

Ornamental Tobacco is a lovely summer bedding plant, producing a wealth of colourful, often scented flowers from early summer to early autumn.

Grow nicotiana in formal displays, for planting in bold groups in borders, and in containers, especially the shorter varieties.

Good varieties include Nicki Formula Mixed', 38cm (15in) high, which is sweetly scented. 'Senation Mixed', 75–90cm (30–36in) high, is also scented and unlike some varieties the flowers open during the day rather than in the evening, as do those of 'Domino Mixed', 30cm (12in) high, in a good range of colours including bi-colours on bushy plants.

It is also possible to buy varieties in separate colours. There are separate colours in the 'Domino' and 'Nicki' series. Probably the most popular single-coloured nicotiana is 'Lime Green' 60cm (24in) in height with greenish yellow flowers.

CULTIVATION
Best results are achieved in a sunny sheltered spot. Nicotiana likes a fertile soil, so prepare the ground well by adding plenty of well-rotted manure or garden compost. Before planting give a base dressing of fertilizer.

PROPAGATION
Sow seeds under glass or indoors during late winter or early spring. Do not cover them with compost. Transplant seedlings to trays, or to 9cm (3½in) pots if preferred, harden thoroughly and plant out when the danger of frost is over.

Papaver nudicaule
Iceland Poppy

Spread 30cm (12in)
Height 45–76cm (18–30in)

HHA HB

Papaver rhoeas
Field Poppy or Shirley Poppy

Spread 30cm (12in)
Height 76–90cm (30–36in)

HA

The Iceland Poppy can be grown either as a half-hardy annual or as a biennial. Strictly speaking it is a short-lived perennial. The flowers are suitable for cutting and a bold group of plants makes a fine show in an annual or mixed border during the summer. The foliage is lobed and light green, a nice background for the large flowers which come in many colours.

Varieties include 'Unwins Giant Coonara', 45cm (18in) high, a mix of bright and pastel colours; 'Champagne Bubbles', 45–60cm (18–24in) high, wide range of colours including shades of red, yellow, pink, orange and white; and 'Oregon Rainbows', height up to 45cm (18in) with strong stems ideal for cutting and flowers in shades of orange, pink, yellow, cream, etc.

The species, which is shown above, is not often grown in gardens but rather the varieties, particularly 'Shirley Double Mixed' with double blooms in shades of red, pink, white, etc. These are produced between early and late summer and make a bright colourful show in the annual or mixed border.

CULTIVATION
Any well-drained soil in full sun will do. Remove dead blooms. Flowers for arranging should be cut just as they are opening and the stem bases dipped in hot water to seal them.

PROPAGATION
To grow as a half-hardy annual sow under glass or indoors in late winter, transplant to small pots, harden and plant out in late spring. To grow as a biennial sow outdoors where the plants are to flower during late spring and thin out the seedlings. Cover with cloches over winter.

CULTIVATION
Any ordinary well-drained soil in full sun will enable Field Poppies to be grown. Dead flowers should be removed regularly.

PROPAGATION
Sow seeds where the plants are to flower during early or mid-spring and thin out the seedlings to the recommended spacing.

Papaver somniferum
Opium Poppy

Spread 30cm (12in)
Height 76–90cm (30–36in)

HA

Pelargonium peltatum
Ive-leaf Geranium

Spread 30cm (12in)
Height 30cm (12in)

HHA

The species has quite attractive pale grey-green lobed leaves, a pleasant contrast to the red, pink, purple or white flowers that are produced from early to late summer. But varieties are usually grown in gardens, particularly 'Paeony-flowered Mixed' with fully double globular flowers in a good mix of colours including shades of pink and red.

The Opium Poppy is best sown in bold groups in the mixed or annual border.

CULTIVATION
Provide a well-drained soil in full sun for best results. Fairly poor soils are suitable, too. Regularly cut off dead flowers.

PROPAGATION
Sow seeds where the plants are to flower during early or mid-spring and thin out the seedlings to the recommended spacing before they start to become overcrowded.

The Ivy-leaf Geranium is popular for summer bedding, for mass planting in formal beds, and for containers such as tubs, urns, window boxes and hanging baskets, flowering continuously from early summer until the autumn frosts. Colours include shades of red, pink and also white.

Prior to the recent introduction of seed-raised varieties one had to buy young plants or raise new ones from cuttings taken in late summer.

The flowers of the F1 hybrid 'Summer Showers' are pink, mauve, red and also white. Completely trailing, the plants are ideal for hanging baskets and window boxes. Plants start coming into flower some 17–18 weeks from sowing and they make a magnificent display.

CULTIVATION
Provide a position in full sun to encourage optimum flowering. Any well-drained soil is suitable if you are planting in beds, provided it is reasonably fertile. If growing in containers use a good-quality potting compost, either soil-based or soilless (peat-based).

PROPAGATION
Seeds must be sown early in the year – mid-winter is recommended if you want plants in flower by early summer. Seeds can be sown under glass or indoors in adequate warmth. Seedlings are transplanted to 7.5cm (3in) pots and if necessary potted on to 12.5cm (5in) pots. Harden well and plant out when the danger of frost is over.

Petunia × hybrida
Petunia

Spread 30cm (12in)
Height 15–38cm (6–15in)

HHA

Petunias are in the top-ten list of summer bedding plants, being used extensively for mass-planting in formal beds with other half-hardy annuals, and in containers such as tubs, urns, window boxes and hanging baskets. Most petunias are bushy plants but some varieties have a somewhat trailing habit and these are especially useful for containers, although the bushy ones are also suitable.

Petunias come in an enormously wide range of colours, in mixtures and separate colours. The flowers are trumpet-shaped and some varieties have double blooms. The flowering period is early summer to autumn when the frosts put a stop to the display.

There are several groups of petunias, including the multiflora varieties which are the best types for bedding, being bushy plants with masses of small flowers. Varieties include the 'Resisto' series, free flowering, the blooms standing up well to wet weather. There is 'Resisto Mixed' in a blend of bright colours; 'Resisto Blue', a beautiful mid-blue; and 'Resisto Rose-pink', the colour being as the name. The 'Jamboree' series is also recommended. Particularly popular is 'Jamboree Mixed' with exceptionally large flowers for a multiflora type, especially recommended for hanging baskets and window boxes as well as for bedding. The 'Madness' series – officially a floribunda – has flowers approaching grandiflora size, with compact habit, but flowers as freely as multiflora types.

The grandiflora petunias are giant-flowered varieties and are especially recommended for tubs and window boxes but are also impressive in beds. They are not quite so weather-resistant as the multifloras – blooms can be marked by rain. The 'Picotee' series is highly recommended,

including 'Red Picotee' in bright scarlet with a broad white picotee edge, and 'Blue Frost' in deep violet-blue with a pure white edge. The 'Flash' series is popular in America for its early flowering and uniform habit with many bright colours.

CULTIVATION
Best flowering achieved in full sun but partial sun is also suitable. Any well-drained soil gives good results as long as it's reasonably fertile. But it must not be too rich, or the plants will make vegetative growth at the expense of flowers. A sheltered site is recommended for the grandiflora petunias. Regularly remove dead flower heads and guard the plants against slugs and snails.

PROPAGATION
Sow seed as under glass or indoors during early spring. The seeds are minute so do not cover them with compost. Transplant seedlings to trays, harden thoroughly and plant out when the danger of frost is over.

Phlox drummondii
Annual Phlox

Spread 20cm (8in)
Height 15–30cm (6–12in)

HHA

Portulaca grandiflora
Sun Plant

Spread 15cm (6in)
Height 15cm (6in)

HHA

Annual Phlox is a bright colourful little plant suitable for mass planting in beds, edging, containers and even for providing colour on the rock garden. It flowers from mid-summer to early autumn and colours include shades of red, pink, purple and white.

Annual Phlox is sold as mixtures of colours and include 'Twinkle Dwarf Star Mixed', 15cm (6in) high, with masses of dainty star-like blooms; and 'Beauty Formula Mixed', 30cm (12in) high, a mixture of brilliantly coloured varieties without the usual contrasting centres.

The Sun Plant is a succulent with fleshy stems and leaves and bears brilliant flowers in shades of red, pink, yellow, etc, from early summer to early autumn. It is an ideal plant for a hot dry bank, the rock garden or for edging beds and borders.

A good variety is 'Sunnyside' Mixed', with large rose-like double blooms in a mix of 12 bright clear colours.

CULTIVATION
Grow Annual Phlox in any reasonably fertile well-drained soil in full sun. The removal of dead flower heads will ensure more blooms to follow. Guard against slugs and snails.

PROPAGATION
Sow seeds under glass or indoors during early spring, transplant the seedlings to trays, harden thoroughly and plant out when the danger of frost is over. Or, sow outdoors in mid spring where the plants are to flower.

CULTIVATION
Full sun is essential together with good drainage – plants thrive in hot dry conditions. There is no need to water in a dry summer unless the plants are obviously flagging. Regularly remove dead flower heads.

PROPAGATION
Sow seeds under glass or indoors during early spring, transplant seedlings to trays, harden well and plant out when the danger of frost is over. Alternatively, sow outdoors during late spring where the plants are to flower and thin out the seedlings to the recommended spacing.

Primula polyantha
Polyanthus

Spread 20cm (8in)
Height 15–22cm (6–9in)   HB

Salvia horminum
Clary

Spread 20cm (8in)
Height 45–60cm (18–24in)   HA

In Britain, Polyanthus are widely grown as spring bedding plants in formal beds and in containers such as tubs and window boxes. In N. America they are grown as pot plants.

Plant them in beds, on their own or with spring bulbs such as dwarf tulips and hyacinths. They bloom over several months in the spring. Plant them in mixed borders or drift them around spring-flowering shrubs in a shrub border.

Some recommended varieties include 'Pacific Giants Mixed', with large blooms in bright colours, and 'Pacific Giants Blue Shades' in various shades of blue – these really need some protection in winter; and 'Crescendo', again with large flowers on vigorous hardy plants, the brilliant colour range including shades of yellow, red and pink.

CULTIVATION
Polyanthus prefer dappled shade cast by trees, and ordinary garden soil as long as it is moisture retentive (though not wet or waterlogged in winter). Add plenty of peat or leafmould to light sandy or chalky soil to help retain moisture. Before planting apply a base dressing of fertilizer. And fill tubs and window boxes with soilless (peat-based) potting compost.

PROPAGATION
Sow seeds in late spring and take care the temperature stays below 18°C/65°F. Transplanted seedlings should be kept cool and shaded in the trays and later in a nursery bed. Plant in final positions in early to mid-autumn.

This easily grown hardy annual makes a fine show in the annual or mixed border from early summer to early autumn. The flower bracts come in various colours such as red, pink, purple, blue and white. The blooms are excellent for cutting and can even be dried for winter decoration.

Good varieties include 'Art Shades', 60cm (24in) high, in shades of pink, rose, blue and white; 'Claryssa', 45cm (18in), a new variety in a wide range of bright colours; 'Claryssa Blue', 'Claryssa Pink' and 'Claryssa White'.

CULTIVATION
Any well-drained soil in full sun gives good results. Regularly cut off dead flower heads to encourage more to follow.

PROPAGATION
Sow seeds in their flowering positions during early to mid-spring and before the seedlings become overcrowded thin them out to the recommended spacing.

Scabiosa atropurpurea
Sweet Scabious

Spread 20cm (8in)
Height 45–90cm (18–36in)

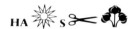

This is an excellent annual for cutting and for providing colour in annual or mixed borders from mid-summer to early autumn. Varieties are usually grown, such as 'Double Mixed', 90cm (36in) high with double scented blooms in shades of blue, purple, red, pink and white; and 'Dwarf Double Mixed', 45cm (18in) high in a similar colour range with fully double scented flowers.

CULTIVATION
Full sun, any fertile well-drained soil is needed for optimum flowering. Watch out for slugs and snails, which are rather partial to Sweet Scabious. Regularly remove dead flower heads to encourage more blooms to follow. Tall varieties may need a few twiggy sticks for support.

PROPAGATION
Sow seeds where the plants are to flower during early or mid-spring and thin the resultant seedlings. Alternatively, make a sowing in early autumn for earlier blooms the following spring and cover the young plants with cloches over winter if you live in a cold area.

Schizanthus pinnatus
Poor Man's Orchid

Spread 30cm (12in)
Height 15–45cm (6–18in)

The Poor Man's Orchid is generally grown as a greenhouse pot plant but it can be bedded out for the summer provided a sunny sheltered spot is chosen. As well as for mass planting in beds, it is also an ideal subject for window boxes and tubs.

It's a bushy plant with ferny foliage, which produces a profusion of multi-coloured flowers between early summer and the autumn.

Most varieties these days are dwarf or comparatively low-growing, such as 'Disco', 30cm (12in) high; 'Hit Parade', 30cm (12in), in a mix of rich and beautiful colours; and 'Star Parade', 15–20cm (6–8in), excellent for mass planting.

CULTIVATION
Choose a sheltered spot in full sun, and a well-drained soil. The plants prefer a light sandy soil which should be improved with bulky organic matter such as peat. Provide twiggy sticks to support the taller varieties.

PROPAGATION
Sow seeds under glass or indoors during early spring and transplant seedlings to small pots. Harden thoroughly and plant outdoors when the danger of frost is over. When plants are 7.5cm (3in) high cut out the growing tips to encourage a bushy habit.

Tropaeolum majus
Nasturtium

Spread 30cm (12in)
Height 30cm to 1.8m (12in to 6ft)

HA

Nasturtium is a favourite hardy annual, flowering from early summer to early autumn, easily grown provided it receives enough sun and especially popular with children. There are both dwarf, bushy varieties and climbing kinds. The latter can also be grown to cascade down a sunny bank, and the bushy kinds are ideal for sowing in bold groups at the front of borders.

Good varieties include 'Alaska Mixed', 30cm (12in) high with a bushy habit and a profusion of brilliant flowers. 'Whirlybird Mixed', 30cm (12in) high, is early flowering and the blooms face upwards, being held well above the leaves so that they show up well. There are other separate colours in the 'Whirlybird' series.

'Jewel Mixed', 30cm (12in) high, produces masses of semi-double flowers in bright shades of yellow, orange and red. The 'Gleam' series contains semi-trailing compact varieties with double or semi-double flowers. All are very effective in hanging baskets.

Among the climbing or trailing varieties suitable for covering a bank, there is 'Tall Mixed' or 'Climbing Mixed'.

CULTIVATION
Provide a sunny spot with well-drained soil. Any kind of soil is suitable, even exceedingly poor soils. Nasturtiums do not mind dry conditions either.

PROPAGATION
Sow seeds during mid-spring where the plants are to flower.

Verbena × hybrida (V. × hortensis)
Vervain

Spread 30cm (12in)
Height 15–45cm (6–18in)

HHA

Vervain can be mass planted, used as an edging or grown in tubs, window boxes and hanging baskets.

Varieties are available in mixtures and in separate colours. There are plenty to choose from in the catalogues, including 'Blaze', 20cm (8in) high, with vivid scarlet blooms on compact plants. This is an excellent variety for bedding out. 'Showtime', 25cm (10in) high, is a mix of bright colours, the plants having a spreading habit – ideal for containers. 'Springtime', 25cm (10in) high is extremely colourful and early flowering, with a dwarf but spreading habit, making it suitable for containers. 'Tropic', 25cm (10in) high, has deep crimson flowers.

Verbena aubletia 'Perfecta', 25cm (10in) high, is well worth growing. The compact rounded plants are exceedingly free flowering and the colour is a pleasing shade of bright rose.

V. venosa (V. rigida) grows up to 30–45cm (12–18in) in height and has slender upright stems carrying heads of purple flowers all summer and into autumn. It is particularly useful as a foil for other plants.

CULTIVATION
Grow in a sunny position with well-drained fertile soil. Regularly remove dead flowers to encourage more blooms to follow.

PROPAGATION
Sow seeds under glass or indoors during late winter or early spring and transplant seedlings to trays. Harden thoroughly and plant out when the danger of frost is over.

Viola × wittrockiana
Garden Pansy

Spread 20cm (8in)
Height 15–22cm (6–9in)

HHA HB

Garden Pansies are highly popular and not difficult to grow. They are as much at home in cottage gardens as in modern plots and there are varieties that bloom in summer as well as winter/spring.

Best effects are achieved by mass planting them in beds or at the front of borders. Winter/spring flowering kinds associate well with bulbs and other spring bedding plants.

Garden pansies are ideal, too, for containers such as tubs and window boxes.

There is a wide range of varieties and mixtures to choose from, as well as separate colours. Some varieties have an attractive black 'face' to each flower.

Recommended summer-flowering varieties include 'Majestic Giants Mixed', vigorous and early flowering with large blooms in a wide range of colours; 'Imperial Pink Shades', bright pink, fading to pale pink then white; 'Imperial Orange Prince', deep pure orange; 'Imperial Sky Blue', azure blue; and 'Roggli Giants Mixed', with large flowers in a wide range of colours.

Good winter-flowering Pansies include 'Floral Dance Mixed', in a wide range of colours; and 'Universal Mixture', in an equally good colour range.

Violas are also well worth growing. They have Pansy-like blooms but are much smaller. They flower from spring to autumn, attain a height of about 15cm (6in), and can be treated as half-hardy annuals or biennials. Try 'Prince Henry', small purple flowers with gold markings; and 'Prince John', clear bright yellow without markings. Grow violas on the rock garden or plant drifts in the shrub border. Also use them for edging beds and borders.

CULTIVATION
Pansies and Violas like a position in sun or partial sun and a moisture-retentive fertile soil. Add bulky organic matter to light sandy or chalky soils.

PROPAGATION
Pansies and Violas can be grown as half-hardy annuals or as biennials. To grow as half-hardy annuals sow under glass or indoors during early spring, transplant to trays and plant out before they become overcrowded, after hardening thoroughly. Winter-flowering Pansies should be sown in early summer and ideally raised in a cold frame. Transplant into a nursery bed and plant in flowering positions in autumn. To grow Pansies and Violas as biennials make the sowing in a cold frame or outdoors in early summer and transplant to a nursery bed. Move to flowering positions in autumn.

Viscaria elegans (Lychnis coeli-rosa)
Rose of Heaven

Spread 15cm (6in)
Height 45cm (18in)

HA

Xeranthemum annuum
Immortelle

Spread 15–20cm (6–8in)
Height 60cm (24in)

HA

This is perhaps not too well known but worth sowing in bold groups in the annual or mixed border where colourful star-shaped blooms will be produced from early to late summer. The species has pinky purple flowers each with a white centre, but normally a mixture of colours is grown, such as 'All Types Mixed' in soft pastel shades of rose, pink, blue, lavender, lilac, white, etc.

CULTIVATION
Full sun or partial sun and any ordinary well-drained soil are recommended.

PROPAGATION
Sow seeds in mid-spring where the plants are to flower and thin out the seedlings to the recommended spacing before they become overcrowded. Alternatively, for earlier flowers the following year make a sowing in early autumn where the plants are to flower. You'll get best results if you live in a mild area and your soil is well drained. Plants can be covered with cloches over winter, particularly if your garden is in a cold part of the country.

This is one of the everlasting flowers, whose blooms are dried and used for winter decoration. The daisy-like flowers are produced freely in summer and colours include shades of pink, lilac, purple and white. Usually sold in a mixture such as 'Double Mixed' with crested double cornflower-like blooms on long stems.

CULTIVATION
Grow in full sun and in a well-drained soil. Light sandy soils are especially suitable. Reasonably fertile soils give best results, so add fertilizer before sowing. The flowers should be cut for drying immediately they have opened. Bundle them loosely and hang them upside down in a cool dry airy place, out of direct sun, for a few weeks to allow them to become thoroughly dry.

PROPAGATION
Seeds are sown where the plants are to flower during early or mid-spring, and the seedlings thinned to the recommended spacing before they start to become overcrowded.

Zinnia elegans
Zinnia

Spread 30cm (12in)
Height 15–75cm (6–30in)

HHA

Zinnias are highly popular both in Britain and America. They have large daisy-like flowers, usually double, in a wide range of colours and are excellent for cutting. The dwarf varieties are ideal for mass planting in beds and the taller ones can be planted in groups in the mixed or annual border. The flowering period is early summer to early autumn.

There are lots of varieties to choose from and the following can be recommended. 'Big Top Mixed', 60cm (24in) high, won't grow well in Britain but popular in America. It has large cactus-dahlia-like blooms in a wide range of bright colours. 'Carved Ivory', 76cm (30in), also has cactus-dahlia-like flowers but in cream. 'Peppermint Stick Mixed', 60cm (24in) high, is a dahlia-flowered mix with striped, blotched and stippled flowers in all sorts of colours. Extremely eye-catching and ideal for cutting. 'Statefair Double Mixed', 60–76cm (24–30in) high, has huge dahlia-like blooms in shades of red, pink, orange, gold, yellow and cream. 'Wild Cherry', 76cm (30in) high, is a cactus-flowered variety with brilliant cherry-rose blooms, Dahlia-flowered hybrids, 60cm (24in) high, with fully double flowers, which can be strongly recommended are 'Gold Sun', 'Red Sun' and 'Sunshine Mixed' in a wide range of colours.

'Envy', 45cm (18in) high, is an unusual colour – chartreuse green. The blooms are like double-flowered dahlias and are much in demand by flower arrangers. An excellent choice of annual for a green and white planting scheme.

'Border Beauty Rose', 45cm (18in) high, unfortunately will not grow well in Britain but it's popular in America. The flowers are a pinky salmon colour, fully double and ideal for cutting. 'Peter Pan Mixed', 22cm (9in) tall, is excellent for bedding and comes in a range of bright colours such as reds, yellows and pinks. 'Pulcino', 22–30cm (9–12in) high, is a mix of many clear colours and it comes into flower early. An improved version is 'Belvedere' with exceptional weather resistance. 'Thumbelina Double Mixed', 15cm (6in) high, is one of the dwarfest of the bedding zinnias and highly popular on account of its wide colour range and free-flowering nature.

CULTIVATION
Grow zinnias in full sun and fertile well-drained soil. Work in plenty of manure or compost and add fertilizer before planting. Remove dead flowers to encourage more blooms.

PROPAGATION
Sow under glass or indoors during early spring, transplant to small pots, harden well and plant out when the danger of frost is over. Or sow outdoors during late spring where the plants are to flower and thin out the seedlings before they become overcrowded.

Flower Gardeners' Reference

Annuals and biennials are easily grown and have minimal needs. Keen gardeners, who spend much time tending them will achieve spectacular results; less assiduous gardeners who give their plants minimum attention will, however, still get very good results. The following tips will help you to raise and grow plants well.

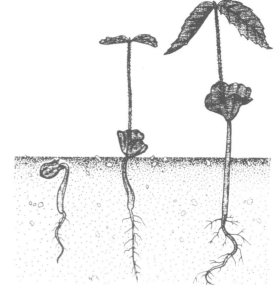

Soils

All soil types are suitable for annuals and biennials provided they are not waterlogged, but most need regular attention to ensure plants flourish.

Digging The best preparation for new beds and borders is digging to two depths of the spade (double digging). If you have the energy, do this where possible every three years. In the intervening years single digging to the depth of the spade will suffice. Dig in autumn ready for spring sowing and planting; or for autumn planting of spring bedding plants.

Alternative to digging Of course, not everyone wants to dig beds; indeed, it may not be possible among permanent plants. So simply fork over the area to be sown or planted to a depth of a few inches, at the same time adding soil improvers (see below), mixing them into the surface.

Improving the soil All soils benefit from the addition of bulky organic matter such as well-rotted manure, garden compost, peat, leafmould, spent hops, spent mushroom compost or pulverized bark. Heavy soils with poor drainage (e.g. clays) benefit from the addition of coarse horticultural sand or grit.

Add these to the trenches while digging, or fork them into the top few inches of soil.

Preparations for sowing outdoors Break down roughly dug soil with a fork. Consolidate by treading. Apply general-purpose fertilizer. Then rake in several directions to break down the soil finely and create about 2.5cm (1in) of loose soil. Prepare soil only when it's dry on the surface but moist below.

The preparation for planting out young plants is the same as for sowing outdoors.

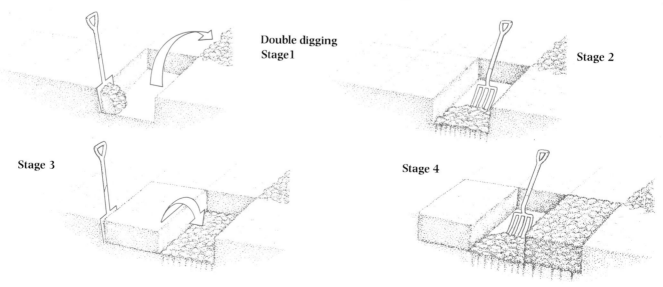

Double digging
Stage 1

Stage 2

Stage 3

Stage 4

Raising and Growing
Hardy Annuals

These are sown in early to late spring in the beds or borders where they are to flower. The state of the soil will dictate exact timing: don't sow when it's cold and wet.

Some hardy annuals can be down in early autumn for earlier blooms next year, provided your garden is in a relatively mild area with well-drained light soil.

Sowing technique Sow each type of annual in a bold informal group – an area of at least 90 × 90cm (3 × 3ft). Sow the seeds in rows of parallel drills or furrows across the area. Spacing of drills varies from about 15cm (6in) apart for small annuals up to 30cm (12in).

Make the shallow drills with a pointed stick or with the corner of a hoe. Most seeds will be happy in 12mm ($\frac{1}{2}$in) deep drills. Sow seeds thinly by trickling them between finger and thumb. None should be touching. Then draw fine soil over them and firm it lightly with the back of a rake if the soil's light and sandy.

Water the seed bed after sowing only if the soil is drying out. You should ideally sow into moist soil. Use a fine sprinkler for watering.

Thinning seedlings Before they become too large seedlings should be thinned out to their correct distance apart. Do a preliminary thinning when seedlings have formed their first true leaves and a second and final thinning when the remainder have further developed but are not yet quite touching each other.

Pull out surplus seedings by hand, placing the fingers of your other hand over the soil around the adjacent seeding that is to remain to prevent it being disturbed. Water remaining seedlings after thinning.

Supporting plants Rain and wind can flatten tall and thinned-stemmed annuals, and supports should be provided to prevent damage. The best supports are twiggy sticks pushed into the ground among and around the plants before they get too tall. The sticks should finish slightly below the ultimate flowering heights of the plants.

Metal plant supports are also suitable for annuals and come in various designs and sizes. Yet another method is to insert three or four bamboo canes around each group and to loop thin gardeners' string around them, to encircle and hold in the stems.

General care Water all annuals in dry weather, applying enough to moisten the soil to a depth of at least 15cm (6in).

The removal of dead flower heads before seeds set is recommended; this encourages more flowers to follow on many plants. Cut them off with flower scissors, leaving virtually all of the flower stems.

At the end of the summer or early in the autumn the display will be over and the plants will start to die, so pull them up and put them on the compost heap. Then dig or fork the bed.

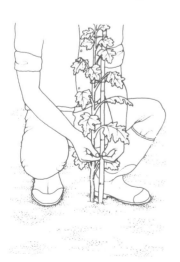

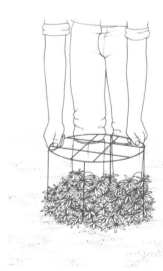

Supporting flowers

Raising and Growing
Half-Hardy Annuals

In temperate (coolish) climates, as in the UK and much of the USA, half-hardy annuals are ideally sown in a frost-free, heated greenhouse or indoors between mid-winter and mid- or late spring according to the plants' growth rates. Slow growers are sown earliest. See also Raising plants indoors.

Sowing techniques Seeds can be sown in full-or half-size seed trays with a depth of 2.5–3.8cm (1–1½in). Use a proprietary soil-based or peat-based seed compost. Firm the compost in the tray with a wooden presser to ensure a smooth level surface on which to sow.

Do sow thinly, so that no seeds are touching. Tiny seeds can be mixed with fine dry silver sand to make sowing easier. Sow the mixture from the palm of one hand, tapping it with the other to slowly release the seeds so that they scatter evenly over the compost surface.

Don't cover tiny seeds with compost but lightly press them into the surface with a wooden presser.

Sow larger seeds in the same way but don't mix them with sand. Very large ones can be spaced out individually. Sift a layer of fine compost or grit over larger seeds. The depth should equal twice the diameter of the seeds.

Then stand the trays in water almost up to their tops until the surface of the compost becomes moist. Add a fungicide to the water to prevent damping-off disease.

Germination conditions The seeds will need a steady temperature of 16–21°C (65–70°F) to germinate. Heat is best provided from below, as with an electrically heated propagating case. Alternatively stand trays on a bench in a heated greenhouse or above a radiator in the house, and cover each with a sheet of glass. When seedlings appear

provide maximum light but shade from sun. An ideal minimum temperature to maintain for growing on is 10°C (50°F).

Transplanting seedlings When large enough to handle easily transplant seedlings to other trays to give them room to grow. Trays ideally should be 5–7.5cm (2–3in) deep. Fill them with proprietary soil-based or peat-based-potting compost.

Space out the seedlings an equal distance apart each way in the trays. A standard-size tray will hold 40 seedlings (five rows of eight). Hold seedlings by the seed leaves and plant in holes made with a pencil or dibber, ensuring each seedling is inserted almost up to its lowest leaves. Firm in gently. Larger plants like dahlias and pelargoniums are better potted into 7.5cm (3in) pots and later moved on to 12.5cm (5in) pots.

Water in seedlings and place on the greenhouse bench. Keep them shaded and steadily moist.

Raising plants indoors If you don't have a greenhouse the plants can be raised indoors. Germinate the seeds in an airing cupboard or in any warm room on a windowsill; a windowsill above a radiator is ideal.

Seedlings must be moved to a light position as soon as germination occurs. Turn the trays regularly to prevent the plants from bending towards the light.

Hardening the plants Before planting outside, the plants must be acclimatized to outdoor conditions. Transfer the trays to a garden frame or a light, protected porch two to three weeks prior to final planting.

Close the frame at night to protect plants from frost or bring the trays indoors to an unheated room. Prior to final

Sowing and hardening off

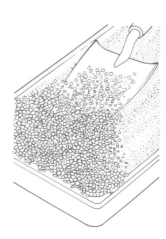
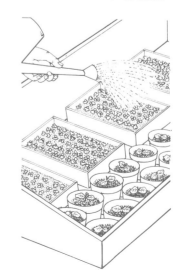

planting, when danger of night frost is over, the night protection should be stopped for a few days.

Buying half-hardy annuals If you buy plants from a garden centre, wait until you are ready to plant, and danger of frost is over.

Good-quality plants should be well hardened; should look sturdy with good, green foliage; and have some flowers plenty of flower buds to follow. Avoid weak spindly plants with pale or blotched leaves. Avoid also plants that have outgrown their containers (yellowing or reddish leaves indicate nutrient deficiency).

Planting out Plant when all danger of frost is over – frost can kill half-hardy annuals.

Containers such as tubs, urns, window boxes and hanging baskets should be filled with soil-based or peat-based potting compost. First put a layer of drainage material in the bottom. Wire hanging baskets should first be lined with sphagnum moss or a proprietary liner, and trailing plants can be planted through the wires and moss in the sides as you fill with compost.

Water plants and containers thoroughly the day before planting out. Gently separate plants in trays by pulling the roots apart or easing them apart with a hand fork. Don't let roots dry out; and make sufficiently large planting holes, with a trowel, to accommodate to roots without cramping. Firm in well with your fingers then water in.

General care When the plants have produced their first flush of flowers you can start a light liquid feeding – not too much or you'll get too much foliage at the expense of flowers. Feeding about once a month will be sufficient, using a proprietary general-purpose or flower-garden fertilizer, high in potash and low in nitrogen for maximum flower production.

Keep plants well watered during dry periods. It's best to use a fine sprinkler, and to apply enough to penetrate to a depth of at least 15cm (6in). Containers must be checked daily (or even twice daily in very hot weather) because they can dry out rapidly.

Regularly remove dead flower heads because this encourages more blooms.

Hanging baskets

Raising and Growing
Hardy Biennials

Most hardy biennials are sown outdoors from late spring to early summer in a prepared seed bed. But very small seeds are best sown in seed trays.

Sow in rows and when seedlings are large enough to handle easily transplant them to a nursery bed to give them room to grow. Plant in rows 30cm (12in) apart with at least 20cm (8in) between seedlings.

Seedlings raised in trays should be pricked out into other trays (as explained for half-hardy annuals) then, before they become overcrowded, transplanted to a nursery bed in the open as outlined above.

The young plants should be kept well watered in dry weather and free from weeds.

Buying plants Hardy biennials can also be bought as young plants from garden centres. The spring and early summer flowering varieties will be available in the autumn.

Some, such as wallflowers, may be sold 'bare-root' in bundles. However, make sure the roots are well wrapped and not dried out. Plant 'bare-root' plants immediately you get them home to prevent roots from becoming dry. Don't buy these plants if the leaves are going yellow as this indicates they have been bundled for too long. Most hardy biennials, however, are sold in trays or strip containers.

The difference between half-hardy annuals and biennials is that the latter will flower in the year after they are bought.

To work out the number of plants you need bear in mind that wallflowers are planted about 30cm (12in) apart each way, so you will need about 16 plants to fill 1m² (1 sq yd). Other smaller plants such as forget-me-nots (myosotis), double daisies (bellis), polyanthus and pansies are planted about 20cm (8in) apart each way, so you will need about 25 plants per m².

Final planting The young plants are set out in their flowering positions in early to mid-autumn, when they should be quite large. Ensure beds and borders are well prepared.

Carefully lift home-grown plants from the nursery bed, and try if possible to retain some soil around the roots. Take out good-sized holes, firm the plants well in, and water.

General care Plants should be checked during winter because a hard frost can partially lift them out of the soil. Re-firm these plants thoroughly.

Large containers do not often dry out and they can be insulated with dry straw or bracken to prevent the compost from freezing and harming the plants, but they should be checked if conditions are bad.

**Pricking out seedlings
raised in trays**

Pests, Diseases and Weeds

Pests Aphids – blackfly and greenfly – may attack the leaves and shoot tips of many plants. When noticed spray plants with a systemic insecticide, such as one containing dimethoate or a combination of permethrin and heptenophos.

Slugs and snails go for any soft plant material, and seedlings and young plants are the most vulnerable. Sprinkle slug pellets, containing methiocarb or metaldehyde, around plants.

Flea beetles attack the leaves of several bedding plants, resulting in masses of small holes. Spray at the first sign of an attack with a systemic insecticide as for aphids.

Caterpillars of various kinds may be found eating holes in leaves, in which case treat the plants with derris dust.

Diseases Club-root disease attacks members of the cabbage family, including ornamental cabbages, wallflowers and stocks. It causes the roots to swell and become deformed, and produces stunted top growth. Preventive treatment involves club-root dip containing thiophanate-methyl, which should be used on the roots of growing plants before planting out.

Wilts and rots – there are several fungal diseases that can cause roots and stems to collapse and/or rot. Plants growing in poor soil conditions are most vulnerable. Try to prevent trouble by improving the soil and treating it with a fungicidal drench of thiophanate-methyl. Dead plants, or dead parts of plants, should be removed and burnt to prevent diseases from spreading.

Rust appears as rust-coloured spots on the leaves of several plants, including hollyhocks. Spray the plants with a fungicide containing copper or propiconazole.

Mildew appears as white powdery patches on leaves and shoot tips of may plants. Grey mould or botrytis can cause rotting of flowers, particularly during a wet summer. Cut off

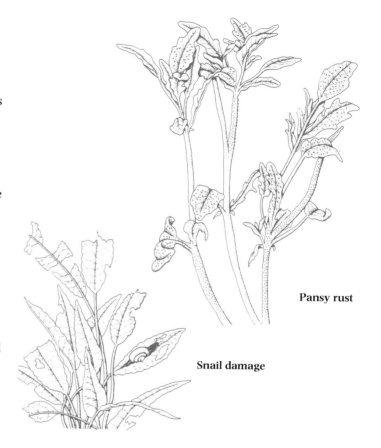

Pansy rust

Snail damage

Blackfly

and burn affected flowers before the disease spreads to healthy parts of the plants. Both diseases can be controlled by a systemic fungicide such as benomyl.

Weeds Weeds must be kept under control at all times because they compete with cultivated plants for food, moisture, air and light. So start off with weed-free beds.

Control seedling weeds among cultivated plants by hoeing them on a dry warm day when the soil surface is dry. The weeds will then quickly dry up and die. To prevent the germination of weed seeds for up to eight weeks, sprinkle propachlor granules over the soil between and around the cultivated plants. The soil must be free from weeds before applying the granules.

Cleaning empty beds of perennial weeds involves spraying with a herbicide containing glyphosphate. And annual weeds can be cleared with paraquate, but again this can only be applied to empty beds.

*I*ndex

A

accent plants, 7
Acroclinium roseum see *Helipterum roseum*
African Daisy, 78
African Marigold, 11, 22, 23, 43
Ageratum, 23, 27
  A. houstonianum, 18, 26
    description and cultivation, 66
  A.h. 'Blue Danube', 66
  A.h. 'Blue Mink', 66
  A.h. 'North Sea', 66
  A.h. 'Ocean', 66
  A.h. 'Summer Snow', 66
Agrostemma githago, description and cultivation, 58
  A.g. 'Milas', 15, 58
Alonsoa grandiflora see *A. warscewiczii*, 50
  A. warscewiczii, 16
    description and cultivation, 50
Althaea chinensis see *A. rosea*, 77
  A. rosea, 20, 28
    description and cultivation, 77
  A.r. 'Majorette', 77
  A.r. 'Summer Carnival', 20, 77
Alyssum maritimum, 15, 22, 27
  description and cultivation, 34
  A.m. 'Carpet of Snow', 34
  A.m. 'Little Dorrit', 34
  A.m. 'Oriental Night', 34
  A.m. 'Rosie O'Day', 34
  A.m. 'Wonderland', 34
Amaranthus caudatus, 10, 18, 21
  description and cultivation, 51
  A. 'Dark Red', 51
  A. tricolor, 10
    description and cultivation, 51
  A.t. 'Flaming Fountains', 51
  A.t. 'Illumination', 21
  A.t. 'Joseph's Coat', 51
  A.t. 'Molten Fire', 51
  A. 'Viridis', 51
Anchusa capensis, 10
  description and cultivation, 67
  A.c. 'Blue Angel', 67
  A.c. 'Blue Bird', 19
Annual Chrysanthemum, 84
Annual Flax, 55
Annual Hollyhock, 77
Annual Mallow, 62
Annual Phlox, 97
Annual Pinks, 59
Antirrhinum majus, 11, 13
  description and cultivation, 77
  A.m. 'Coronette', 77
  A.m. 'Double Madame Butterfly', 77
  A.m. 'Little Darling', 77
  A.m. 'Monarch', 77
aphids, 109
Apple of Peru, 74
Arctotis x *hybrida*, description and cultivation, 78
Argemone mexicana, 18
  description and cultivation, 38
Australian Everlasting, 61

B

Baby Blue Eyes, 74

Baby's Breath, 35
banks, 29
Bartonia aurea see *Mentzelia lindleyi*
baskets, hanging, 27
Bedding Calceolaria, 39
beds:
  spring bedding schemes, 24–5
  sub-tropical, 21
  summer bedding schemes, 22–3
Begonia semperflorens, 18, 21, 22, 23, 26
  description and cultivation, 52
  B.s. 'Cocktail', 52
  B.s. 'Coco Bright Scarlet', 52
  B.s. 'Coco Ducolor', 52
  B.s. 'Coco Mixed', 52
  B.s. 'Coco Pink', 52
  B.s. 'Organdie', 52
  B. x *tuberhybrida*, 26, 27
    description and cultivation, 78
  B. x *t.* 'Clips', 78
  B. x *t.* 'Nonstop', 78
Bellis perennis, 18, 26
  description and cultivation, 79
  B.p. 'Goliath', 79
  B.p. 'Pomponette' 79
Bells of Ireland, 20
Berberis, 19
biennials:
  definition, 6
  mixed borders, 18
  raising, 108
  sowing, 7, 108
Black-eyed Susan (*Rudbeckia hirta*), 42
Black-eyed Susan (*Thunbergia alata*), 46
blackfly, 109
Blanket Flower, 87
Blazing Stars, 41
blue borders, 14
blue flowers:
  descriptions, 66–76
  use of, 12
Blue Lace Flower, 69
Blue Thimble Flower, 70
borders, 18–20
  annual, 18
  cottage-garden style, 20
  mixed, 18–19
Brachycome iberidifolium, description and cultivation, 63
  B.i. 'Purple Splendour', 63
Brassica oleracea capitata, description and cultivation, 79
  B.o.c. 'Coral Prince', 79
  B.o.c. 'Coral Queen', 79
  B.o.c. 'Osaka Red', 79
Briza, 15
  B. maxima, 14, 18, 31
Brompton Stock, 91
Burning Bush, 32
Busy Lizzie, 21, 26, 54

C

Calceolaria 'Golden Bunch', 39
  C. integrifolia, description and cultivation, 39
  C. rugosa, 39
  C. 'Sunshine', 39

Calendula officinalis, 11, 16, 19, 20
  description and cultivation, 47
  C.o. 'Fiesta Gitanna', 47
  C.o. 'Orange King', 47
  C.o. 'Pacific Beauty', 47
  C.o. 'Touch of Class', 47
Californian Bluebell, 75
Californian Poppy, 18, 28, 48
Callistephus chinensis, description and cultivation, 80
  C.c. 'Duchess Mixed', 80
  C.c. 'Milady Super Mixed', 80
  C.c. 'Ostrich Feather Mixed', 80
  C.c. 'Powderpuffs', 80
  C.c. 'Thousand Wonders Mixed', 80
  C.c. 'Thousand Wonders Rose', 80
  C.c. 'Totem Pole', 80
Campanula medium, 18, 20
  description and cultivation, 81
  C.m. 'Bells of Holland', 81
  C.m. 'Cup and Saucer Mixed', 81
Canary Creeper, 18, 29
Candytuft, 20, 28, 61
Canna, 14
  C. x *generalis*, 21, 22, 23
    description and cultivation, 81
  C. x *g.* 'Giant Hybrids', 81
  C. x *g.* 'Seven Dwarfs', 81
Canterbury Bells, 18, 20, 81
Castor Oil Plant, 23, 57
caterpillars, 109
Celosia plumosa, 21
  description and cultivation, 82
  C.p. 'Apricot Brandy', 82
  C.p. 'Century Mixed', 82
  C.p. 'Fairy Fountains', 82
Centaurea cyanus, 16, 20
  description and cultivation, 67
  C.c. 'Blue Diadem', 19, 67
  C.c. 'Jubilee Gem', 67
  C.c. 'Polka Dot Mixed', 67
  C. moschata, description and cultivation, 82
  C.m. 'Giant Imperial Mixed', 82
Cheiranthus allionii, 25, 26
  description and cultivation, 83
  C.a. 'Golden Bedder', 83
  C.a. 'Orange Bedder', 83
  C.a. 'Yellow Bedder', 83
  C. cheiri, 20, 25, 26
    description and cultivation, 82
  C.c. 'Fair Lady Mixed', 17, 83
  C.c. 'Golden Bedder', 83
  C.c. 'Orange Bedder', 83
  C.c. 'Primrose Bedder', 83
  C.c. 'Scarlet Bedder', 83
China Aster, 80
Chrysanthemum carinatum, 19
  description and cultivation, 84
  C. multicaule 'Gold Plate', 84
  C. paludosum, 84
  C. parthenium, description and cultivation, 36, 42
  C.p. 'Golden Ball', 36
  C.p. 'Golden Fleece', 42

C.p. 'Golden Moss', 42
C.p. 'Snow Dwarf', 36
C.p. 'Snowball', 36
C.p. 'White Stars', 36
C. tricolor see *C. carinatum*
Cineraria maritima, 13, 15, 22, 23, 26, 27
  description and cultivation, 35
  C.m. 'Cirrus', 35
  C.m. 'Silver Dust', 35
Clarkia elegans, 19
  description and cultivation, 58
  C. pulchella, 58
Clary, 98
Cleome spinosa, 15, 18
  description and cultivation, 58
  C.s. 'Colour Fountains', 59
  C.s. 'Rose Queen', 59
climbing plants, 7, 29
club root, 109
Cobaea scandens, 29
  description and cultivation, 63
Coix lacryma-jobi, 15, 14, 18
  description and cultivation, 31
Coleus blumei, 21, 27
  description and cultivation, 52
  C.b. 'Carefree', 52
  C.b. 'Dragon', 52
  C.b. 'Fashion Parade', 52
  C.b. 'Red Monarch', 52
  C.b. 'Rose Wizard', 52
  C.b. 'Saber', 52
  C.b. 'Scarlet Poncho', 52
  C.b. 'Wizard Mixed', 52
colour:
  colour wheel, 9
  contrasts, 11
  effective use, 12
  harmony, 10
  multi-coloured flowers, 17
  perspective and, 13
  primary, 9
  principles of using, 9
  rainbow effect, 16
  restricted use of, 14–15
  strong, 15, 16
conifers, 9
containers, 26
Convolvulus minor see *C. tricolor*
  C. tricolor, 11, 28
    description and culture, 68
  C.t. 'Blue Flash', 68
  C.t. 'Ensign', 68
Coreopsis tinctoria, description and cultivation, 39
Corn Cockle, 58
Cornflower, 20, 67
Cosmos bipinnatus, description and cultivation, 53
  C.b. 'Candystripe', 53
  C.b. 'Sensation', 53
  C. sulphureus 'Bright Lights', 53
  C.s. 'Diablo', 53
  C.s. 'Sunny Gold', 53
  C.s. 'Sunny Red', 53
Cotinus, 19
cottage-garden borders, 20
crazy paving, 28
Cucurbita pepo ovifera, 29
  description and cultivation, 84
  C.p.o. 'Small Fruit Mixed', 84
Cup and Saucer Vine, 64
Cup Flower, 65

D

Dahlia variabilis, 13, 14, 18
  description and cultivation, 85
  D.v. 'Coltness Hybrids', 85
  D.v. 'Redskin', 85
  D.v. 'Rigoletto', 85
  D.v. 'Unwins Dwarf Hybrids', 85
Daisy, double, 17, 18, 24, 26, 79
Delphinium chinensis, description and cultivation, 86
  D.c. 'Blue Mirror', 86
  D. consolida, 20, 19
    description and cultivation, 86
  D.c. 'Double Mixed', 86
  D.c. 'Dwarf Hyacinth-flowered, 86
  D.c. 'Giant Imperial', 86
Dianthus barbatus, 18, 20
  description and cultivation, 86
  D.b. 'Auricula-eyed Mixed', 86
  D.b. 'Extra Dwarf Double Mixed', 86
  D. caryophyllus, 59
  D. 'Chabaud's Giant Mixed', 59
  D. chinensis, 19, 20, 28
    description and cultivation, 59
  D.c. 'Laced Mixed', 59
  D.c. 'Magic Charms', 59
  D.c. 'Telstar', 59
  D. 'Scarlet Luminette', 59
Didiscus caerulea, description and cultivation, 69
digging, 104
Digitalis purpurea, 18, 20, 28
  description and cultivation, 60
  D.p. 'Excelsior Strains', 18, 20, 60
Dimorphotheca aurantiaca, 28
  description and cultivation, 48
diseases, 109
distance, illusions of, 13
Double Daisy, 17, 18, 24, 26, 79
Dusty Miller, 26
Dwarf Morning Glory, 68

E

Echium lycopsis see *E. plantagineum*
  E. plantagineum, description and cultivation, 87
  E.p. 'Dwarf Hybrids', 87
Eschscholzia californica, 18, 19, 28
  description and cultivation, 48
  E.c. 'Ballerina', 48
  E.c. 'Monarch Art Shades Mixed', 48
Euphorbia marginata, 13, 15, 18
  description and cultivation, 32
  E.m. 'White Icicle', 32

F

Feather Cockscomb, 21
Felicia bergerana, description and cultivation, 69
fences, 7, 29
fertilizers, 104
Feverfew, 36

Flame Nettle, 52
flea beetles, 109
Floss Flower, 66
focal points, 7, 13, 28
Forget-me-not, 19, 20, 24, 26, 73
Forsythia, 19
Four O'Clock Plant, 18, 92
Foxgloves, 19, 20, 28, 60
French Marigolds, 26, 27, 44
fungal diseases, 109

G
Gaillardia pulchella, description and cultivation, 87
G.p. 'Double Mixed', 87
Garden Pansy, 101
Gazania x *hybrida*, 26, 28
description and cultivation, 88
G. x *h.* 'Daybreak', 88
G. x *h.* 'Mini-star Mixed', 88
G. x *h.* 'Mini-star Tangerine', 88
G. x *h.* 'Sundance', 88
Gilia capitata, 18
description and cultivation, 70
Glaucium corniculatum, 18
description and cultivation, 53
Godetia grandiflora, 19
description and cultivation, 60
G.p. 'Azalea-flowered Mixed', 60
G.p. 'Double Mixed', 60
G.p. 'Monarch', 60
Golden Feather, 42
Golden Philadelphus, 19
Golden Pyrethrum, 22
Gourds, Ornamental, 29, 84
Greater Quaking Grass, 31
green and white borders, 15
green plants:
descriptions, 31–3
use of, 12
greenfly, 109
grey plants, use of, 12
Gypsophila elegans, 13, 15, 16, 19
description and cultivation, 36
G.e. 'Giant White', 36
G.e. 'Monarch Strain', 36

H
half-hardy annuals:
as bedding plants, 7
buying, 107
care of, 107
containers, 26
definition, 6
hanging baskets, 27
hardening, 106–7
planting out, 107
sowing, 106
transplanting, 106
hanging baskets, 27
hardy annuals:
borders for, 18
care of, 107
definition, 6
mixed borders, 18
sowing techniques, 105
supporting, 105
thinning, 105
hedges, 9
Helianthus annuus, 19, 28
description and cultivation, 40

H.a. 'Giant Single, 40
H. cucumerifolius 'Bouquet Mixed', 40
Helichrysum bracteatum, description and cultivation, 88
H.b. 'Bright Bikinis', 88
H.b. 'Double Mixed', 88
H.b. 'Hot Bikini', 88
Heliotropium arborescens, 10, 18, 26, 27, 70
description and cultivation, 70
H.a. 'Marine', 22, 23, 70
H. peruvianum see *H. arborescens*, 70
Helipterum roseum, 16, 18, 61
Hollyhock 28, 77
Honesty, 18, 19, 20, 64
Horned Poppy, 53
Hunnemannia fumariifolia, description and cultivation, 41

I
Iberis umbellata, 19, 20, 28
description and cultivation, 61
I.u. 'Fairy Maid', 61
I.u. 'White Pinnacle', 61
Iceland Poppy, 94
Immortelle, 102
Impatiens holstii see *I. walleriana*
I. walleriana, 21, 26, 27
description and cultivation, 54
I.w. 'Accent', 54
I.w. 'Blitz', 54
I.w. 'Confection Mixed', 54
I.w. 'Lipstick', 54
I.w. 'Novette Mixed', 54
I.w. 'Rosette Hybrids', 54
I.w. 'Super Elfin', 54
improving soils, 104
Indian Shot, 14, 81
Ionopsidium acaule, 28, 71
Ipomoea rubrocoerulea see *I. tricolor*, 71
I. tricolor, 29
description and cultivation, 71
I.t. 'Flying Saucers', 71
I.t. 'Heavenly Blue', 71
Ivy-leaved Geraniums (Pelargoniums), 95

J
Job's tears, 31
Joseph's Coat, 51

K
Kingfisher Daisy, 69
Kochia scoparia 'Trichophylla', 14
description and cultivation, 32
K.s. 'Acapulco', 13
K.s. 'Childsii', 32

L
Larkspur, 20, 86
Lathyrus odoratus, 20, 29
description and cultivation, 89
L.o. 'Bijou Mixed', 89
L.o. 'Early Mammoth Mixed', 89
L.o. 'Early Wonder Mixed', 89
L.o. 'Galaxy Mixed', 89

L.o. 'Jet Set Mixed, 89
L.o. 'Knee Hi', 89
L.o. 'Snooper Mixed', 89
L.o. 'Supersnooper Mixed', 89
Lavatera 'Loveliness', 15
L. rosea see *L. trimestris*
L. trimestris, description and cultivation, 61
L.t. 'Mont Blanc', 62
L.t. 'Silver Cup', 19, 62
Libaria maroccana, 28
Limonium sinuatum, description and cultivation, 90
L.s. 'Blue River', 90
L.s. 'Mixed Hybrids', 90
Linaria maroccana, description and cultivation, 90
Linum grandiflorum, 14
description and cultivation, 55
L.g. 'Rubrum', 16, 18, 19, 55
Linus grandiflorum, 14
Livingstone Daisy, 91
Lobelia, 26, 27
L. erinus, 10, 18, 26
description and cultivation, 72
L.e. 'Blue Cascade', 72
L.e. 'Blue Stone', 72
L.e. 'Cambridge Blue', 72
L.e. 'Colour Cascade', 72
L.e. 'Crystal Palace Compacta', 72
L.e. 'Sapphire', 72
L.e. 'String of Pearls', 72
Lobularia maritima see *Alyssum maritimum*
Love Lies Bleeding, 18, 21, 51
Love-in-a-mist, 20, 75
Lunaria annua, 18, 20
description and cultivation, 64
L.a. 'Munstead Purple', 64
L. biennis see *L. annua*
Lupinus texensis, 13, 18, 19
description and cultivation, 73
Nemophila insignis see *N. menziesii*
Lychnis coeli-rosa see *Viscaria elegans*

M
Maize, Ornamental, 33
Malcomia maritima, 18, 19, 20, 28
description and cultivation, 62
Mallow, 62
Mallow-wort, 65
Malope trifida 'Grandiflora', 18
description and cultivation, 65
marigolds, 22
Mask Flower, 50
Mathithiola incana, 20
description and cultivation, 91
M.i. 'Giant Excelsior' 91
Matricaria eximea see *Chrysanthemum parthenium*
Matthiola bicornis, 91
M. incana, description and cultivation, 91
M.i. 'Large Flowered Ten Week Mixed', 91
M.i. 'Park Stocks', 91
Mentzelia lindleyi, 18, 19
description and cultivation, 41
Mesembryanthemum criniflorum, description and cultivation, 91

M. oculatum 'Yellow Lunette', 91
Mesemesia strumosa, 28
Mexican Sunflower, 49
Mexican Tulip Tree, 41
Mignonette, 20, 37
mildew, 109
Mimulus, 27
M. x *hybridus*, 26
M. x *h.*, description and cultivation, 92
M. x *h.* 'Calypso', 92
M. x *h.* 'Malibu', 92
Mirabilis jalapa, 18
description and cultivation, 92
mixed borders, 18–19
Mock Orange, 19
Molucella laevis, 20
description and cultivation, 33
Monarch of the Veldt, 50
Monkey Flower, 92
Morning Glory, 71
Dwarf, 68
Mullein, 38
multi-coloured flowers, description 77–103
Myosotis, 25
M. oblongata see *M. sylvatica*
M. sylvatica, 18, 20, 26
description and cultivation, 73
M.s. 'Blue Bird', 73
M.s. 'Blue Cloud', 73
M.s. 'Marine', 73
M.s. 'Royal Blue', 25, 73

N
Nasturtium, 29, 100
Nemesia strumosa, description and cultivation, 93
N.s. 'Carnival Mixed', 93
N.s. 'Funfair', 93
N.s. 'Triumph Mixed', 93
Nemophila insignis see *N. menziesii*
N. menziesii, 18, 19, 28
description and cultivation, 74
Nicandra physaloides, description and cultivation, 74
Nicotiana, 23
N. affinis see *N. alata*
N. alata, 18, 26
description and cultivation, 93
N.a. 'Domino Mixed', 93
N.a. 'Domino Scarlet', 14
N.a. 'Lime Green', 15, 22, 18, 93
N.a. 'Nicki Formula Mixed', 93
N.a. 'Sensation Mixed', 93
Nierenbergia caerulea, description and cultivation, 65
N.c. 'Purple Robe', 65
N. hippomanica see *N. caerulea*
Nigella damascena, 11, 20
description and cultivation, 75
N.d. 'Miss Jekyll', 19, 75
N.d. 'Persian Jewels', 75
Night-scented Stock, 91
Nodding Catchfly, 63

O
Onopordum acanthium, 13, 14, 15, 18–19, 28
description and cultivation, 37

Opium Poppy, 95
orange plants:
descriptions, 47–50
use of, 12
Ornamental Cabbage, 79
Ornamental Gourd, 29, 84
Ornamental Kale, 79
Ornamental Maize, 33
Ornamental Tobacco, 93

P
Pansy, 10, 11, 19, 20, 101
winter-flowering, 24, 25, 26
Papaver nudicaule, 19
description and cultivation, 93
P.n. 'Champagne Bubbles', 94
P.n. 'Oregon Rainbows', 94
P.n. 'Unwins Giant Coonara', 94
P.rhoeas, description and cultivation, 94
P.r. 'Shirley Double Mixed', 94
P. somniferum, description and cultivation, 95
P.s. 'Paeony-flowered Mixed', 95
pastel colours, 9, 15
patios, 26, 27, 28
paved areas, 28
Pelargonium, 13, 22, 23, 26, 27
P. x *hortorum*, 26, 27
description and cultivation, 56
P. x *h.* 'Cherry Diamond', 56
P. x *h.* 'Diamond', 56
P. x *h.* 'Hollywood Star', 56
P. x *h.* 'Orange Orbit', 23, 56
P. x *h.* 'Rose Diamond', 56
P. x *h.* 'Scarlet Diamond', 56
P. x *h.* 'Scarlet Orbit Improved', 56
P. x *h.* 'Sprinter', 56
P. x *h.* 'Video', 56
P. x *h.* 'White Orbit', 56
P. peltatum, description and cultivation, 95
P.p. 'Summer Showers', 95
perennials:
mixed borders, 18
treated as biennials, 6
pergolas, 27
perspective, 12
pests, 109
Petunia x *hybrida*, 10, 13, 22, 23, 26
description and cultivation, 96
P. x *h.* 'Blue Frost', 96
P. x *h.* 'Flash', 96
P. x *h.* 'Jamboree', 96
P. x *h.* 'Madness', 96
P. x *h.* 'Plum Picotee', 10
P. x *h.* 'Red Picotee', 96
P. x *h.* 'Resisto Blue', 96
P. x *h.* 'Resisto Mixed', 96
P. x *h.* 'Resisto Rose-pink', 96
Phacelia campanularia, 18, 19, 28
description and cultivation, 75
Philadelphus, 19
Phlox drummondii, 28
description and cultivation, 97
P.d. 'Beauty Formula Mixed', 97
P.d. 'Twinkle Dwarf Star Mixed', 97

pillars, 29
pink and silver borders, 15
pink flowers:
    descriptions, 58–63
    use of, 12
planning, 8–29
    borders, 18–20
    colour contrast, 11
    containers, 26
    cottage-garden borders, 20
    hanging baskets, 27
    harmony, 10
    multi-coloured flowers, 17
    perspective, 13
    planting schemes, 18–29
    rainbow effect, 16
    restricted use of colour,
        14–15
    spring bedding schemes,
        24–5
    strong colours, 15
    sub-tropical beds, 21
    suitable sites, 9
    summer bedding schemes,
        22–3
    use of colour, 9, 12
    wild areas, 29
planting schemes, 18–29
    borders, 18–20
Polyanthus, 19, 24, 25, 26, 98
Poor Man's Orchid, 99
Portulaca grandiflora, 28
    description and cultivation,
        97
    P.g. 'Sunnyside Mixed', 97
Pot Marigold, 47
Prickly Poppy, 38
primary colours, 9
Primula polyantha, 19, 26
    description and cultivation,
        98
    P.p. 'Crescendo', 98
    P.p. 'Pacific Giants Blue
        Shades', 98
    P.p. Pacific Giants Mixed', 17,
        98
Prince of Wales Feathers, 82
protection, 9
purple flowers:
    descriptions, 63–5
    use of, 12
Pyrethrum parthenicum see
    Chysanthemum parthenicum

Q
quaking grass, 31

R
rainbow effect, 16
red borders, 14
red flowers:
    descriptions, 50–7
    use of, 12
Reseda odorata, 20
    description and cultivation,
        37
    R.o. 'Fragrant Beauty', 36
    R.o. 'Machet', 37
    R.o. 'Red Monarch', 19, 37
Ricinus communis, 18, 23, 28
    description and cultivation,
        57
    R.c. 'Gibsonii', 14, 23, 57
    R.c. 'Impala', 21, 57
rock gardens, 28
Rose of Heaven, 102
rots, 109
Rudbeckia hirta, description and
    cultivation, 42
    R.h. 'Goldilocks', 42
    R.h. 'Marmalade', 42

R.h. 'Rustic Dwarfs', 42
rusts, 109

S
Salvia farinacea 'Victoria',
    description and cultivation,
        76
    S. horminum, 19, 98
        description and cultivation,
            98
    S.h. 'Shades', 98
    S. splendens, 10, 13, 22, 26
        description and cultivation,
            57
    S.s. 'Blaze of Fire', 57
    S.s. 'Caramba', 57
    S.s. 'Carbiniere', 57
    S.s. 'Dress Parade Mixed', 57
    S.s. 'Laser Purple', 57
    S.s. 'Red Hot Sally', 57
    S.s. 'Red Riches', 57
Scabiosa atropupurea, 20
    description and cultivation,
        99
    S.a. 'Double Mixed', 99
    S.a. 'Dwarf Double Mixed', 99
Scarlet Sage, 57
Schizanthus pinnatus, description
    and cultivation, 99
    S.p. 'Disco', 99
    S.p. 'Hit Parade', 99
    S.p. 'Star Parade', 99
Scotch Thistle, 13, 19, 37
Sea Lavender, 90
seed:
    catalogues, 7
    sowing, 7, 105, 106
Senecio cineraria, 14
shade, 9
shelter, 9
shrubs, 9
    mixed borders, 18
Siberian wallflowers, 26, 83
Silene pendula, 15, 18, 19
    description and cultivation,
        63
silver and pink borders, 15
silver plants, use of, 12
Silver-leaved Cineraria, 35
site planning see planning
Slipperwort, 39
slugs, 109
snails, 109
Snapdragon, 77
Snow on the Mountain, 32
soils, 104
sowing techniques:
    half-hardy annuals, 106
    hardy annuals, 105
specimen plants, 28
Spider Flower, 59
spring bedding plants, 7
    definition, 6
    schemes for, 24–5
Star of the Veldt, 28, 48
Statice sinuata see Limonium
    sinuatum
Stock, 20, 91
Strawflower, 88
strong colours, 15
    separating, 16
sub-tropical beds, 21
summer bedding plants:
    definition, 6
    schemes for, 22–3
Summer Forget-me-not, 67
sun, 9
Sun Plant, 97
Sunflower, 28, 40
supports, 105

Swan River Daisy, 63
Sweet Alyssum, 34
Sweet Pea, 20, 29, 89
Sweet Scabious, 99
Sweet Sultan, 82
Sweet William, 18, 20, 86

T
Tagetes erecta:
    description and cultivation,
        43
    T.e. 'Climax', 43
    T.e. 'Diamond Jubilee', 43
    T.e. 'Gold Galore', 43
    T.e. 'Golden Jubilee', 43
    T.e. 'Inca Gold', 43
    T.e. 'Inca Orange', 43
    T.e. 'Inca Yellow', 22, 43
    T.e. 'Jubilee Mixed', 43
    T.e. 'Perfection Gold', 43
    T.e. 'Toreador', 43
    T.e. 'Yellow Galore', 43
    T. patula, 26
        description and cultivation,
            44
    T.p. 'Bonanza', 44
    T.p. 'Boy-o-Boy Mixed', 44
    T.p. 'Cinnabar', 44
    T.p. 'Honeycomb', 44
    T.p. 'Orange Boy', 44
    T.p. 'Queen Mixture', 44
    T.p. 'Queen Sophia', 44
    T.p. 'Scarlet Sophia', 44
    T.p. 'Seven Star Red', 44
    T.p. 'Susie Wong', 44
    T.p. 'Yellow Jacket', 44
    T. signata see T. tenuifolia
    T. tenuifolia, 26, 27, 28
        description and cultivation,
            45
    T.t. pumila 'Golden Gem', 45
    T.t.p. 'Lemon Gem', 45
    T.t.p. 'Paprika', 45
    T.t.p. 'Starfire', 45
    T.t.p. 'Tangerine Gem', 45
terraces, 26
Texas Blue Bonnet, 73
thinning seedlings, 105
Throatwort, 76
Thunbergia alata, 29
    description and cultivation,
        46
    T.a. 'Susie Mixed', 46
Tickseed, 39
Tithonia rotundifolia,
    description and cultivation,
        48
    T.r. 'Goldfinger', 49
    T.r. 'Torch', 49
    T. speciosa see T. rotundifolia
Toadflax, 90
Tobacco, Ornamental, 93
Trachelium caeruleum,
    description and cultivation,
        76
trailing plants, 26, 27
Treasure Flower, 88
trees, 9
trelliswork, 29
Tropaeolum canariense see T.
    peregrinum
    T. majus, 20, 29
        description and cultivation,
            100
    T.m. 'Alaska Mixed', 100
    T.m. 'Gleam', 100
    T.m. 'Jewel Mixed', 100
    T.m. 'Whirlybird Mixed', 100
    T. peregrinum, 18, 29
        description and cultivation,
            47

Tuberous Begonia, 26, 78
tubs, 26
Tulipa, 25, 26

U
Urns, 26
Ursinia pulchra, 49
    U. versicolor see U. pulchra

V
Venidium fatuosum, description
    and cultivation, 50
Verbascum bombyciferum, 14,
    16, 20, 28
    description and cultivation,
        38
    V. 'Broussa', 38
Verbena, 13, 27
    V. aubletia 'Perfecta', 100
    V. x hortensis see V. x hybrida
    V. x hybrida, 18,26
        description and cultivation,
            100
    V. x h. 'Blaze', 100
    V. x h. 'Showtime', 100
    V. x h. 'Springtime', 100
    V. x h. 'Tropic', 100
    V. rigida, 10, 100
    V. venosa, 10, 22, 100
Viola 'Prince Henry', 101
    V. 'Prince John', 101
    V. x wittrockiana, 19, 20, 26,
        28
        description and cultivation,
            101
    V. x w. 'Floral Dance
        Mixture', 17, 101
    V. x w. 'Imperial Orange
        Prince', 101
    V. x w. 'Imperial Sky Blue',
        101
    V. x w. 'Imperial White
        Shades', 101
    V. x w. 'Majestic Giant
        Mixed', 101
    V. x w. 'Roggli Giants Mixed',
        101
    V. x w. 'Universal Mixture',
        101
Violet Cress, 71
violet plants, use of, 12
Viper's Bugloss, 87
Virginian Stock, 18, 20, 28, 62
Viscaria elegans, description and
    cultivation, 102

W
Wallflower, 11, 20, 24, 26, 83
walls, 7, 29
    hanging baskets, 27
Wax Begonia, 52
weeds, 109
white and green borders, 15
white plants:
    descriptions, 34–8
    use of, 12
wild areas, 29
wild flowers, 29
wilts, 109
windbreaks, 9
window boxes, 26
winds, 9
winter cold, 9
woodland areas, 29

X
Xeranthemum annuum,
    description and cultivation,
        102

Y
yellow borders, 14
yellow plants:
    descriptions, 38–46
    use of, 12

Z
Zea mays, 18, 23, 28
    description and cultivation,
        33
    Z.m. 'Gigantea Quadricolor',
        33
    Z.m. 'Japonica Multicolor', 33
    Z.m. 'Strawberry Corn', 33
Zinna elegans, description and
    cultivation, 103
    Z.e. 'Belvedere', 103
    Z.e. 'Big Top Mixed', 103
    Z.e. 'Border Rose Beauty',
        103
    Z.e. 'Carved Ivory', 103
    Z.e. 'Envy', 15, 103
    Z.e. 'Gold Sun', 103
    Z.e. 'Peppermint Stick Mixed',
        103
    Z.e. 'Peter Pan Mixed', 103
    Z.e. 'Pulcino', 103
    Z.e. 'Red Sun', 103
    Z.e. 'Statefair Double Mixed',
        103
    Z.e. 'Sunshine Mixed', 103
    Z.e. 'Thumbelina Double
        Mixed', 103
    Z.e. 'Wild Cherry', 103
Zonal Geraniums, 22, 27, 56

Acknowledgements
Photographers
HEATHER ANGEL: 29, 31, 33R,
38, 64L, 75R, 94R, 95L; PAT
BRINDLEY: 63L, 71L; LINDA
BURGESS: 28, 59R, 73R;
BRUCE COLEMAN LTD: 73L;
KELLY FLYNN: 31, 66R, 83L,
83R, 86R, 101R; SUE HALL:
40; MARSHALLS SEEDS LTD:
39R, 100L; TANIA MIDGELEY:
37L, 46R, 51L, 53R, 54R, 61L,
64R, 65L, 68, 74R, 77L, 90L;
CLAY PERRY: 28, 29; HARRY
SMITH COLLECTION: 32L, 37R,
40L, 49R, 59L, 65R, 67R, 69,
70L, 76R, 81, 82R, 92R, 102R;
UNWINS SEEDS LTD: 11, 29,
32, 33, 34, 35, 36, 39, 40R,
42, 43, 44, 45, 46, 47, 48, 49L,
50R, 51, 52, 53L, 54L, 55, 56,
57, 58, 60, 61R, 62, 63R, 66L,
67L, 70R, 71R, 72, 74L, 75L,
76L, 77L, 78, 79, 80, 82L, 83C,
84, 85, 86L, 87, 88, 89, 90R,
91, 92L, 93L, 94L, 95R, 96,
97L, 98, 99, 100R, 101L,
102L, 103; MICHAEL WARREN
AIIP: 93R; JEREMY
WHITAKER: 8

Illustrator
NICOLA GREGORY: 1, 3, 5, 7,
10, 11, 13, 14, 15, 16, 17, 18,
19, 20, 21, 22, 23, 24, 25, 26,
27.

T = Top   B = Bottom
C = Centre